D1051682

*Through the Grand Canyon
from Wyoming to Mexico*

THE MACMILLAN COMPANY
NEW YORK · BOSTON · CHICAGO · DALLAS
ATLANTA · SAN FRANCISCO

MACMILLAN & CO., LIMITED
LONDON · BOMBAY · CALCUTTA
MELBOURNE

THE MACMILLAN CO. OF CANADA, LTD.
TORONTO

A NOTE ABOUT THE 2007 EDITION

TIMES have changed since the Kolb brothers made their historic river trip down the Green and Colorado rivers in 1911–12. But *Through the Grand Canyon from Wyoming to Mexico*, Ellsworth Kolb's classic tale of running the major rivers of the West and filming their adventure, remains a thrilling part of Grand Canyon history.

The Grand Canyon Association, which supports education and scientific research at Grand Canyon National Park, often publishes books that teach about the canyon but are not of interest to commercial publishers, so it is no surprise that the association decided to bring out a new edition of the Kolb classic. But the association's ties to the Kolb brothers stretch back some seventy-five years. The association operates a bookstore and a gallery of changing art exhibits in Kolb Studio (the first part of which was built in 1904), the home of the Kolbs on the South Rim of the Grand Canyon. The association funded the restoration of Kolb Studio, and Emery Kolb was even one of the association's founding board members in 1932. If any book fits our mission of teaching about the canyon, this adventure tale does.

The book is reproduced here in nearly the same form as the original book in 1914. There has been no editing of the text and the photographs are largely the same as those in the original (and many are reprinted from the original glass-plate or nitrate negatives). This book is reproduced exactly how Ellsworth Kolb originally wanted it to be published. We hope you enjoy it.

Todd R. Berger
Managing Editor
Grand Canyon Association

Copyright by Kolb Bros.

THE GRAND CANYON AT THE MOUTH OF HA VA SU CREEK

Through the Grand Canyon from Wyoming to Mexico

By

E. L. Kolb

With a Foreword by Owen Wister

With 48 Plates from Photographs
by the Author and his brother

New York
The Macmillan Company
1914

All rights reserved

GRAND CANYON ASSOCIATION
P.O. Box 399, Grand Canyon, AZ 86023-0399
(800) 858-2808
www.grandcanyon.org

Copyright © 2007 by the Grand Canyon Association

All Rights Reserved. Published 2007
No portion of this book may be reproduced in whole or in part, by any means (with the exception of short quotes for the purpose of review), without permission of the publisher.

Printed in the United States
Todd R. Berger, Managing Editor
Ron Short, Art Director

11   10   09   08   2   3   4   5

Library of Congress Cataloging-in-Publication Data

Kolb, E. L. (Ellsworth Leonardson), b. 1876.
  Through the Grand Canyon from Wyoming to Mexico / by E.L. Kolb ; with
a foreword by Owen Wister ; with 48 plates from photographs by the
author and his brother.
     p. cm.
  Originally published: New York : MacMillan, 1914.
  ISBN-13: 978-0-938216-96-4 (alk. paper)
  ISBN-10: 0-938216-96-1 (alk. paper)
  1. Colorado River (Colo.-Mexico)--Pictorial works. 2. Grand Canyon
(Ariz.)--Pictorial works. 3. Green River (Wyo.-Utah)--Pictorial works.
4. Colorado River (Colo.-Mexico)--Description and travel. 5. Grand
Canyon (Ariz.)--Description and travel. 6. Green River
(Wyo.-Utah)--Description and travel. 7. Boats and boating--Colorado
River (Colo.-Mexico)--History--20th century. 8. Boats and
boating--Green River (Wyo.-Utah)--History--20th century. 9. Kolb, E. L.
(Ellsworth Leonardson), b. 1876--Travel--Arizona--Grand Canyon. 10.
Kolb, Emery Clifford, 1881-1976--Travel--Arizona--Grand Canyon. I.
Kolb, Emery Clifford, 1881-1976. II. Title.
  F788.K84 2007
  979.1'32--dc22
                              2007033988

It is the mission of the Grand Canyon Association to cultivate knowledge, discovery, and stewardship for the benefit of Grand Canyon National Park and its visitors.

Proceeds from the sale of this book will be used to support the educational goals of Grand Canyon National Park.

Printed in the United States of America on recycled paper using soy-based inks.

Dedication

TO THE MANY FRIENDS

WHO "PULLED" FOR US, IF NOT WITH US

DURING THE ONE HUNDRED ONE DAYS OF OUR RIVER TRIP

THIS VOLUME

IS RESPECTFULLY DEDICATED

FOREWORD

IT is a twofold courage of which the author of this book is the serene possessor — shared equally by his daring brother; and one side of this bravery is made plain throughout the following pages. Every youth who has in him a spark of adventure will kindle with desire to battle his way also from Green River to the foot of Bright Angel Trail; while every man whose bones have been stiffened and his breath made short by the years, will remember wistfully such wild tastes of risk and conquest that he, too, rejoiced in when he was young.

Whether it deal with the climbing of dangerous peaks, or the descent (as here) of some fourteen hundred miles of water both mysterious and ferocious, the well-told tale of a perilous journey, planned with head and carried through with dauntless persistence, always holds the attention of its readers and gives them many a thrill. This tale is very well told. Though it is the third of its kind, it differs from its predecessors more than enough to hold its own: no previous explorers have attempted to take moving pictures of the Colorado River with themselves weltering in its foam. More than this: while the human race lasts it will be true, that any man who is lucky enough to fix upon a hard goal and win it, and can in direct and simple words tell us how he won it, will write a good book.

Perhaps this planet does somewhere else contain a thing like the Colorado River — but that is no matter; we at any rate in our continent possess one of nature's very vastest works. After The River and its tributaries have done with all sight of the upper world, have left behind the bordering plains and streamed through the various gashes which their floods have sliced in the mountains that once stopped their way, then the culminating wonder begins. The River has been flowing through the loneliest part which remains to us of that large space once denominated " The Great American Desert" by the vague maps in our old geographies. It has passed through regions of emptiness still as wild as they were before Columbus came; where not only no man lives now nor any mark is found of those forgotten men of the cliffs, but the very surface of the earth itself looks monstrous and extinct. Upon one such region in particular the author of these pages dwells, when he climbs up out of the gulf in whose bottom he has left his boat by the River, to look out upon a world of round gray humps and hollows which seem as if it were made of the backs of huge elephants. Through such a country as this, scarcely belonging to our era any more than the mammoth or the pterodactyl, scarcely belonging to time at all, does the Colorado approach and enter its culminating marvel. Then, for 283 miles it inhabits a nether world of its own. The few that have ventured through these places and lived are a handful to those who went in and were never seen again. The white bones of some have been found on the shores; but most were drowned; and in this water no bodies ever rise, because the thick sand that its torrent churns along clogs and sinks them.

This place exerts a magnetic spell. The sky is there above it, but not of it. Its being is apart; its climate; its light; its own. The beams of the sun come into it like visitors. Its own winds blow through it, not those of outside, where we live. The River streams down its mysterious reaches, hurrying ceaselessly; sometimes a smooth sliding lap, sometimes a falling, broken wilderness of billows and whirlpools. Above stand its walls, rising through space upon space of silence. They glow, they gloom, they shine. Bend after bend they reveal themselves, endlessly new in endlessly changing veils of colour. A swimming and jewelled blue predominates, as of sapphires being melted and spun into skeins of shifting cobweb. Bend after bend this trance of beauty and awe goes on, terrible as the Day of Judgment, sublime as the Psalms of David. Five thousand feet below the opens and barrens of Arizona, this canyon seems like an avenue conducting to the secret of the universe and the presence of the gods.

Is much wonder to be felt that its beckoning enchantment should have drawn two young men to dwell beside it for many years; to give themselves wholly to it; to descend and ascend among its buttressed pinnacles; to discover caves and waterfalls hidden in its labyrinths; to climb, to creep, to hang in mid-air, in order to learn more and more of it, and at last to gratify wholly their passion in the great adventure of this journey through it from end to end? No siren song could have lured travellers more than the siren silence of the Grand Canyon: but these young men did not leave their bones to whiten upon its shores. The courage that brought them out whole is plain throughout this narrative, in spite of its modesty; but they have had to exert and maintain an equal courage against another danger.

The Atchison, Topeka & Santa Fe Railway is the most majestic system between Chicago and the Pacific. Years in advance of its imitators, it established along its course hotels and restaurants where both architecture and cooking made part of an immense plan that was something not far from genius. The very names of these hotels, chosen from the annals of the Spanish explorers, stamp them with distinction. Outside and in, they conform alike to climate and tradition. They are like shells in the desert, echoing the tale of Coronado, the legend of the Indian. No corporation equals the Santa Fe in its civilized regard for beauty. To any traveller asking what way to go to California for scenery, comfort, pleasure, and good food, I should answer, by this way.

But is the Santa Fe wise in its persecution of the brothers Kolb? Of course it has made the Grand Canyon accessible to thousands where only scores could go before. And for the money and the enterprise spent upon this, nobody but a political mad-dog would deny the railroad's right to a generous return. But why try to swallow the whole canyon? Why, because the brothers Kolb are independent, crush their little studio, stifle their little trade, push these genuine artists and lovers of nature away from the Canyon that nobody has photographed or can photograph so well? This isn't to regard Beauty. You're hurting your own cause.

The attempt, so far, has failed to extinguish these independent brothers. But is such an attempt wise? Isn't it a good specimen of that high-handed disregard of everybody but yourself, which has bred (and partly justified) the popular rage that now undiscriminatingly threatens honest and dishonest dollars alike, so that the whole nation is at the mercy of laws passed by the overdone emotions and the underdone intelligence of the present hour?

OWEN WISTER.

PREFACE

THIS is a simple narrative of our recent photographic trip down the Green and Colorado rivers in rowboats — our observations and impressions. It is not intended to replace in any way the books published by others covering a similar journey. Major J. W. Powell's report of the original exploration, for instance, is a classic, literary and geological; and searchers after excellence may well be recommended to his admirable work.

Neither is this chronicle intended as a handbook of the territory traversed — such as Mr. F. S. Dellenbaugh's two volumes: "The Romance of the Grand Canyon," and "A Canyon Voyage." We could hardly hope to add anything of value to his wealth of detail. In fact, much of the data given here — such as distances, elevations, and records of other expeditions — is borrowed from the latter volume. And I take this opportunity of expressing our appreciation to Mr. Dellenbaugh for his most excellent and entertaining books.

We are indebted to Mr. Julius F. Stone, of Columbus, Ohio, for much valuable information and assistance. Mr. Stone organized a party and made the complete trip down the Green and Colorado rivers in the fall and winter of 1909, arriving at Needles, California, on November 27, 1909. He freely gave us the benefit of his experience and presented us with the complete plans of the boats he used.

One member of this party was Nathan Galloway, of Richfield, Utah. To him we owe much of the success of our journey. Mr. Galloway hunts and traps through the wilds of Utah, Colorado, and Arizona, and has a fame for skill and nerve throughout this entire region. He makes a yearly trip through the upper canyons, usually in a boat of his own construction; and in addition has the record of being the only person who has made two complete trips through the entire series of canyons, clear to Needles. He it is who has worked out the type of boats we used, and their management in the dangerous waters of the Colorado.

We have tried to make this narrative not only simple, as we say, but truthful. However, no two people can see things in exactly the same light. To some, nothing looks big; to others, every little danger is unconsciously magnified out of all proportion. For instance, we can recall rapids which appeared rather insignificant at first, but which seemed decidedly otherwise after we had been overturned in them and had felt their power — especially at the moment when we were sure we had swallowed a large part of the water that composed them.

The reader will kindly excuse the use of the first person, both singular and plural. It is our own story, after all, and there seems to be no other way than to tell it as you find it here.

CONTENTS

ILLUSTRATIONS

Through the Grand Canyon
from Wyoming to Mexico

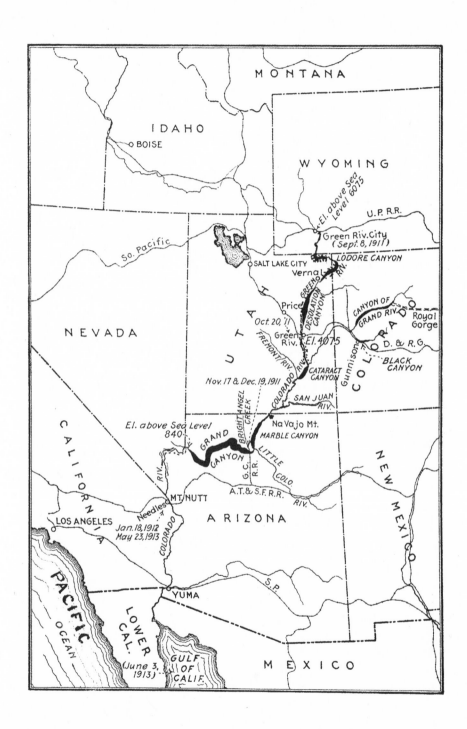

THROUGH THE GRAND CANYON FROM WYOMING TO MEXICO

CHAPTER I

PREPARATIONS AT GREEN RIVER CITY, WYOMING

EARLY in September of 1911 my brother Emery and I landed in Green River City, Wyoming, ready for the launching of our boats on our long-planned trip down the Green and Colorado rivers.

For ten years previous to this time we had lived at the Grand Canyon of Arizona, following the work of scenic photography. In a general way we had covered much of the country adjacent to our home, following our pack animals over ancient and little-used trails, climbing the walls of tributary canyons, dropping over the ledges with ropes when necessary, always in search of the interesting and unusual.

After ten years of such work many of our plans in connection with a pictorial exploration of the Grand Canyon were crowned with success. Yet all the while our real ambition remained unsatisfied.

B   1

We wanted to make the "Big Trip" — as we called it; in other words, we wanted a pictorial record of the entire series of canyons on the Green and Colorado rivers.

The time had come at last, after years of hoping, after long months of active preparation.

We stood at the freight window of the station at Green River City asking for news of our boats. They had arrived and could be seen in their crates shoved away in a corner. It was too late to do anything with them that day; so we let them remain where they were, and went out to look over the town.

Green River City proved to be a busy little place noisy with switch engines, crowded with cattle-men and cowboys, and with hunting parties outfitting for the Jackson Hole country. A thoroughly Western town of the better sort, with all the picturesqueness of people and surroundings that the name implies.

It was busier than usual, even, that evening; for a noisy but good-natured crowd had gathered around the telegraph office, eager for news of a wrestling match then taking place in an Eastern city. As we came up they broke into a cheer at the news that the American wrestler had defeated his foreign opponent. There was a discussion as to what constituted the "toe-hold," three boys ran an impromptu foot-race, there was some talk on the poor condition of the range, and the party began to break up.

Copyright by Kolb Bros.

AFTER A DIFFICULT PICTURE. E. C. KOLB ON THE ROPE.

The little excitement over, we returned to the hotel; feeling, in spite of our enthusiasm, somewhat lonesome and very much out of place. Our sleep that night was fitful and broken by dreams wherein the places we had known were strangely interwoven with these new scenes and events. Through it all we seemed to hear the roar of the Rio Colorado.

We looked out of the window the next morning, on a landscape that was novel, yet somehow familiar. The river, a quarter of a mile away, very clear and unruffled under its groves of cottonwood, wound through low barren hills, as unlike as could be to the cliffs and chasms we knew so well. But the colours — gray, red, and umber, just as Moran has painted them — reassured us. We seemed not so far from home, after all.

It was Wyoming weather, though; clear and cold, after a windy night. When, after breakfast, we went down to the river, we found that a little ice had formed along the margin.

The days of final preparation passed quickly — with unpacking of innumerable boxes and bundles, checking off each article against our lists; and with a long and careful overhauling of our photographic outfit.

This last was a most important task, for the success of our expedition depended on our success as photographers. We could not hope to add anything of importance to the scientific and topographic knowledge of the canyons already existing: and merely to come out alive at the other end did not make a strong appeal to our vanity. We were there as scenic photographers in love with their work, and determined to reproduce the marvels of the Colorado's canyons, as far as we could do it.

In addition to three film cameras we had 8 × 10 and 5 × 7 plate cameras; a plentiful supply of plates and films; a large cloth dark-room; and whatever chemicals we should need for tests. Most important of all, we had brought a motion-picture camera. We had no real assurance that so delicate an apparatus, always difficult to use and regulate, could even survive the journey — much less, in such inexperienced hands as ours, reproduce its wonders. But this, nevertheless, was our secret hope, hardly admitted to our most intimate friends — that we could bring out a record of the Colorado as it is, a live thing, armed as it were with teeth, ready to crush and devour.

There was shopping to do; for the purchases of provisions, with a few exceptions, had been left to the last. There were callers, too — an embarrassing number of them. We had camped on a small island near the town, not knowing when we did so that it had recently been put aside for a public park. The whole of Green River City, it seemed, had learned of our project, and came to inspect, or advise, or jeer at us. The kindest of them wished us well; the other sort told us "it would serve us right"; but not one of our callers had any encouragement to offer. Many were the stories of disaster and death with which they entertained us. One story in particular, as it seems never to have reached print — though unquestionably true — ought to be set down here.

Three years before two young men from St. Louis had embarked here, intending to follow the river throughout its whole course. They were expert canoeists, powerful swimmers, and equipped with a steel boat, we were told, built somewhat after the style of a canoe. They chose the time of high water — not knowing, probably, that while high water decreases the labour of the passage, it greatly increases the danger of it. They came to the first difficult rapid in Red Canyon, seventy odd miles below Green River City. It looked bad to them. They landed above it and stripped to their underclothing and socks. Then they pushed out into the stream.

Almost at once they lost control of the boat. It overturned; it rolled over and over; it flung them off and left them swimming for their lives. In some way, possibly the currents favouring, they reached the shore. The boat, with all its contents, was gone. There they were, almost naked, without food, without weapons, without the means of building a fire; and in an uninhabited and utterly inhospitable country.

For four days they wandered, blistered by the sun by day; nearly frozen at night, bruised by the rocks, and torn by the brambles. Finally they reached the ranch at the head of the canyons and were found by a half-breed Indian, who cared for them. Their underwear had been made into bindings for their lacerated feet; they were nearly starved, and on the verge of mental collapse. After two weeks' treatment in the hospital at Green River City they were partially restored to health. Quite likely they spent many of the long hours of their convalescence on the river bank, or on the little island, watching the unruffled stream glide underneath the cottonwoods.

Such tales as this added nothing to our fears, of course — for the whole history of the Colorado is one long story of hardship and disaster, and we knew, even better than our advisors, what risks lay before us. We told our new-found friends, in fact, that we had lived for years on the brink of the Grand Canyon itself, a gorge deeper and more awful, even, than Lodore; with a volume of water ten times greater. We knew, of course, of the river's vast length, of the terrible gorges that confined it, of the hundreds of rapids through which a boat would have to pass.

We knew, too, how Major Powell, undismayed by legends of underground channels, impassable cataracts, and whirlpools; of bloodthirsty tribes haunting its recesses, — had passed through the canyons in safety, measuring and surveying as he went. We also knew of the

Copyright by Kolb Bros.

IN THE GRAND CANYON NEAR THE LITTLE COLORADO.

many other attempts that had been made — most of them ending in disaster or death, a very few being successful.

Well, it had been done; [1] it could be done again — this was our answer to their premonitions.

We had present worries enough to keep us from dwelling too much on the future. It had been our intention to start two weeks earlier, but there had been numerous unavoidable delays. The river was low; "the lowest they had seen it in years" they told us, and falling lower every day. There were the usual difficulties of arranging a lot of new material, and putting it in working order.

At last we were ready for the boats, and you may be sure we lost no time in having them hauled to the river, and launching them.

They were beauties — these two boats of ours — graceful, yet strong in line, floating easily, well up in the water, in spite of their five hundred pounds' weight. They were flat-bottomed, with a ten-inch rake or raise at either end; built of white cedar, with unusually high sides; with arched decks in bow and stern, for the safe storing

---

[1] The various expeditions which are credited with continuous or complete journeys through all the canyons and the dates of leaving Green River, Wyoming, are as follows:

Major Powell, 1st journey. May 24, 1869.

Major Powell, 2nd journey. May 22, 1871. Discontinued at Kanab Canyon in the Grand Canyon.

Galloway. Sept. 20, 1895 and 1896.

Flavell. Aug. 27, 1896.

Stone. Sept. 12, 1909.

Kolb. Sept. 8, 1911.

For a more complete record of the earlier parties see appendix.

of supplies. Sealed air chambers were placed in each end, large enough to keep the boats afloat even if filled with water. The compartment at the bow was lined with tin, carefully soldered, so that even a leak in the bottom would not admit water to our precious cargoes. We had placed no limit on their cost, only insisting that they should be of materials and workmanship of the very best, and strictly in accordance with our specifications. In every respect but one they pleased us. Imagine our consternation when we discovered that the hatch covers were anything but water-tight, though we had insisted more upon this, perhaps, than upon any other detail. Loose boards, with cross-pieces, fastened with little thumbscrews — there they were, ready to admit the water at the very first upset.

There was nothing to be done. It was too late to rebuild the hatches even if we had had the proper material. Owing to the stage of water it was imperative that we should start at once. Bad as it would be to have water in our cargo, it would be worse to have too little water in the rock-obstructed channels of Red Canyon, or in the "flats" at Brown's Park for instance.

Certainly the boats acted so beautifully in the water that we could almost overlook the defective hatches. Emery rowed upstream for a hundred yards, against a stiff current, and came back jubilant.

"They're great — simply great!" he exclaimed.

We had one real cause for worry, for actual anxiety, though; and as each hour brought us nearer to the time of our departure, we grew more and more desperate. What about our third man?

We were convinced that a third man was needed; if not for the duties of camp making, helping with the cooking and portaging; at least, for turning the crank of the motion-picture camera. Emery and I could not very well be running rapids, and photographing ourselves in the rapids at the same time. Without a capable assistant, therefore, much of the real purpose would be defeated.

Our first move, accordingly, had been to secure the services of a strong, level-headed, and competent man. Friends strongly advised us to engage a Canadian canoe-man, or at least some one familiar with the management of boats in rough water. It was suggested, also, that we might secure the help of some one of the voyagers who had been members of one of the previous expeditions.

But — we may as well be frank about it — we did not wish to be piloted through the Colorado by a guide. We wanted to make our own trip in our own way. If we failed, we would have no one but ourselves to blame; if we succeeded, we would have all the satisfaction that comes from original, personal exploration. In other words, we wanted a man to execute orders, not to give them. But that man was hard to find!

There had been many applicants; some of them from

distant parts of the country. One by one they were sifted out. At length we decided on one man; but later he withdrew. We turned elsewhere, but these applications were withdrawn, until there remained but a single letter, from a young man in San Francisco. He seemed in every way qualified. We wrote accepting his application, but while waiting to hear from us a civil service position had been offered and accepted. "He was sorry"; and so were we, for his references proved that he was a capable man. Later he wrote that he had secured a substitute. We replied on the instant, by wiring money for transportation, with instructions for the new man to report at once at Green River. We took very much for granted, having confidence in our friends' sincerity and knowledge of just what was required.

The time had passed, two days before; but — no sign of our man! We wrote, we telegraphed, we walked back and forth to every train; but still he did not come. Had this man, too, failed us?

Then "Jimmy" came — just the night before we were to leave. And never was a man more heartily welcome!

With James Fagen of San Francisco our party was complete. He was an Irish-American, aged 22 years, a strong, active, and willing chap. To be sure, he was younger, and not so experienced at "roughing it" as we had hoped. But his good qualities, we were sure, would make up for what was lacking.

THE START AT GREEN RIVER, WYOMING.

FIRE HOLE CHIMNEYS.

Evening found us encamped a half mile below the town, near the county bridge. Our preparations were finished — even to the final purchase of odds and ends; with ammunition for shot-gun and rifle. We threw our sleeping-bags on the dry ground close to the river's edge, and, all our anxieties gone, we turned our faces to the stars and slept.

At daybreak we were aroused by the thunder of hoofs on the bridge above us, and the shouts of cowboys driving a large herd of half-broken horses. We tumbled into our clothes, splashed our faces with ice-cold water from the river, and hurried over to the hotel for a last breakfast.

Then we sat down — in the little hotel at Green River City — as others had done before, to write last messages to those who were nearest and dearest to us. A telegram to our parents in an Eastern city; and another to Emery's wife and little girl, at Bright Angel, more than eight hundred miles down this self-same river — these, somehow, took longer to write than the letters themselves. But whatever we may have felt, we finished this final correspondence in silence, and hurried back to the river.

Something of a crowd had gathered on the bridge to wish us *bon voyage*. Shouting up to them our thanks for their hospitality, and telling them to "look pleasant," we focussed the motion-picture camera on them, Emery turning the crank, as the boat swung out into the current.

So began our journey, on Friday, September the 8th, 1911, at 9.30 A.M., as entered in my journal.

CHAPTER II

ALL this preparation — and still more, the vexatious delays — had been a heavy tax upon us. We needed a vacation. We took it — six pleasant care-free days — hunting and fishing as we drifted through the sixty miles of southern Wyoming. There were ducks and geese on the river to test our skill with the shot-gun. Only two miles below Green River City Emery secured our first duck, a promise of good sport to follow. An occasional cottontail rabbit was seen, scurrying to cover through the sage-brush, when we made a detour from the boats. We saw many jack-rabbits too — with their long legs, and exaggerated ears — creatures swifter, even, than the coyotes themselves.

We saw few people, though an occasional rancher hailed us from the shore. Men of the open themselves, the character of our expedition appealed to them. Their invitations to "come up to the ranch, and spend the evening" were always hearty, and could seldom be refused if the day was nearly gone.

The Logan boys' ranch, for instance, was our first camp; but will be one of the last to be forgotten. The two Logan boys were sturdy, companionable young men, full of pranks, and of that bubbling, generous humour that flourishes in this Western air. We were amused by their kindly offer to allow Jimmy to ride "the little bay" — a beautiful animal, with the shifty eye of a criminal. But Jimmy, though city-bred, was not to be trapped, and declined; very wisely, as we thought. We photographed their favourite horses, and the cabin; also helped them with their own camera, and developed some plates in the underground storm-cellar, — a perfect dark-room, as it happened.

We took advantage of this pleasant camp to make a few alterations about our boats. Certain mechanical details had been neglected in our desire to be off, our intention being to look after them as occasion demanded. Our short run had already shown us where we were weak or unprepared. The rowlocks needed strengthening. One had come apart in our first brush with a little riffle. The rowlocks were of a little-used type, but very serviceable in dangerous waters. Inside the usual rowlock a heavy ring was hung, kept in place by strong set-screws, but allowing full play in every direction. These rings were slipped over the oars; then the usual leather collar was nailed on the oar, making it impossible for the rings to become separated from the oars. The holes for the set-screws were too shallow, so we went over the entire lot to deepen them. We foresaw where a break might occur, and hung another lock of the open type on a cord, beside each oar, ready for instant use in case of emergency.

The Logan boys, seeing our difficulties in making some of these changes, came to our relief. "Help yourselves to the blacksmith shop," they said heartily. Here was an opportunity. Much time was consumed in providing a device to hold our extra oars — out of the way on top of the deck, but available at a moment's notice. Thanks to the Logan boys and their blacksmith shop, these and many other little details were corrected once for all; and we launched our boats in confidence on the morning of September 10.

A few miles below we came to the locally famous Fire Hole Chimneys, interesting examples of the butte formation, so typical of the West. There were several of these buttes, about 800 feet high, composed of stratified rock; in colour quite similar to the rocks at Green River City, but capped with rock of a peculiar burnt appearance, though not of volcanic origin. Some of the buttes sloped up from the very edge of the river; others were separated from the river by low flats, covered with sage-brush and bunch-grass, — that nutritious food of the range stock. At the water's edge was the usual fringe of willows, cottonwoods, and shrubs innumerable, — all mirrored in the limpid surface of Green River.

At the foot of the cliffs were a number of wild burros, old and young — fuzzy little baby-burros, looking ridiculously like jack-rabbits — snorting their indignation at our invasion of their privacy. Strange, by the way, how quickly these wild asses lose their wildness of carriage when broken, and lapse into the utmost docility!

Just below the Chimneys Emery caught sight of fish gathered in a deep pool, under the foliage of a cottonwood tree which had fallen into the river. Our most tempting bait failed to interest them; so Emery, ever clever with hook and line, "snagged" one just to teach them better manners. It was a Colorado River salmon or whitefish. That evening I "snagged" a catfish and used this for salmon bait, a fourteen-pound specimen rewarding the attempt.

These salmon were old friends of ours, being found from one end to the other of the Colorado, and on all its tributaries. They sometimes weigh twenty-five or thirty pounds, and are common at twenty pounds; being stockily built fish, with large, flat heads. They are not gamey, but afford a lot of meat with a very satisfying flavour.

On September 11, about forty miles below Green River, we passed Black's Fork, a tributary entering from the west. It is a stream of considerable length, but was of little volume at that time. The banks were cliffs about 300 feet high, rugged, dark, and overhanging. Here were a half dozen eagles and many old nests — proof enough, if proof were needed, that we were in a little visited country. What strong, splendid birds they were; how powerful and graceful their flight as they circled up, and up, into the clear blue sky !

Our next camp was at the Holmes' ranch, a few miles below Black's Fork. We tried to buy some eggs of Walter Holmes, and were told that we could have them on one condition — that we visit him that evening. This was a price we were only too glad to pay, and the evening will linger long in our memories.

Mr. Holmes entertained us with stories of hunting trips — after big game in the wilds of Colorado; and among the lakes of the Wind River Mountains, the distant source of the Green River. Mrs. Holmes and two young ladies entertained us with music; and Jimmy, much to our surprise, joined in with a full, rich baritone. It was late that night when we rolled ourselves in our blankets, on the banks twenty feet above the river.

Next morning we were shown a group of Mrs. Holmes' pets — several young rabbits and a kitten, romping together in the utmost good fellowship. The rabbits had been rescued from a watery grave in an irrigation ditch and carefully nursed back to life. We helped her search for a lame wild duck that had spurned the offer of a good home with civilized ducklings, and had taken to the sage-brush. Mrs. Holmes' love of wild animals, however, failed to include the bald-headed eagle that had shown such an appetite for her spring chickens.

A few miles below this ranch we passed Bridger Crossing, a ford on an old trail through southern Wyoming. In pioneer days Jim Bridger's home was on this very spot. But those romantic days are long since past; and where this world-famous scout once watched through the loopholes of his barricade, was an amazed youngster ten or eleven years old who gazed on us, then ran to the cabin and emerged with a rifle in his hands. We thought little of this incident at the time, but later we met the father of the boy and were told that the children had been left alone with the small boy as their only protector, and that he stood ready to defend the home against any possible marauders. No doubt we looked bad enough to him.

Just below the ford the channel widened, and the river became very shallow, the low rolling hills falling away into a wide green prairie. We camped that night on a small island, low and treeless, but covered with deep, rank grass. Next morning our sleeping-bags were wet with frost and dew. A hard pull against a heavy wind between gradually deepening rocky banks made us more than glad to pitch camp at noon a short distance above the mouth of Henry's Fork, a considerable stream flowing from the west. In the afternoon Emery and I decided to walk to Linwood, lying just across the Utah line, four

c

miles up Henry's Fork. Jimmy preferred to remain with the boats.

Between the river and a low mesa lay a large ranch of a different appearance from those others which we had passed. Those past were cattle ranches, with stock on the open range, and with little ground fit for cultivation, owing to the elevation. Here we found great, broad acres, fenced and cultivated, with thoroughbred stock — horses and cattle — contentedly grazing.

This pastoral scene, with a background of rugged mountains, appealed strongly to our photographic instincts. After three or four exposures, we climbed the farthest fence and passing from alfalfa to sage-brush in one step, were at the foot of the mesa.

Climbing to the summit, we beheld the village in the distance, in a beautiful green valley — a splendid example of Mormon irrigation and farming methods. Linwood proved to be the market-place for all the ranchers of this region. Dotting the foot-hills where water was less plentiful were occasional cabins, set down in the middle of hay ranches. All this husbandry only emphasized the surrounding desolation. Just beyond, dark in the southern sky, rose the great peaks of the Uintah range, the mountains we were so soon to enter.

Storm-clouds had been gathering about one great snow-covered peak, far in the distance. These clouds spread and darkened, moving rapidly forward. We had taken the hint and were already making all possible haste toward the town, hoping to reach it before the storm broke. But it was useless.   Long before we had gained the edge of the valley the rain had commenced in the mountains, — small local storms, resembling delicate violet-coloured veils, hung in the dense pall of the clouds.   There were far flashes of lightning, and the subdued roar of distant thunder, rapidly growing louder as the storm approached. Unable to escape a drenching, we paused a moment to wonder at the sight; to marvel — and shrink a little too — at the wild, incessant lightning.   The peaks themselves seemed to be tumbling together, such was the continuous roar of thunder, punctuated by frequent deafening crashes.

Then the storm came down upon us.   Such torrents of rain we have seldom witnessed : such gusts of driving wind !   At times we could scarcely make headway against it, but after most strenuous effort we neared the village. We hoped to find shelter under a bridge, but found innumerable muddy streams running through the planks. So we resumed our plodding, slipping and sliding in the black, bottomless mud.

The storm by this time had passed as quickly as it came.   Wet to our skins, we crawled into the little store and post-office combined, and found it filled with ranch hands, waiting for the weekly mail.   We made a few purchases, wrote some letters, then went to a large boarding-house near by and fortified ourselves with a generous, hot supper.

There were comments by some of the men on our venture, but they lacked the true Green River tang. Here, close to the upper canyons, the unreasonable fear of the rapids gave way to a reasonable respect for them. Here we heard again of the two young men from St. Louis, and the mishaps that had befallen them. Here too we were to hear for the first time of the two Snyders, father and son, and the misfortunes that had overtaken them in Lodore Canyon, twenty years before. We were to hear more of these men later.

We made what haste we could back to our boats, soon being overtaken by a horseman, a big-hearted Swede who insisted on carrying our load as long as we were going in his direction. How many just such instances of kindliness we were to experience on our journey down the river! How the West abounds with such men! It was dark when he left us a mile from the river. Here there was no road to follow, and we found that what had been numerous dry gullies before were now streams of muddy water. Two or three of these streams had to be crossed, and we had a disagreeable half hour in a marsh. Finally we reached the river, but not at the point where we had left our boats. We were uncertain whether the camp was above or below us, and called loudly for Jimmy, but received no answer.

E. L. KOLB. EMERY KOLB. H. LAUZON. *Copyright by Kolb Bros.*

BOATS AND CREW. PHOTO TAKEN IN THE GRAND CANYON.

Emery felt sure that camp was upstream. So up-stream we went, keeping back of the bushes that fringed the banks, carefully searching for a sign. After a few minutes' hunt we heard a sound : a subdued rumble, not unlike the distant thunder heard that afternoon, or of boats being dragged over the pebbles. What could it be ? We listened again, carefully this time, and dis-covered that it came from a point about thirty feet away, on the opposite side of the bushes. It could be only one thing. Jimmy's snore had brought us home !

Hurriedly securing some dry clothes from the rubber sacks, which contained our sleeping-bags as well, we made a quick change, and slid into the beds, inflating the air mattresses with our lungs after we were inside. Then we lay down contentedly to rest.

CHAPTER III

WE awoke the next morning full of anticipation. Something new lay ahead of us, a promise of variety. In plain sight of our camp lay the entrance to Flaming Gorge, the gateway to the entire series of canyons. Hurriedly finishing our camp duties, we loaded the boats, fastened down the hatches, and shoved off into the current, eager to be on our way.

It was cloudy overhead and looked as if we were to have more rain. Even then it must have been raining away to the north, for a dirty, clay-colored torrent rushed through the dry arroyo of the night before, a stream large enough to discolour the water of the Green itself. But we thought little of this. We were used to seeing muddy water in the Colorado's gorges ; in fact we were surprised to find clear water at all, even in the Green River. Rowing downstream we found that the country sloped gently towards the mountains. The river skirted the edge of these foot-hills as if looking for a possible escape, then turned and entered the mountain at a sharp angle. The walls sloped back considerably at first, and there was a little shore on either side.

Somewhere near this point runs the dividing line of Wyoming and Utah.

We considered the gateway a subject worthy of a motion picture, if taken from the deck of the boat; but doubted if it would be a success owing to the condition of the light and the motion of the boat. Still it was considered worthy of a trial, and the film was run through.

The colour of the rocks at the entrance was a light red, but not out of the ordinary in brilliancy. The rock formation was stratified, but displaced; standing at an angle and flexed over on top with a ragged break here and there, showing plainly the great pressure to which the rocks had been subjected. The upheaval was not violent, the scientists tell us, but slow and even, allowing the river to maintain its old channel, sawing its way through the sandstone. The broken canyon walls, when well inside the gorge, were about 600 to 700 feet high. The mountains beyond and on either side were much higher. The growth on the mountain sides was principally evergreen; Douglas fir, the bull-pine and yellow pine. There was a species of juniper, somewhat different from the Utah juniper, with which we were familiar at the Grand Canyon. Bushes and undergrowth were dense above the steep canyon walls, which were bare. Willows, alder-thickets, and a few cottonwood trees lined the shores.

Meanwhile the current had quickened, almost imperceptibly at first, but enough to put us on our guard. While there were no rapids, use was made of what swift water we found by practising on the method we would use in making a passage through the bad rapids. As to this method, unused as yet by either of us, we had received careful verbal instruction from Mr. Stone, who had made the trip two years before our own venture; and from other friends of Nathan Galloway, the trapper, the man who first introduced the method on the Green and Colorado rivers.

Our experience on water of any kind was rather limited. Emery could row a boat, and row it well, before we left Green River, but had never gone over any large rapids. While he was not nearly so large or heavy as I, — weighing no more than 130 pounds, while I weighed 170 pounds, — he made up for his lighter weight by a quickness and strength that often surprised me. He was always neat and clever in his method of handling his boat, taking a great deal of pride in keeping it free from marks, and avoiding rocks when making a landing. I had done very little rowing before leaving Green River, so little that I had difficulty in getting both oars in the water at the same time. Of course it did not take me long to learn that; but I did not have the knack of making clean landings, and bumped many rocks that my brother missed. Still I was improving all the time and was anxious to get into the rough water, feeling sure I would get through somehow, but doing my best in the meantime to get the knack of handling the boat properly before the rough water was reached.

An occasional rock would stick up above the surface; the swift water would rush up on it, or drive past on either side. Instead of pulling downstream with might and main, and depending on a steersman with a sweep-oar to keep us clear of obstructions — the method usually adopted on large rivers, and by the earlier parties on the Colorado — by our method the single oarsman reversed his boat so that it was turned with the stern downstream, giving the oarsman a view of what was ahead; then by pulling upstream the boat was held in check. We allowed ourselves to be carried in a direct line with the rocks ahead, approaching them as closely as we dared; then, with a pull on one oar, the boat was turned slightly at an angle to the current, and swung to one side or the other; just as a ferry is headed into the current, the water itself helping to force it across. The ferry is held by a cable; the boat, by the oarsman; the results are quite similar.

The boats, too, were somewhat unusual in design, having been carefully worked out by Galloway after much experience with the problem, and after building many boats. He finally settled on the design furnished us by Mr. Stone. The flat bottom, sloping up from the centre to either end, placed the boats on a pivot one might say, so that they could be turned very quickly, much more quickly than if they had had a keel. There was a four-foot skag or keel under the stern end of the boat, but this was only used when in quiet water; and as it was never replaced after being once removed we seldom refer to it. Being flat-bottomed, they drew comparatively little water, a matter quite important on low water such as we found in the Green River. While each boat carried a weight of seven hundred pounds in addition to its own five hundred pounds, they often passed over rocks less than ten inches below the surface, and did so without touching. While the boats were quite large, the arched decks made them look even larger. A considerable amount of material could be stored under these decks. The only part of the boat that was entirely open or un-protected from the waves was the cockpit, or mid-section occupied by the oarsman. This was only large enough for one man. A second man had to sit on the deck behind the oarsman, with his feet hanging into the cockpit. Jimmy occupied this place of honour as we drifted through the placid water; first on one boat, then on the other, entertaining us meanwhile with his songs.

We encountered two splashy little rapids this day, but with no rocks, or any dangerous feature whatever. Any method, or none at all, was safe enough in these rapids.

Copyright by Kolb Bros.

TILTED ROCKS AT KINGFISHER CANYON.

Copyright by Kolb Bros.

INSIDE OF THE FIRST CANYONS.

The colouring of the rocks changed as we proceeded, and at the lower end of the short canyon we saw the flaming patch of colour that had suggested its name to Major Powell, forty-two years before.   Intensified on that occasion by the reflected light of a gorgeous sunset, it must have been a most brilliant spectacle.

Two beavers slid into the water when we were close beside them, then rose to the surface to stare curiously when we had passed.   We left them undisturbed.   Some geese decoyed us into an attempt to ambush them, but they kept always just out of reach of our guns.   Wise fellows, those geese !

A geological fault accompanied by the breaking down of the walls marks the division between Flaming Gorge and Horseshoe Canyon, which immediately follows. We nooned here, opposite a deserted cabin.   A trail dropped by easy stages over the slope on the east side; and fresh tracks showed that sheep had recently been driven down to the water's edge.

Passing through Horseshoe, — another very short canyon, — we found deep, placid pools, and sheer, light red walls rising about four hundred feet on either side, then sloping back steeply to the tree-covered mountains. In the middle of this canyon Emery was startled out of a day-dream by a rock falling into the water close beside him, with never a sound of warning.   Years spent in the canyons had accustomed Emery and me to such occurrences; but Jimmy, unused to great gorges and towering cliffs, was much impressed by this incident. After all, it is only the unusual that is terrible. Jimmy was ready enough to take his chances at dodging bricks hurled by a San Francisco earthquake, but never got quite used to rocks descending from a source altogether out of sight. Small wonder, after all! Later we were to experience more of this thing, and on a scale to startle a stoic!

We halted at the end of Horseshoe, early in the afternoon of September 14, 1911, one week out from Green River City. Camp No. 6 was pitched on a gravelly shore beside Sheep Creek, a clear sparkling stream, coming in from the slopes of the Uintah range. Just above us, on the west, rose three jagged cliffs, about five hundred feet high, reminding one by their shape of the Three Brothers of Yosemite Valley. Here, again, we were treated to another wonderful example of geologic displacement, the rocks of Horseshoe Canyon lying in level strata; while those of Kingfisher, which followed, were standing on end. Sheep Creek, flowing from the west, finds an easy course through the fault, at the division of the canyons. The balance of this day was spent in carefully packing our material and rearranging it in our boats, for we expected hard work to follow.

Tempted by the rippling song of the brook, and by tales of fish to be found therein, we spent two hours fishing from its banks on the morning of the 15th. But the foliage of overhanging trees and shrubs was dense, making it difficult to cast our lines, or even to climb along its shores, and our small catch of two trout, which were fried with a strip of bacon to add flavour, only whetted our appetites for more.

It was a little late in the season for many birds. Here in Kingfisher Canyon were a few of the fish-catching birds from which the canyon took its name. There were many of the tireless cliff-swallows scattered all through these canyons, wheeling and darting, ever on the wing. These, with the noisy crested jays, an occasional "camp-robber," the little nuthatches, the cheerful canyon wren with his rollicking song, the happy water-ousel, "kill-deer," and road-runners and the water birds, — ducks, geese, and mud-hens, with an occasional crane, — made up the bird life seen in the open country and in these upper canyons. Earlier in the season it must be a bird's paradise, for berries and seeds would then be plentiful.

We resumed our journey at 10 A.M., a very short run bringing us to the end of Kingfisher Canyon. The three canyons passed through approximate hardly more than ten miles in length, different names being given for geological reasons, as they really form only one canyon. The walls at the end were broken down, and brilliantly tinted talus of many hues covered the slopes, the different colours intermingling near the bottom. The canyon-walled river turned southeast here, and continued in this general direction for many miles, but with many twists and turns.

We had previously been informed that Red Canyon, the next to follow, while not considered bad when compared to others, gave one the experience most necessary to combat the rapids farther down. It was not without danger, however, as a review of previous expeditions showed : some had lost their lives, still others, their boats; and one of Major Powell's parties had upset a boat in a Red Canyon rapid. The stage of water was so different on these previous attempts that their experiences were of little value to us one way or the other. A reference to pictures taken by two of these parties showed us there was considerable more water when they went through — six, and even eight feet higher in places. Possibly this would be the best stage on which to make the voyage in heavy boats. The unfortunate ones had taken the spring rise, or flood water, with disastrous results to themselves or their boats.

We soon found that our passage was to be hard on account of having too little water. In the quiet water above we had been seldom bothered with shoals; but now that we were in swifter water, there was scarcely any depth to it at all, except in the quiet pools between the rapids.

For a description of our passage through this upper end of Red Canyon we refer to our journal : sketchy notes jotted down, usually in the evening just before retiring, by the light of a camp-fire, or the flickering flame of a candle. Under the date of Friday, September the 15th, we find the following :

"End of Kingfisher : long, quiet pools and shoals where we grounded a few times ; several small, splashy rapids ; then a larger one near an old boat landing. Looked the rapid over from the shore. Jim remained at the lower end with a life-preserver on a rope, while we ran the rapid. Struck one or two rocks, lightly ; but made the run in safety."

"At the third rapid we saw some geese — but they got away. At noon we ate a cold lunch and because of the low water removed the skags, carrying them in the cockpit. The scenery in upper Red Canyon is impressive : pines and fir come down on the sloping sides to the river's edge ; the rocks are reddish brown in colour, often broken in squares, and looking like great building blocks piled one upon another. The canyon is about fifteen hundred feet deep ; the river is clear again, and averages about two hundred feet in width. We have seen a few deer tracks, but have not seen any deer. We also saw some jumping trout in a splashy little rapid. Doubtless they came from a little creek, close by, for we never heard of trout being found in the Green River."

"We made a motion picture, while dropping our boats down with lines, over the first rapid we considered bad.

Emery remained in the boats, keeping clear of the rocks with a pole. Powell's second party records an upset here."

"We passed Kettle Creek about 5 P.M. In the fifth rapid below Kettle Creek I got on the wrong side of the river and was carried into a very rocky rapid — the worst so far encountered. I touched a rock or two at the start, but made the run in safety; while Emery ran the opposite side without trouble. We camped beside a small stream on the south, where there were signs of an old camp."

"*Saturday, September 16.* Clear and cold in the early morning. Started about 9 A.M. Lined our boats past a difficult rapid. Too many rocks, not enough water. Two or three miles below this I had some difficulty in a rapid, as the pin of a rowlock lifted out of the socket when in the middle of rough water. Emery snapped a picture just as it happened. A little later E. C.[1] ran a rocky rapid, but had so much trouble that we concluded to line my boat. Noon. Just a cold lunch, but with hot coffee from the vacuum bottles. Then at it again."

"The scenery is wonderful; the canyon is deeper than above; the river is swift and has a decided drop. We proceed cautiously, and make slow progress. We camp

---

[1] The initials E. C. apply to my brother, Emery C. Kolb; E. L. to myself. These initials are frequently used in this text. For several years the nick-name "Ed" has been applied to me, and in my brothers' narratives I usually figure as Ed.

for the day on the north side close to a little, dry gully, on a level sage and bunch-grass covered bottom back from the river's edge. An abruptly descending canyon banked with small cottonwood trees coming in from the opposite side contains a small stream. Put up our tent for the second time since leaving Green River, Wyoming. We are all weary, and glad to-morrow is Sunday — a day of rest."

"*Sunday, September 17.* E. C. and I follow a fresh deer track up a game trail and get — a rabbit. Climb out about 1300 feet above the river to the top of the narrow canyon. Here is a sloping plateau, dotted with bunch-grass and grease-wood, a fourth of a mile wide. Then rounded mountains rise beyond the plateau, some of the peaks reaching a height of 4000 feet above the river. The opposite side is much the same, but with a wider plateau. We had no idea before what a wonderful country this is. It is a picture to tempt an artist. High on the mountain tops is the dark blue-green of pines and firs, reds and yellows are mixed in the quaking aspen, — for the frost comes early enough to catch the sap in the leaves; little openings, or parks with no trees, are tinted a beautiful soft gray; 'brownstone fronts' are found in the canyon walls; and a very light green in the willow-leafed cottonwoods at the river's edge, and in all side canyons where there is a running stream. The river glistens in the sunlight, as it winds around the base of the

D

wall on which we stand, and then disappears around a bend in the canyon. Turn where we will, we see no sign of an opening, nothing but the rounded tops of wooded mountains, red and green, far as the eye can reach, until they disappear in the hazy blue. Finally Emery's keen eyes, aided by the binoculars, discover a log cabin at the foot of a mountain, on the plateau opposite us, about three miles away."

"We hurry back to camp and write some letters; then Jim and I cross the river and climb out over the rocky walls to the plateau above. In two hours we reach the cabin. It is new — not yet finished. A woman and four children are looking over a garden when we arrive. They are a little frightened at first, but soon recover. The woman gladly promises to take out our mail when they go to the nearest town, which happens to be Vernal, Utah, forty-five miles away. Three other families live near by, all recently moved in from Vernal. The woman tells us that Galloway hunts bear in these timbered mountains, and has killed some with a price on their heads — bear with a perverted taste for fresh beef."[1]

---

[1] It is not unusual for certain individual animals to be outlawed or to have a price set on their heads by the stockmen's associations, in addition to the regular bounty paid by the counties. At the time this is written there is a standing reward of $200 for a certain "lobo," or timber wolf which roams over the Kaibab Forest directly opposite our home in the Grand Canyon. In addition to this there is a bounty of $10 offered by the county. This wolf has taken to killing colts and occasional full-grown horses, in addition to his regular diet of yearling calves.

"Thanking the woman, we make our way back to the river. We see some dried-out elk horns along our trail; though it is doubtful if elk get this far south at present. A deer trail, leading down a ravine, makes our homeward journey much easier. It has turned quite cold this evening, after sunset. We finish our notes and prepare to roll into our beds a little earlier than usual."

CHAPTER IV

SUSPICIOUS HOSTS

WE awoke bright and early the next morning, much refreshed by our day of rest and variety. With an early start we were soon pulling down the river, and noon found us several miles below the camp, having run eleven rapids with no particular difficulty. A reference in my notes reads: "Last one has a thousand rocks, and we could not miss them all. My rowing is improving, and we both got through fairly well." In the afternoon they continued to come — an endless succession of small rapids, with here and there a larger one. The canyon was similar to that at our camp above, dark red walls with occasional pines on the ledges, — a most charming combination of colour. At 2.30 P.M. we reached Ashley Falls, a rapid we had been expecting to see for some time. It was a place of singular beauty. A dozen immense rocks had fallen from the cliff on the left, almost completely blocking the channel — or so it seemed from one point of view. But there was a crooked channel, not more than twelve

36

Copyright by Kolb Bros

"IMMENSE ROCKS HAD FALLEN FROM THE CLIFF."

feet wide in places, through which the water shot like a stream from a nozzle.

We wanted a motion picture of our dash through the chute. But the location for the camera was hard to secure, for a sheer bank of rock or low wall prevented us from climbing out on the right side. We overcame this by landing on a little bank at the base of the wall and by dropping a boat down with a line to the head of the rapid, where a break occurred in the wall. Jimmy was left with the camera, the boat was pulled back, and we prepared to run the rapid.

We first had to pass between two square rocks rising eight feet above the water so close together that we could not use the oars; then, when past these, pull ten feet to the right in order to clear the large rock at the end of the main dam, or barrier, not more than twenty feet below. To pull down bow first and try to make the turn, would mean to smash broadside against this rock. It could only be done by dropping stern first, and pulling to the right under the protection of the first rocks; though it was doubtful if even this could be accomplished, the current was so swift. The *Defiance* was ready first, the *Edith* was to follow as closely as safety allowed.

Almost before I knew it I was in the narrow channel, so close to the right rock that I had to ship that oar, and pull altogether on the left one. As soon as I was through I made a few quick strokes, but the current was too strong for me; and a corner of the stern struck with a bang when I was almost clear. She paused as a wave rolled over the decks, then rose quickly; a side current caught the boat, whirling it around, and the bow struck. I was still pulling with all my might, but everything happened so quickly, — with the boat whirling first this way, then that, — that my efforts were almost useless. But after that second strike I did get in a few strokes, and pulled into the quiet pool below the line of boulders.

Emery held his boat in better position than I had done, and it looked for a while as if he would make it. But the *Edith* struck on the stern, much as mine had done. Then he pulled clear and joined me in the shelter of the large rock, as cool and smiling as if he had been rowing on a mill-pond. We were delighted to find that our boats had suffered no damage from the blows they had received. Striking on the ends as they did, the shock was distributed throughout the whole boat.

This completed our run for that day, and we went into camp just below the "Falls." Emery painted the name *Edith* on the bow of his boat, at this camp. The name was given in honour of his four-year-old daughter, waiting for us at the Grand Canyon. I remarked that as no one loved me, I would name my boat the *Defiance*. But I hesitated about putting this name on the bow. I would look rather foolish, I thought, if the *Defiance* should be wrecked in the first bad rapid.

So the christening of my boat was left until such time as she should have earned the title, although she was constantly referred to as the *Defiance*.

We remained until noon of the following day at Ashley Falls, exploring, repairing, and photographing this picturesque spot. The canyon walls here dropped down to beautiful, rolling foot-hills eight or nine hundred feet high, tree covered as before but more open. The diversity of rocks and hills was alluring. There was work to be done and no pleasanter spot could be found in which to do it. Among other things that had to be looked after were some adjustments to the motion-picture camera — usually referred to by us as the M. P. C. — this delicate work always falling to Emery, for he alone could do it.

There was much to interest us here. Major Powell reported finding the name "Ashley" painted under an overhanging rock on the left side of the river. Underneath was a date, rather indistinct, but found to have been 1825, by Dellenbaugh, after carefully tracing the career of Colonel Ashley who was responsible for the record. Accompanied by a number of trappers, he made the passage through this canyon at that early day. We found a trace of the record. There were three letters — A-s-h — the first two quite distinct, and underneath were two black spots. It must have been pretty good paint to leave a trace after eighty-six years !

Resuming our journey we passed into deep canyon again, — the deepest we had found up to this time, — with steeply sloping, verdure-covered walls about 2700 feet high. The rapids still continued. At one rapid the remark was made that "Two feet of water would cover two hundred rocks so that our boats would pass over them." But we did not have the two feet needed.

We had previously been informed that some of these mountains were the hiding-places of men who were "wanted" in the three states which bordered near here. Some escaping prisoners had also been traced to the mountains in this direction; then all tracks had ceased. The few peaceable ranchers who lived in these mountains were much alarmed over these reports. We found one such rancher on the plateau above the canyon, whom we will call Johnson for convenience, — living in one of the upper canyons. He sold us some provisions. In return he asked us to help him swim some of his horses across the river. He said the high water had taken out his own boat. The horses were rounded up in a mountain-hidden valley and driven into the water ahead of the boat. After securing the horses, Johnson's welcome seemed to turn to suspicion and he questioned our reasons for being there, wanting to know what we could find in that wild country to interest us. Johnson's sons, of whom there were several, seemed to put in most of their time at hunting and trapping, never leaving the house without a gun.

Copyright by Kolb Bros

THE ROCKS WERE DARK RED: OCCASIONAL PINES GREW ON THE LEDGES, MAKING
A CHARMING COMBINATION OF COLOUR.

The cabin home looked like an arsenal, revolvers and guns hanging on all the walls — even his daughters being familiar with their use. Although we had been very well treated after all, Mrs. Johnson especially having been very kind to us, we felt just a little relieved when the Johnson ranch was left behind. We use, in fact, a fictitious name, not caring to visit on them the suspicions we ourselves felt in return.

Another morning passed in repairing the M. P. camera, and another afternoon's work was necessary to get us out of the walls and the rapids of Red Canyon. But on the evening of the 20th, we did get out, and pulled into an open country known as Brown's Park, one week after entering Flaming Gorge. It had not been very fast travelling; but we were through, and with no mishap more serious than a split board on the side of my boat. Under favourable conditions, and in experienced hands, this distance might have been covered in three days. But meanwhile, we were gaining a lot of experience.

About the lower end of Red Canyon the river turned directly east, paralleling the northern boundary of Utah, and continued to flow in this general direction until it crossed into Colorado.

On emerging from Red Canyon we spied a ranch house or log cabin close to the river. The doors were open and there were many tracks in the sand, so we thought some one must be about. On approaching the house, however, we found the place was deserted, but with furniture, books, and pictures piled on the floor in the utmost confusion, as if the occupants had left in a great hurry. This surmise afterward proved to be correct; for we learned that the rancher had been murdered for his money, his body having been found in a boat farther down the river. Suspicion pointed to an old employee who had been seen lurking near the place. He was traced to the railroad, over a hundred miles to the north; but made his escape and was never caught.

We found Brown's Park, once known as Brown's Hole, to be a beautiful valley several miles in width, and thirty-five or forty miles in length. The upper end of the valley was rugged in places, with rocky hills two or three hundred feet high. To the south, a few miles away, were the mountains, a continuation of those we had come through. We saw many cattle scattered over some of these rocky hills, grazing on the bunch-grass. At one place our course led us through a little canyon about two miles long, and scarcely more than two hundred feet deep. This was Swallow Canyon — a name suggested by the many birds of that species which had covered the canyon's walls with their little clay nests. The openings of some of these nests were so small that it scarcely seemed possible for a bird to enter.

The water was deep and quiet in this short canyon, and a hard wind blowing up the stream made it difficult for us to gain any headway. In this case, too, the forms of the boat were against us. With the keel removed and with their high sides catching the wind, they were carried back and forth like small balloons. Well, we could put up with it for a while, for those very features would prove most valuable in the rough-water canyons which were to follow!

Emerging from the canyon at last, we saw a ferry loaded with sheep crossing the stream. On the left shore was a large corral, also filled with sheep which a half dozen men were driving back and forth into different compartments. Later these men told us there were 2400 sheep in the flock. We took their word for it, making no attempt to count them. The foreman of the ranch agreed to sell us some sugar and honey, — these two articles being a welcome addition to our list of supplies, which were beginning to show the effects of our voracious appetites.

We found many other log cabins and ranches as we proceeded. Some of them were deserted; at others men were busily engaged in cutting hay or the wild grass that grew in the bottoms. The fragrance of new-mown hay was in the air. Young boys and women were among these busy workers, some of the women being seated on large harvesters, handling the horses with as much dexterity as any of the men.

The entire trip through this pretty valley was full

of interest. We were hailed from the shore by some of the hay ranchers, it being a novel sight to them to see a river expedition. At one or two of these places we asked the reason for the deserted ranches above, and were given evasive answers. Finally we were told that cattle rustlers from the mountains made it so hard for the ranchers in the valleys that there was nothing for them to do but get out. They told us, also, that we were fortunate to get away from Johnson's ranch with our valuables! Our former host, we were told, had committed many depredations and had served one term for cattle stealing. Officers, disguised as prospectors, had taken employment with him and helped him kill and skin some cattle; the skins, with their telltale brands, having been partially burned and buried. On this evidence he was afterwards convicted.

Our cool welcome by the Johnsons, their suspicions of us, the sinister arsenal of guns and pistols, all was explained! Quite likely some of these weapons had been trained against us by the trappers on the chance that we were either officers of the law, or competitors in the horse-stealing industry. For that matter we were actually guilty of the latter count, for come to think of it, we ourselves had helped them steal eight horses and a colt!

The entire trip through this pretty valley was full of interest. It was all so different from anything seen above.

There were great bottoms that gave evidence of having recently been overflooded, though now covered with cottonwood trees, gorgeous in their autumn foliage. We had often wondered where all the driftwood that floated down the Colorado came from; but after seeing those unnumbered acres of cottonwoods we ceased to wonder.

There were many beaver slides on the banks; and in places, numberless trees had been felled by these industrious animals. On one or two occasions we narrowly escaped splitting the sides of our boats on snags of trees which the beavers had buried in the bottom of the stream. We saw no beaver dams on the river; they were not necessary, for deep, quiet pools existed everywhere in Brown's Park. We saw two beavers in this section. One of these rose, porpoise-like, to the top of the water, stared at us a moment, then brought his tail down with a resounding smack on the top of the water, and disappeared, to enter his home by the subterranean route, no doubt.

The river was gradually losing its clear colour, for the sand-bars were beginning to "work out," or break, making the water quite roily. In some sections of Brown's Park we grounded on these sand-bars, making it necessary for us to get out into the water, pushing and pulling on the boats until deeper water was reached. Sometimes the deep water came when least expected, the sand-bars having a disconcerting way of dropping off abruptly on the downstream side. Jimmy stepped off the edge of one of these hidden ledges while working with a boat, and was for some time in no condition to appreciate our ill-concealed mirth.

Often we would be passing along on perfectly smooth water, when suddenly a turmoil would rise all about us, as though a geyser had broken out below the surface. If we happened to be directly over it, the boat would be rocked back and forth for a while; then all would be peaceful again. This was most often caused by the ledges of sand, anywhere from three to ten feet high, breaking down or falling forward as their bases were undermined. In a single night a bar of this kind will work upstream for a distance of several feet; then the sand will be carried down with the current to lodge again in some quiet pool, and again be carried on as before. This action gives rise to long lines of regular waves or swells extending for some distance down the stream. These are usually referred to as sand-waves. These waves increase in size in high water; and the monotonous thump, thump of the boat's bottom upon them is anything but pleasant, especially if one is trying to make fast time.

So, with something new at every turn, we pulled lazily through Brown's Park, shooting at ducks and geese when we came near them, snapping our cameras when a picture presented itself, and observing the animal life along the stream.

We stopped at one hay-ranch close to the Utah-Colorado line and chatted awhile with the workers. A pleasant-faced woman named Mrs. Chew asked us to deliver a message at a ranch a mile or two below. Here also was the post-office of Lodore, Colorado, located a short distance above the canyon of the same name. Mrs. Chew informed us that they had another ranch at the lower end of Lodore Canyon and asked us to look them up when we got through, remarking:

"You may have trouble, you know. Two of my sons once tried it. They lost their boat, had to climb out, and nearly starved before they reached home."

The post-office at the ranch, found as described, without another home in sight, was a welcome sight to us for several reasons. One reason was that it afforded shelter from a heavy downpour of rain that greeted us as we neared it, and a better reason still was, that it gave us a chance to write and mail some letters to those who would be most anxious to hear from us.

Among the messages we mailed was a picture post-card of Coney Island at night. In some way this card had slipped between the leaves of a book that I had brought from the East. I sent it out, addressed to a friend who would understand the joke; writing underneath the picture, "We have an abundance of such scenery here." The young woman who had charge of the office looked at the card in amazement. It was evidently something new to her. She told us she had never been to the railroad, and that her brother took the mail out on horseback to Steamboat, Colorado, 140 miles distant.

The rain having ceased, we returned to our boats, pausing to admire a rainbow that arched above the canyon in the mountains, toward which we were headed. We remarked, jokingly, to Jimmy that this was a good sign. He replied without smiling that he "hoped so." Jimmy's songs had long since ceased, and we suspected him of homesickness. With the exception of a short visit to some friends on a large ranch, Jimmy had never been away from his home in San Francisco. This present experience was quite a contrast, to be sure! We did what we could to keep him cheered up, but with little success. Jimmy had intimated that he would prefer to leave at the first opportunity to reach a railroad, and we willingly agreed to help him in every possible way. Emery and I also agreed between ourselves that we would not take any unnecessary risks with him; but would leave him out of the boats at all rapids, if there was any passage around them.

The river had taken a sharp turn to the south soon after passing the post-office, heading directly towards the mountains. Camp was pitched just above the mouth of Lodore. This twenty-mile canyon bears a very unsavory reputation, having a descent of 425 feet in that short distance, the greater part of the fall occurring

Copyright by Kolb Bros.

"WE STOPPED AT ONE HAY RANCH CLOSE TO THE UTAH–COLORADO LINE."

in a space of twelve miles. This would mean wild water somewhere!

We were camped on a spot recently occupied by some engineers of the United States Conservation Department, who had been trying to determine if it was feasible to dam the river at this place. The plan was to flood the whole of Brown's Park and divert the water through the mountains by a tunnel to land suitable for cultivation, and in addition, allow the muddy water to settle and so prevent the vast amount of silt from being washed on down, eventually to the mouth of the Colorado. The location seemed admirably suited for this stupendous project. But holes drilled beside the river failed to find bottom, as nothing but quicksand existed even at a depth of nearly three hundred feet; and without a strong foundation, such a dam would be utterly useless.

E

CHAPTER V

CAMP routine was hurriedly disposed of the next morning, Saturday, September the 23d. Everything was made snug beneath the hatches, except the two guns, which were too long to go under the decks, and had to be carried in the open cockpits. "Camp No. 13, at the head of Lodore," as it is entered in my journal, was soon hidden by a bend in the river. The open, sun-lit country, with its pleasant ranches and its grazing cattle, its rolling, gray, sage-covered hills and its wild grass and cottonwood-covered bottoms, was left behind, and we were back in the realm of the rock-walled canyon, and beetle-browed, frowning cliffs with pines and cedars clutching at the scanty ledges.

We paused long enough to make a picture or two, with the hope that the photographic record would give to others some idea of the geological and scenic wonder — said to be the greatest known example of its kind — which lay before us. Here is an obstructing mountain raised directly in the river's path. Yet with no deviation

Copyright by Kolb Bros.

REMARKABLE ENTRANCE TO LODORE CANYON.

whatever the stream has cut through the very centre of the peak! The walls are almost sheer, especially at the bottom, and are quite close together at the top. A mile inside, the mountain on the left or east side of the gorge is 2700 feet high. Geologists say that the river was here first, and that the mountain was slowly raised in its pathway — so slowly that the river could saw away and maintain its old channel. The quicksand found below the present level would seem to indicate that the walls were once even higher than at present, and that a subsidence had taken place after the cutting.

The river at the entrance of this rock-walled canyon was nothing alarming, four small rapids being passed without event. Then a fifth was reached that looked worse. The *Edith* was lined down. This was hard work, and dangerous too, owing to the strength of the current and the many rocks; so I concluded that my own boat, the *Defiance*, must run the rapid. Jimmy went below, with a life-preserver on a rope. Emery stood beside the rapid with a camera and made a picture as I shot past him. Fortunately I got through without mishap. I refused to upset even to please my brother.

We were beginning to think that Lodore was not so bad after all. Rapid followed rapid in quick succession, and all were run without trouble; then we came to a large one. It was Upper Disaster Falls; so named by Major Powell, for it was here that one of his boats was wrecked on his first voyage of exploration. This boat failed to make the landing above the rapid and was carried over. She struck a rock broadside, turned around and struck again, breaking the boat completely in two. This boat was built of $\frac{3}{4}$-inch oak reënforced with bulkheads. When this fact is taken into consideration, some idea may be had of the great power of these rapids. The three men who occupied the boat saved themselves by reaching an island a short distance below.

This all happened on a stage of water much higher than the present one, so we did not let the occurrence influence us one way or the other, except to make us careful to land above the rapid. We found a very narrow channel between two submerged boulders, the water plunging and foaming for a short distance below, over many hidden rocks. Still, there was only one large rock near the lower end that we greatly feared, and by careful work that might be avoided.

The *Edith* went first and grazed the boulder slightly, but no harm was done as E. C. held his boat well in hand. I followed, and struck rocks at the same instant on both sides of the narrow channel with my oars. It will be remembered that we ran all these dangerous rapids facing downstream. The effect of this was to shoot the ends of both oars up past my face. The operator said that I made a grimace just as he took a picture of the scrimmage.

We landed on the island below and talked of camping there for the night, as it was getting late; but the island was so rocky and inhospitable that we concluded to try the lower part of the rapid. This had no descent like the upper end; but it was very shallow, and we soon found ourselves on rocks, unable to proceed any farther. It took an hour of hard labour to work our heavy boats safely to the shore.

We had been hoping for a rest the next day — Sunday — but the island was such a disagreeable place to camp that it seemed necessary to cross to the mainland at least. A coil of strong, pliable wire had been included in our material. Here was a chance to use it to advantage. The stream on the left side of the island could be waded, although it was very swift; and we managed to get the wire across and well fastened at both ends. Elevating the wire above the water with cross-sticks, our tent and camp material were run across on a pulley, and camp was pitched a hundred yards below, on the left shore of the river.

There were fitful showers in the afternoon, and we rested from our labour, obtaining a great deal of comfort from our tent, which was put up here for the third time since leaving Green River City. Always, when the weather was clear, we slept in the open.

Monday, the 25th, found us at the same camp. Having concluded that Disaster Falls was an ideal place for a moving picture, we sent the balance of the material across on the pulley and wire, making a picture of the operation; stopping often because it continued to shower. Between showers we resumed our work and picture making.

The picture was to have been concluded with the operation of lining the boat across. E. C. stood on the shore about sixty feet away, working with the camera; Jimmy was on the island, paying out the rope; while I waded in the water, holding the bow of the boat as I worked her between the rocks. Having reached the end of the rope, I coiled it up, advising Jimmy to go up to a safe crossing and join my brother while I proceeded with the boat. All was going well, and I was nearing the shore, when I found myself suddenly carried off my feet into water beyond my depth, and drifting for the lower end of the rapid. Meanwhile I was holding to the bow of the boat, and calling lustily to my brother to save me. At first he did not notice that anything was wrong, as he was looking intently through the finder. Then he suddenly awoke to the fact that something was amiss, and came running down the boulder-strewn shore, but he could not help me, as we had neglected to leave a rope with him. Things were beginning to look pretty serious, when the boat stopped against a rock and I found myself once more with solid footing under me. It was too good a picture to miss; and I found the operator at the machine, turning the crank as I climbed out.

We developed some films and plates that evening, securing some satisfactory results from these tests. It continued to rain all that night, with intermittent showers the next morning. The rain made little difference to us, for we were in the water much of the following day as the boats were taken along the edge of another unrunnable rapid, a good companion rapid for the one just passed.

This was Lower Disaster Falls, the first of many similar rapids we were to see, but this was one of the worst of its kind. The swift-rushing river found its channel blocked by the canyon wall on the right side, the cliff running at right angles to the course of the stream. The river, attacking the limestones, had cut a channel under the wall, then turned and ran with the wall, emerging about two hundred feet below. Standing on a rock and holding one end of a twenty-five foot string we threw a stone attached to the other end across to the opposite wall. The overhanging wall was within two feet of the rushing river; a higher stage of water would hide the cut completely from view. Think what would happen if a boat were carried against or under that wall! We thought of it many times as we carefully worked our boats along the shore.

Between the delays of rain, with stops for picture making, portaging our material, and "lining" our boats, we spent almost three days in getting past the rapids called Upper and Lower Disaster Falls, with their combined fall of 50 feet in little more than half a mile. On the evening of September the 26th we camped almost within sight of this same place, at the base of a 3000-foot sugarloaf mountain on the right, tree-covered from top to bottom.

Things were going too easily for us, it seemed; but we were in for a few reverses. It stormed much of the night and still drizzled when we embarked on the following morning. The narrow canyon was gloomy and darkened with shreds of clouds drifting far below the rim. The first rapid was narrow, and contained some large boulders. The *Edith* was caught on one of these and turned on her side, so that the water flowed in, filling the cockpit. The boat was taken off without difficulty, and bailed out. We found that the bulkheads failed to keep the water out of the hatches. Some material from the *Edith* was transferred to the *Defiance*. A bed, in a protecting sack of rubber and canvas, was shoved under the seat and we proceeded.

Less than an hour later I repeated my brother's performance, but I was not so fortunate as he. The *Defiance* was carried against one rock as I tried to pull clear of another, and in an instant she was on her side, held by the rush of water. I caught the gunwale, and, climbing on to the rock that caused the disaster, I managed to catch the rope and held the boat. In the meantime Emery was in a whirlpool below, trying to

Copyright by Kolb Bros.

"EVERYTHING WAS WET."

Copyright by Kolb Bros.

"THE RIVER CUT A CHANNEL UNDER THE WALLS" AT
LOWER DISASTER FALLS.

land on the right side; but was having a difficult
time of it. Jimmy stood on the shore unable to
help. The bed was washed out of the boat and went
bobbing over the waves, then before I knew what had
happened, the rope was jerked from my hands and I was
left stranded on my rock. Seeing this, Jimmy ran with
all his might for a pool at the end of the rapid, bravely
rescuing the boat and the bed as well, just as the *Edith*
was landed. A rope was soon thrown to me, after the
inevitable picture was made. Then I jumped and was
pulled to shore.

On making an inventory we found that our guns were
lost from the boat. Being too long to go under the
hatches, they had been left in the cockpit. The *Defiance* had an ugly rap on the bottom, where she
struck a rock, the wood being smashed or jammed, but not
broken out. Nearly all material in the two boats was wet,
so we took everything out and piled it on a piece of canvas, spread out on the sand. We worked rapidly, for
another storm had been threatening all the morning.

We were engaged in putting up our little tent when
a violent wind which swept up the canyon, followed
by a downpour of rain interrupted our work; and if
anything missed a soaking before, it certainly received
it then. The sand was beaten into our cameras and
everything was scattered helter-skelter over the shore.
We were fortunate in only one respect. The wind was

away from the river instead of toward it. We finally got the tent up, then threw everything into it in an indiscriminate pile, and waited for the storm to pass. Emery proposed that we do a song and dance just to show how good we felt; but any appearance of merriment was rather forced.

Had the builders of the boats been there, we fear they would have had an uncomfortable half-hour; for nearly all this loss could have been avoided had our instructions regarding the hatch covers been followed. And for the sake of their saving a few dollars we had to suffer!

The rain soon passed and we went to work, first starting a fire and getting a hurried lunch, for we had not eaten our noon meal, and it was then 4 P.M. We put up our dark-room tent, then went to work to find what was saved, and what was lost. We were surprised to find that all our small films and plates had escaped a soaking. Protected in tin and cardboard boxes, wrapped with adhesive tape, and covered with a coating of paraffine melted and poured over them, they had turned the water in nearly every instance. The motion-picture film was not so fortunate. The paraffine had worn off the tin boxes in spots, the water soaked through the tape in some instances, and entered to the film. One roll, tightly wrapped, became wet on the edges; the gelatine swelled and stuck to the other film, thus sealing the inner portion or picture part of the film, so that roll was saved.

The motion-picture camera was filled with water, mud, and sand; and the other cameras fared likewise. We cleaned them out as best we could, drying them over a small alcohol lamp which we had included in our duffle. Our job seemed endless. Jimmy had retired early, for he could help us but little in this work. It rained again in torrents, and the wind howled about the tent. After midnight, as we still toiled, a land-slide, loosened by the soaking rains, thundered down the mountain side about a fourth of a mile below our camp. We hoped Jimmy would not hear it. We retired soon after this. Smaller slides followed at intervals, descending over the 3000-foot precipices. Thunder reverberated through the canyon, and altogether it was a night long to be remembered. These slides made one feel a little uncomfortable. "It would be most inconvenient," as we have heard some one say, "to wake in the morning and find ourselves wrapped up in a few tons of earth and rock."

Emery woke me the next morning to report that the river had risen about six feet; and that my boat — rolled out on the sand but left untied — was just on the point of going out with the water. It had proven fortunate for us all Emery was a light sleeper! There was no travelling this day, as the boat had to be repaired. Emery, being the ship's carpenter, set to work at once, while Jimmy and I stretched our ropes back and forth, and hung up the wet clothes. Then we built a number of fires underneath and soon had our belongings in a steam. Things were beginning to look cheerful again. The rain stopped, too, for a time at least.

A little later Jimmy ran into camp with a fish which he had caught with his hands. It was of the kind commonly called the bony-tail or humpback or buffalo-fish, a peculiar species found in many of the rivers of the Southwest. It is distinguished by a small flat head, with a hump directly behind it; the end of the body being round, very slender, and equipped with large tail-fins. This specimen was about sixteen inches long, the usual length for a full-grown fish of this species.

Now for a fish story! On going down to the river we found a great many fish swimming in a small whirl-pool, evidently trying to escape from the thick, slimy mud which was carried in the water. In a half-hour we secured fourteen fish, killing most of them with our oars. There were suckers and one catfish in the lot. You can judge for yourself how thick the water was, that such mudfishes as these should have been choked to helplessness. Our captured fish were given a bath in a bucket of rain-water, and we had a fish dinner.

In the afternoon we made a test of the water from the river, and found that it contained 20 per cent of an alkaline silt. When we had to use this water, we bruised the leaf of a prickly pear cactus, and placed it in a bucket of water. This method, repeated two or three times, usually clears the muddiest water. We also dug holes in the sand at the side of the river. The water, filtering through the sand, was often clear enough to develop the tests we made with our films.

Jimmy continued to feel downhearted; and this afternoon he told us his story. Our surmise about his being homesick was correct, but it was a little more than that. He had an invalid mother, it seemed, and, aided by an older brother, he had always looked after the needs of the family. When the proposition of making the river trip came up, serious objections were raised by the family; but when the transportation arrived he had determined to go, in spite of their objections. Now he feared that his mother would not live, or that we would be wrecked, and he would not know where to turn, or what to do. No wonder he felt blue!

All we could do was to promise to help him leave the river at the very first opportunity. This would quite likely be at Jensen, Utah, still fifty miles farther downstream.

It continued to rain by spells that night and the next morning. About 11 A.M. we resumed our work on the river. A short distance below our camp we saw the land-slide which we heard the night before — tons of earth and shattered rock wrapped about the split and stripped trunks of a half-dozen pines. The slide was started by the dislodged section of a sheer wall close to the top of the 2700-foot cliff. We also saw a boat of crude construction, pulled above the high-water mark; evidently abandoned a great while before. Any person who had to climb the walls at that place had a hard job to tackle, although we could pick out breaks where it looked feasible; there were a few places behind us where it would be next to impossible. We had only gone over a few rapids when we found a long pool, with driftwood eddying upstream, and knew that our run for the day was over — the Triplet Rapids were ahead of us. We found this rapid to be about a fourth of a mile long, divided into three sections as its name indicated, and filled with great boulders at the base of a sheer cliff on the right — another unrunnable rapid.

Taking the camp material from the boats, we carried it down and pitched our tent first of all, then, while Emery prepared supper, Jimmy and I carried the remaining duffle down to camp. One of the boats was lined down also. Then after supper we enjoyed the first rest we had taken for some time.

Camp Ideal we called it, and it well deserved the name. At the bottom of a tree-covered precipice reaching a height of 2700 feet, was a strip of firm, level sand, tapering off with a slope down to the water, making a perfect landing and dooryard. A great mass of driftwood, piled up at the end of the rapid, furnished us with all the fuel we needed with small effort on our part. Our tent was backed against a large rock, while other flat rocks near at hand made convenient shelves on which to lay our camp dishes and kettles. It started to drizzle again that night, but what cared we? With a roaring fire in front of the tent we all cleaned up for a change, sewed patches on our tattered garments, and, sitting on our beds, wrote the day's happenings in our journals. Then we crawled into our comfortable beds, and I was soon dreaming of my boyhood days when I "played hookey" from school and went fishing in a creek that emptied into the Allegheny River, or climbed its rocky banks; to be awakened by Jimmy crying out in his sleep,

"There she goes over the rapids."

Jimmy was soon informed that he and the boats were perfectly safe, and I was brought back to a realization of the fact that I was not going to get a "whaling" for going swimming in dog-days; but instead was holed up in Lodore Canyon, in the extreme northwestern corner of Colorado.

CHAPTER VI

WE began our work the next morning where we left off the night before by bringing the remaining boat down along the edge of the "Triplets." Then, while Emery cooked the breakfast, Jimmy and I "broke camp." The beds came first. The air had been released from the mattresses before we got up, — one way of saving time. A change of dry clothing was placed with each bed, and they were rolled as tightly as the two of us could do it, after which they were strapped, placed in a rubber sack, with a canvas sack over that, both these sacks being laced at the top. The tent — one of those so-called balloon silk compositions — made a very small roll; the dark-room tent, with its three plies of cloth, made the largest bundle of the lot. Everything had been taken from the boats, and made quite a pile of dunnage, when it was all collected in a pile ready for loading. After the dishes were washed they were packed in a box, the smoke-covered pots and pans being placed in a sack. Everything was sorted and piled before the loading

Copyright by Kolb Bros.

"THE CANYON WAS GLOOMY, AND DARKENED WITH SHREDS OF CLOUDS."

commenced. An equal division of nearly everything was made, so that the loss of one boat and its cargo would only partially cripple the expedition. The photographic plates and films, in protecting canvas sacks, were first disposed of, being stored in the tin-lined hatches in the bow of the boats. Two of the smaller rolls containing bedding, or clothing; a sack of flour, and half of the cameras completed the loads for the forward compartments. Five or six tin and wooden boxes, filled with provisions, went into the large compartments under the stern. A box containing tools and hardware for the inevitable repairs, and the weightier provisions — such as canned milk and canned meats — went in first. This served as ballast for the boats. Then the other provisions followed, the remaining rolls of bedding and tents being squeezed in on top. This compartment, with careful packing, would hold as much as two ordinary-sized trunks, but squeezing it all in through the small hatchway, or opening on top, was not an easy job. One thing we guarded very carefully from this time on was a waterproofed sack containing sugar. The muddy water had entered the top of this sack in our upset, and a liquefied sugar, or brown-coloured syrup, was used in our coffee and on our breakfast foods after that. It gradually dried out, and our emptied cups would contain a sediment of mud in the bottom.

Such was our morning routine, although it was not

F

often that everything was taken from the boats, and it only happened in this case because we made a portage the night before.

Our work was all undone an hour later, when we came to the sharp descent known as Hell's Half Mile. A section of a cliff had fallen from above, and was shattered into a hundred fragments, large and small; gigantic rocks were scattered on both shores and through the river bed, not an orderly array of rocks such as that found at Ashley Falls, but a riotous mass, looking as though they had been hurled from the sky above. The stripped trunk of an eight-foot tree, with roots extending over the river, had been deposited by a recent flood on top of the principal barrier. All this was found about fifty yards below the beginning of the most violent descent in Lodore Canyon. It would have been difficult enough without this last complication; the barrier seemed next to insurmountable, tired and handicapped with heavy boats as we were.

With a weary sigh we dropped our boats to the head of the rapid and prepared to make the portage. Our previous work was as nothing to this. Rounded limestone boulders, hard as flint and covered with a thin slime of mud from the recent rise, caused us to slip and fall many times. Then we dragged ourselves and loads up the sloping walls. They were cut with gullies from the recent rains; low scraggy cedars caught at our loads, or tore our clothes, as we staggered along; the muddy earth stuck to our shoes, or caused our feet to slip from under us as we climbed, first two or three hundred feet above the water, then close to the river's edge. Three-fourths of a mile of such work brought us to a level place below the rapid. It took nine loads to empty one boat.

Darkness came on before our boats were emptied, so they were securely tied in quiet water at the head of the rapid, and left for the morning.

The next day found Emery and me at work on the boats, while Jimmy was stationed on the shore with the motion-picture camera. This wild scene, with its score of shooting currents, was too good a view to miss. With life-preservers inflated and adjusted, Emery sat in the boat at the oars, pulling against the current, lessening the velocity with which the boat was carried down toward the main barrier, while I followed on the shore, holding a rope, and dropped him down, a little at a time, until the water became too rough and the rocks too numerous. All directions were given with signals; the human voice was of little avail in the turmoil. We kept the boats in the water as long as it was safe to do so, for it greatly lessened the hard work of a portage. With one end of the boat floating on the water, an ordinary lift would take the other end over a rock with insufficient water above it to float the boat. Then the boat was balanced on the rock, the opposite end was lifted, she was shoved forward and dropped in the water again, and another threatening rock was passed. Foot by foot we fought our way, now on the shore, now waist deep in the water below some protecting boulder, threatened every moment by the whirling water that struggled to drag us into the torrent. The sand and water collecting in our clothes weighted us down; the chill of standing in the cold water numbed our limbs. Finally the barrier was reached and the boats were run out close to the end, and tied in a quiet pool, while we devised some method of getting them past or over this obstruction.

Directly underneath and beyond the roots of the tree were large rounded boulders, covered with slippery mud. Past this barrier the full force of the water raced, to hurl itself and divide its current against another rock. It was useless to try to take a boat around the end of the rock. The boat's sides, three-eighths of an inch thick, would be crushed like a cardboard box. If lifted into the V-shaped groove, the weight of the boats would wedge them and crush their sides. Fortunately an upright log was found tightly wedged between these boulders. A strong limb, with one end resting on a rock opposite, was nailed to this log; a triangle of stout sticks, with the point down, was placed opposite this first limb, on the same level, and was fastened to the upright log with still another piece; and another difficulty was overcome.

Copyright by Kolb Bros.

"AN UPRIGHT LOG WAS FOUND WEDGED BETWEEN THE BOULDERS."

Copyright by Kolb Bros.

"IT TOOK NINE LOADS TO EMPTY ONE BOAT."

With a short rope fastened to the iron bar or hand-hold on the stern, this end was lifted on to the cross-piece, the bow sticking into the water at a sharp angle. The short rope was tied to the stump, so we would not lose what we had gained. The longer rope from the bow was thrown over the roots of the tree above, then we both pulled on the rope, until finally the bow was on a level with the stern. She was pulled forward, the ropes were loosened and the boat rested on the cross-pieces. The motion-picture camera was transferred so as to command a view of the lower side of the barrier, then the boat was carefully tilted, and slid forward, a little at a time, until she finally gained headway, nearly jerking the rope from our hands, and shot into the pool below.

We enjoyed the wildest ride we had experienced up to this time in running the lower end of this rapid. The balance of the day was spent in the same camp below the rapid. Our tent was put up in a group of box elder trees, — the first trees of this species we had seen. Red cedar trees dotted the rocky slopes, while the larger pines became scarce at the river's edge, and gathered near the top of the canyon's walls. The dark red rocks near the bottom were covered with a light blue-tinted stratum of limestone, similar to the fallen rocks found in the rapid above. In one land-slide, evidently struck with some rolling rock, lay the body of a small deer. We saw many mountain sheep tracks, but failed to see the sheep. Many dead fish, their gills filled with the slimy mud from the recent rise, floated past us, or lay half buried in the mud. These things were noticed as we went about our duties, for we were too weary to do any exploring.

The next morning, Monday, October the 2d, saw us making arrangements for the final run that would take us out of Lodore Canyon. No doubt it was a beautiful and a wonderful place, but none of us seemed sorry to leave it behind. For ten days we had not had a single day entirely free from rain, and instead of having a chance to run rapids, it seemed as if we had spent an entire week in carrying our loads, or in lining our boats through the canyon. The canyon walls lost much of their precipitous character as we neared the end of the canyon.

A short run took us over the few rapids that remained, and at a turn ahead we saw a 300-foot ridge, brilliantly tinted in many colours, — light and golden yellows, orange and red, purple and lavender, — and composed of numberless wafer-like layers of rock, uptilted, so that the broken ends looked like the spines of a gigantic fish's back. A sharp turn to the left soon brought us to the end of this ridge, close to the bottom of a smooth, sheer wall. Across a wide, level point of sand we could see a large stream, the Yampa River, flowing from the East to join its waters with those of the Green. This was the end of Lodore Canyon.

CHAPTER VII

JIMMY GOES OVER THE MOUNTAIN

THE Yampa, or Bear River, was a welcome sight to us in spite of its disagreeable whitish yellow, clay colour; quite different from the red water of the Green River. The new stream meant more water in the channel, something we needed badly, as our past tribulations showed. The recent rise on the Green had subsided a little, but we now had a much higher stage than when we entered Lodore. Quite likely the new conditions gave us six feet of water above the low water on which we had been travelling. Would it increase or diminish our dangers? We were willing, Emery and I, even anxious, to risk our chances on the higher water.

Directly opposite the Yampa, the right shore of the Green went up sheer about 700 feet high, indeed it seemed to overhang a trifle. This had been named Echo Cliffs by Powell's party. The cliffs gave a remarkable echo, repeating seven words plainly when shouted from the edge of the Yampa a hundred yards away, and would doubtless repeat more if shouted from the farther shore of the Yampa. Echo Cliffs, we found, were in the form of a peninsula and terminated just below this point where we stood, the river doubling back on the other side of the cliff. On the left side of the river, the walls fell back, leaving a flat, level space of about twenty-five acres. Here was a little ranch of which Mrs. Chew had told us. The Chew ranch lay back from the river on top of the cliffs. We found no one at home here at this first ranch, but there was evidence of recent habitation. There were a few peach trees, and a small garden, while beyond this were two buildings, — little shacks in a dilapidated condition. The doors were off their hinges and leaned against the building, a few logs being placed against the doors. Past the dooryard, coming out of a small canyon above the ranch, ran a little brook; up this canyon was a trail, the outlet to the ranch above. We camped near the mouth of the stream.

It had been agreed upon the night before, that we should endeavour to make arrangements to have Jimmy taken out on horseback over the mountains. Before looking for the ranch, however, we asked him if he did not wish to reconsider his decision to leave here. We pointed out that Jensen, Utah, was only fifty miles away, half that distance being in quiet water, and that the worst canyon was behind us. But he said he had enough of the river, and preferred to see what could be done. While I busied myself about camp, he and Emery left for the ranch.

About seven o'clock that evening they returned in great spirits. They had found the ranch without any trouble, nearly three miles from our camp. Mrs. Chew was there and gave them a hearty welcome. She had often wondered what had become of us. She invited the boys to remain for supper, which they did. They talked over the matter of transportation for Jimmy. As luck would have it, Mrs. Chew was going to drive over to Jensen, and Vernal, Utah, in two days' time, and agreed to take Jimmy along.

Early the next morning two boys, one about fourteen years old the other a little older, rode down from the ranch. Some of their horses were pastured across the river and they had come after these. After a short visit they got into the *Edith* with Emery and prepared to cross over to the pasture, which was a mile or more downstream. They were soon out of our sight. Jimmy and I remained at the camp, taking pictures, packing his belongings, and finding many odd jobs to be done. In about three hours the boys returned with their horses. The horses were quite gentle, and they had no difficulty in swimming them across. A young colt, too feeble to swim, placed its fore feet on its mother's flanks and was ferried across in that way. Then they were driven over a narrow trail skirting the cliff, 300 feet above the river. No one, looking from the river, would have imagined that any trail, over which horses could be driven, existed.

The boys informed us that we were expected at the ranch for dinner, and would listen to no refusal, so up we went, although we would have to make a second trip that day. The view of the ranch was another of those wonderful scenic changes which we were to meet with everywhere in this region. The flat on which we stood was simply a pocket, shut in by the round-domed mountains, with a pass, or an opening, to the east side. A small stream ran down a mountain side, spreading over the rocks, and glistening in the sunlight. This same stream passed the ranch, and ran on down through the narrow canyon up which we had come. The ranch itself was refreshing. The buildings were new, some were under construction; but there was considerable ground under cultivation. Cattle were scattered up the valley, or dotted the rocky slopes below the mountains. A wild spot this, on the borderland of the three states. None but people of fortitude, or even of daring, would think of taking up a homestead in this secluded spot. The same rumours of the escaped prisoners had drifted in here. It was Mr. Chew who gave us the information we have previously quoted concerning the murdered man. He had found the body in the boat, in front of the post-office. He further stated that others in the mountains would not hesitate at anything to drive out those who were trying to improve a homestead as he was doing, and that it was a common event to find the carcasses of his own horses

Copyright by Kolb Bros.

END OF ECHO CLIFFS. THE MOUTH OF THE YAMPA
RIVER IS ON THE RIGHT.

Copyright by Kolb Bros.

ECHO CLIFFS. "THIS WAS THE END OF LODORE."

or cattle which had been ruthlessly slaughtered. This was the reason for putting the horses across the river. There they were safe, for none could approach them save by going past the ranch, or coming through Lodore Canyon.

Mr. Chew also told us of the Snyders, who had lost their boat in upper Lodore Canyon, and of how he had given them a horse and provisions to aid them in reaching the settlements. This did not prevent the elder Snyder from coming back to trap the next year, much to Mr. Chew's disgust. He thought one experience should be enough for any man.

While we were talking, a very old, bearded man rode in on a horse. He was Pat Lynch, the owner of the little ranch by the river. He was a real old-timer, having been in Brown's Park when Major Powell was surveying that section of the country. He told us that he had been hired to get some meat for the party, and had killed five mountain sheep. He was so old that he scarcely knew what he was talking about, rambling from one subject to another; and would have us listening with impatience to hear the end of some wonderful tale of the early days, when he would suddenly switch off on to an entirely different subject, leaving the first unfinished.

In spite of his years he was quite active, having broken the horse on which he rode, bareback, without assistance. We were told that he placed a spring or trap gun in his houses at the river, ready to greet any prying marauder. The last we saw of him he was on his way to the post-office, miles away, to draw his pension for service in the Civil War.

Returning to the transportation of Jimmy, it was settled that the Chews were to leave early the next morning. They also agreed to take out our exposed films and plates for us — something we had not counted on, but too good a chance to lose. We all three returned to the boats and packed the stuff that was to go out; then went back to the ranch with Jimmy. It was late — after midnight — when we reached there, and we did not disturb any one. Jimmy's blankets were unrolled in the wagon, so there would be no question about his going out. He was to go to Jensen, or Vernal, and there await us, keeping our films until we arrived. We knew they were in good hands. It was with some difficulty that we found our way back to our camp. The trail was difficult and it was pitch dark. My boat had been taken down to where Emery left the *Edith* when the horses were driven across, and this extra distance was added to our walk.

We were laggard the next morning, and in no hurry to resume our work. We rearranged our loads in the boats; with one less man and considerable less baggage as well, they were lighter by far. Our chances looked much more favourable for an easier passage. Not only were these things in our favour, but in addition we felt that we had served our apprenticeship at navigation in rapid water, and we were just as capable of meeting the rapids to follow as if we had years of experience to our record. On summing up we found that the river had dropped 1000 feet since leaving Green River, Wyoming, and that 5000 feet remained, to put us on a level with the ocean. Our difficulties would depend, of course, on how this fall was distributed. Most of the fall behind was found in Lodore and Red canyons. It was doubtful indeed if any section would have a more rapid fall than Lodore Canyon.

There is a certain verse of wisdom which says that "Pride goeth before a fall," but perhaps it was just as well for us if we were a little bit elated by our past achievements as long as we had to go through with the balance of our self-imposed task. Confidence, in a proper degree, is a great help when real difficulties have to be surmounted. We were full of confidence that day when we pulled away about noon into Whirlpool Canyon, Whirlpool Canyon being next on the list. The camp we were about to leave was directly opposite Lodore Canyon, where it ran against the upended cliff. The gorgeous colours were the same as those on the opposite side, and, to a certain degree, were also found in Whirlpool Canyon.

Our two and a half hours' dash through the fourteen miles of rapid water in Whirlpool Canyon put us in a joyful frame of mind. Rapid after rapid was left behind us without a pause in our rowing, with only a hasty survey standing on the deck of the boats before going over. Others that were free from rocks were rowed into bow first, the big waves breaking over our boats and ourselves. We bailed while drifting in the quiet stretches, then got ready for the next rapids. Two large rapids only were looked over from the shore and these were run in the same manner. We could hardly believe it was true when we emerged from the mountain so quickly into a little flat park or valley sheltered in the hills. This was Island or Rainbow Park, the latter name being suggested by the brilliant colouring of the rocks, in the mountains to our left. Perhaps the form of the rocks themselves helped a little, for here was one end of the rainbow of rock which began on the other side of the mountains. Jagged-edged canyons looking almost as if their sides had been rent asunder came out of these mountains. There was very little dark red here except away on top, 2300 feet above, where a covering of pines made a soft background for light-cream and gorgeous yellow-coloured pinnacles, or rocky walls of pink and purple and delicate shades of various hues. Large cottonwoods appeared again along the river banks, in brilliant autumn colours, adding to the beauties of the scene. Back from the river, to the west, stretched the level park, well covered with bunch-grass on which some cattle grazed, an occasional small prickly pear cactus, and the ever present, pungent sage.

Copyright by Kolb Bros.

"HERE WAS ONE END OF THE RAINBOW OF ROCK WHICH BEGAN ON THE OTHER SIDE OF THE MOUNTAINS."

Verdure-covered islands dotted the course of the stream, which was quiet and sluggish, doubling back and forth like a serpent over many a useless mile. Nine miles of rowing brought us back to a point about three miles from the mouth of Whirlpool Canyon; where the river again enters the mountain, deliberately choosing this course to one, unobstructed for several miles, to the right.

The next gorge was Split Mountain Canyon, so named because the stream divided the ridge lengthwise, from one end to the other. It was short, only nine miles long, with a depth of 2700 feet in the centre of the canyon. Three miles of the nine were put behind us before we camped that evening. These were run in the same manner as the rapids of Whirlpool, scarcely pausing to look them over, but these rapids were bigger, much bigger. One we thought was just formed or at least increased in size by a great slide of rock that had fallen since the recent rains. We just escaped trouble in this rapid, both boats going over a large rock with a great cresting wave below, and followed by a very rough rapid. Emery was standing on top of a fifteen-foot rock below the rapid when I went over, and for a few moments could see nothing of my boat, hardly believing it possible that I had come through without a scratch. These rapids with the high water looked more like rapids we had seen in the Grand Canyon, and were very unlike the shallow water of a week previous. We had only travelled a half day, but felt as if it had been a very complete day when we camped at the foot of a rock slide on the right, just above another big rapid.

On Thursday, October 5, Camp No. 20 was left behind. The rapid below the camp was big, big enough for a moving picture, so we took each other in turns as we ran the rapid. More rapids followed, but these were not so large. A few sharp-pointed spires of tinted rock lifted above us a thousand feet or more. Framed in with the branches of the near-by cottonwood trees, they made a charming picture. Less than three hours brought us to the end of Split Mountain Canyon, and the last bad water we were to have for some time. Just before leaving the canyon, we came to some curious grottos, or alcoves, under the rock walls on the left shore. The river has cut into these until they overhang, some of them twenty-five feet or over. In one of these was a beaver lying on a pile of floating sticks. Although we passed quite close, the beaver never moved, and we did not molest it.

Another shower greeted us as we emerged into the Uinta Valley as it is called by the Ute Indians. This valley is eighty-seven miles long. It did not have the fertileness of Brown's Park, being raised in bare rolling hills, runnelled and gullied by the elements. The water was quiet here, and hard rowing was necessary to make any progress. We had gone about seven miles when we spied a large placer dredge close to the river. To the uninitiated this dredge would look much like a dredging steamboat out of water, but digging its own channel, which is what it really does.

Great beds of gravel lay on either side of the river and placer gold in large or small quantities, but usually the latter is likely to exist in these beds. When a dredge like the one found here is to be installed, an opening is made in the river's bank leading to an excavation which has been made, then a large flatboat is floated in this. The dredging machinery is on this float, as well as most of the machinery through which the gravel is passed accompanied by a stream of water; then with quicksilver and rockers of various designs, the gold is separated from the gravel and sand.

Numerous small buildings were standing near the dredge, but the buildings were empty, and the dredge lay idle. We saw many fresh tracks of men and horses and were welcomed by a sleek, well-fed cat, but found the place was deserted. All buildings were open and in one was a telephone. We were anxious to hear just where we were, so we used the telephone and explained what we wanted to know. The "Central" informed us that we were about nine miles from Jensen, so we returned to the boats and pulled with a will through a land that was no longer barren, but with cozy ranch houses, sur-

G

rounded by rows of stately poplars, bending with the wind, for it was storming in earnest now. About six o'clock that evening we caught sight of the top of the Jensen bridge; then, as we neared the village, the sun broke through the pall of cloud and mist, and a rainbow appeared in the sky above, and was mirrored in the swollen stream, rainbow and replica combined nearly completing the wondrous arc. There was a small inn beside the bridge, and arrangements were made for staying there that night. We were told that Jim and Mrs. Chew had passed through Jensen about four hours before we arrived. They had left word that they would go on through to Vernal, fifteen miles distant from the river.

CHAPTER VIII

AN INLAND EXCURSION

JENSEN was a small village with two stores and a post-office. A few scattered houses completed the village proper, but prosperous-looking ranches spread out on the lowland for two or three miles in all directions on the west side of the river. Avenues of poplar trees, fruit trees, and fields of alfalfa gave these ranches a different appearance from any others we had passed.

We found some mail awaiting us at the post-office, and were soon busily engaged in reading the news from home. We conversed awhile with the few people at the hotel, then retired, but first made arrangements for saddle horses for the ride to Vernal.

Next morning we found two spirited animals, saddled and waiting for us. We had some misgivings concerning these horses, but were assured that they were "all right." A group of grinning cowboys and ranch hands craning their necks from a barn, a hundred yards distant, rather inclined us to think that perhaps our informant might be mistaken. Nothing is more amusing to these men of the range than to see a man thrown from his horse, and a horse that is "all right" for one of them might be anything else to persons such as we who never rode anything except gentle horses, and rode those indifferently. We mounted quickly though, trying to appear unconcerned. The horses, much to our relief, behaved quite well, Emery's mount rearing back on his hind legs, but not bucking. After that, all went smoothly.

Leaving the irrigated ranches on the bottom lands, we ascended a low, rolling mesa, composed of gravel and clay, unwatered and unfertile, from which we caught occasional glimpses of the mountains and the gorge from which we had emerged, their brilliant colours softened and beautified by that swimming blue haze which belongs to this plateau region. Then we rode down into the beautiful Ashley Valley, watered by Ashley Creek, a good-sized stream even after it was used to irrigate all the country for miles above. The valley was several miles wide. The stream emptied into the river about a mile below Jensen. All parts of the valley were under cultivation. It is famous for its splendid deciduous fruits, apples, pears, peaches; splendid both in appearance and flavour. It excelled not only in fruits, however, but in all products of the field as well. "Vernal honey," which is marketed far and near, has a reputation for fine flavour wherever it is known. A thick growth of the bee-blossom or bee-weed crowded the road sides and

Copyright by Kolb Bros.

EACH BED WAS PLACED IN A RUBBER AND A CANVAS SACK. PHOTO TAKEN
IN MARBLE CANYON.

hugged the fences. The fragrance of the flower can easily be noticed in the sweetness of the honey. The pity of it was that bushels of fruit lay rotting on the ground, for there were no transportation facilities, the nearest railroad being 90 miles distant. There were stock ranches too, with blooded stock in the fence-enclosed fields. Some of the splendid horses paced along beside us on the other side of the fence. We heard the rippling song of some meadow-larks this day, the only birds of this species we remember having seen on the Western plateaus.

All these ranches were laid out in true Mormon style, that is, squared off in sections, fenced, and planted with shade-trees before being worked. The roads are usually wide and the streets exceptionally so. Except in the business streets, a large garden usually surrounds the home building, each family endeavouring to raise all their own vegetables, fruits, and poultry. They usually succeed.

The shade trees about Vernal were Lombardy poplars. They attained a height that would give ample shade under most conditions, and too much when we were there, for the roads were very muddy, although they had dried in all other sections. Nearing Vernal, we passed Nathan Galloway's home, a cozy place set back some distance from the road. We had hoped to meet Galloway and have an opportunity of talking over his experiences with him, but found he was absent on a hunting trip, in fact was up in the mountains we had come through.

On nearing the town we were greeted by a busy scene. Numerous wagons and horses stood in squares reserved for that purpose, or were tied to hitching posts in front of the many stores. Ranchers and their families were everywhere in evidence; there were numerous prospectors in their high-topped boots just returning from the mountains, and oil men in similar garb, muddy from head to foot. Later we learned that oil had recently been discovered about forty miles distant, this fact accounting for much of the activity.

The town itself was a surprise; we found it to be very much up-to-date considering its isolated position. Two of the streets were paved and oiled and were supplied with drinking fountains. There were two prosperous looking banks, two well-stocked and up-to-date drug stores, several mercantile stores, and many others, all busy. Many of the buildings were of brick; all were substantial.

Near a hotel we observed a group of men surrounding some one who was evidently keeping them interested. On approaching them we found it was Jimmy, giving a graphic description of some of our difficulties. His story was not finished, for he saw us and ran to greet us, as pleased to see us as we were to see him. He had little idea we would be along for two or three days and naturally was much surprised.

On entering the hotel we were greeted by an old Grand Canyon friend, a civil engineer named Duff, who with a crew of men had been mapping the mountains near Whirlpool Canyon. You can imagine that it was a gratifying surprise to all concerned to find we were not altogether among strangers, though they were as hospitable as strangers could be. The hotel was a lively place that night. There was some musical talent among Duff's men, and Duff himself was an artist on the piano. Many of the young people of the town had dropped in that evening, as some one had passed the word that there might be an impromptu entertainment at the hotel. There was. Duff played and the boys sang. Jimmy was himself again and added his rich baritone. The town itself was not without musical talent, and altogether it was a restful change for us.

Perhaps we should have felt even better if we had been dressed differently, for we wore much the same clothes as those in which we did our work on the river — a woollen shirt and overalls. Besides, neither Emery nor I had shaved since starting, and it is quite likely that we looked just a little uncouth. Appearances count for little with these people in the little-settled districts, and it is a common enough sight to them to see men dressed as we were. They did everything they could to make us feel at ease. As one person remarked,

"The wealthiest cattle man, or the owner of the richest

mine in the country, usually looks worse than all others after a month on the range or in the hills."

If wealth were indicated on an inverse ratio to one's good appearance, we should have been very wealthy indeed. We felt as if it would take us a week to get rested, and lost little time in getting to bed when the party broke up. We imagine most of the residents of Vernal were Mormons. It is part of their creed to give "the stranger within their gates" a cordial welcome. This, however, was accorded to us, not only among the Mormons, but in every section of our journey on the Green and Colorado rivers.

The following day was a busy one. Arrangements had been made with a local photographer to get the use of his dark room, and we proceeded to develop all plates and many of our films. These were then to be packed and shipped out. We were informed at the local express office, that it might be some time before they would go, as the recent rains had been very bad in Colorado and had washed out most of the bridges.

Vernal had passenger transportation to the railway — a branch of the D. & R. G. running north into Colorado — by automobile, the route lying across the Green and also across the White River, a tributary to the Green. A steel structure had been washed away on the White River, making it impossible to get through to the station. The high water below here must have been a flood, judging from all reports. About ten bridges, large and small, were reported as being washed away on numerous branch streams leading into the Green River. Fortunately Vernal had another means of communication. This was a stage running southwest from Vernal, over 125 miles of rough road to Price, Utah — Price being a station on the main line of the D. & R. G.

Jimmy concluded that he would take this road, in preference to the uncertainties of the other route, and noon that day found him on board the stage. He promised to write to us, and was anxious to hear of our success, but remarked that when he once got home he would "never leave San Francisco again." There was a final hand clasp, a cheer from the small group of men, and the stage drove away with Jimmy, a happy boy indeed.

Our work on the developing progressed well, and with very satisfying results on the whole, and that evening found us with all plates packed ready for shipment to our home. The moving-picture film was also packed and shipped to be developed at once. This was quite a load off our minds.

The following day we prepared to depart, but did not leave until the afternoon. Then, with promises to let them know the outcome of our venture, we parted from our friends and rode back to Jensen.

We planned on leaving the following morning. The river had fallen one foot since we had landed, and we were anxious to have the benefit of the high water. We were told that it was six feet above the low-water stage of two weeks before.

On Monday, October the 9th, after loading our boats with a new stock of provisions, — in which was included a few jars of honey, and a few dozen of eggs, packed in sawdust, — we began what might be called the second stage of our journey; the 175-mile run to Blake or Green River, Utah, a little west of south from Jensen. Ten miles below Jensen was a ferry used by the auto and wagons. Here also was a ranch house, with a number of people in the yard. We were invited to land and did so. They had been informed by telephone of our coming and were looking for us; indeed they had even prepared dinner for us, hoping we would reach there in time. Not knowing all this, we had eaten our cold lunch half an hour before. The women were busy preserving fruits and garden truck, and insisted on us taking two or three jars along. This was a welcome change to the dried fruit, which was one of our principal foods. These people made the usual request —

"Drop us a post card if you get through."

The memory of these people that we met on this journey will linger with us as long as we live. They were always anxious to help us or cheer us on our way.

We passed a dredge that evening and saw a man at work with a team and scoop shovel, the method being to scoop up the gravel and sand, then dump it in an iron car. This was then pulled by the horses to the top of a derrick up a sloping track and dumped. A stream of water pumped up from the river mixed with the gravel, the entire mass descended a long zigzagging chute. We paused a few minutes only and did not examine the complicated process of separating the mineral from the gravel. This dredge had been recently installed. We camped early, half a mile below the dredge.

Emery had been feeling poorly all this day. He blamed his indisposition to having eaten too many good things when in Vernal — a break in training, as it were. This was our excuse for a short run that day. I played nurse and gave him some simple remedy from the little supply that we carried; and, after he was in his sleeping bag, I filled some hot-water bags for the first time on the trip, and soon had him feeling quite comfortable.

A hard wind came up that night, and a little rain fell. I had a busy half-hour keeping our camp from being blown away. The storm was of short duration, and all was soon quiet again. On the following morning Emery felt so good that I had a hard time in keeping up with him, and I wondered if he would ever stop. Towards evening, after a long pull, we neared the reservation of the Uinta Utes, and saw a few Indians camped away from the river. Here, again, were the cottonwood bottoms, banked by the barren, gravelly hills. We had been informed that there was a settlement called Ouray, some distance down the river, and we were anxious to reach it before night. But the river was sluggish, with devious and twisting channels, and it was dark when we finally landed at the Ouray ferry.

CHAPTER IX

CANYON OF DESOLATION

OURAY, Utah, consisted of a large store to supply the wants of the Indians and ranchers, a small hotel, and a few dwellings. The agency proper was located some distance up the Uinta River, which stream emptied into the Green, just below Ouray.

Supper was taken at the hotel, after which we visited a young man in charge of the store, looking over his curios and listening to tales of his life here among these Indians. They were peaceable enough now, but in years gone by were a danger to be reckoned with. We slept in our own beds close to our boats by the river.

The following morning, when we were ready to leave, a small crowd gathered, a few Indians among them. Most of the Indians were big, fat, and sleepy-looking. Apparently they enjoyed the care of the government. A mile below we passed several squaws and numerous children under some trees, while on a high mound stood a lone buck Indian looking at us as we sped by, but without a single movement that we could see. He still stood there as we passed from sight a mile below. It might be interesting if one could know just what was in his mind as he watched us.

A mile below the Uinta River, which entered on the west, we passed another stream, the White River, entering from the east, the two streams adding considerable water to the Green River. We passed another idle dredge, also some mineral workings in tunnels, and saw two men camped on the shore beside them. We saw numerous Indian carvings on the rocks, but judged they were recent because horses figured in most of them. In all the open country the river was fringed with large cottonwood trees, alders and willow thickets. A number of islands followed, one of them very symmetrical in shape, with cottonwood trees in the centre, while around the edge ran a fringe of bushes looking almost like a trimmed hedge. The autumn colouring added to its beauty. The hedge, as we called it, was dark red, brown, yellow, and green; the cottonwoods were a light yellow. After we had passed this island, a deer, confused by our voices, jumped into the river fifty yards behind us, leaping and swimming as he made for the shore. We had no gun, but Emery had the moving-picture camera at hand, and turned it on the deer. The hour was late, however, and we had little hopes of its success as a picture. The country back from the river stretched in rolling, barren

E. L. KOLB. EMERY KOLB. *Copyright by Kolb Bros.*

"NOW FOR A FISH STORY!"

hills 200 or 300 feet high — a continuation of the Bad Lands of Utah, which lay off to the west.

With the next day's travel the hills lost some of their barren appearance. Some cattle were seen early in the afternoon of the following day. We passed a cattle man working at a ferry, who had just taken some stock across, which other men had driven on ahead. He was busy, so we did not interrupt him, merely calling to him from the boats, drifting meanwhile with the current. Soon we saw him riding down the shore and waited for him to catch up. He invited us to camp with him that evening, remarking that he had "just killed a beef." We thanked him, but declined, as it was early and we had only travelled a short distance that day. We chatted awhile, and he told us to look out for rapids ahead. He was rather surprised when he learned that we had started at Green River, Wyoming, and had already come through a few rapids.

"Where are you going to stop?" he then asked.

On being told that our destination was Needles, California, he threw up his hands with an expressive gesture, then added soberly, "Well, boys, I sure wish you luck," and rode back to his camp.

We had difficulty in making a suitable landing that evening, as the high water had deposited great quantities of black mud over everything, making it very disagreeable when we left the boats. We finally found a place with less mud to wade through than on most of the banks seen, and tied up to the roots of a tree.

While lying in our beds that night looking at the starlit sky — such a sky as is found only on these high plateaus — we discovered a comet directly above us. An astronomer would have enjoyed our opportunities for observing the heavens. No doubt this comet had been heralded far and wide, but we doubt if any one saw it to better advantage than did we.

Later, some coyotes, possibly in chase of a rabbit, gave vent to their yodeling cry, and awakened us from a sound sleep. They were in a little lateral canyon, which magnified and gave a weird, organ-like echo to their calls long after the coyotes themselves had passed from hearing.

The nights were getting warmer as we travelled south, but not so warm that we were bothered with insects. The same reason accounted for the absence of snakes or scorpions, for no doubt there were plenty of both in warm weather in this dry country. When there was no wind, the silence of the nights was impressive, with no sound save the lapping of the water against the banks. Sometimes a bird in the trees above would start up with a twitter, then quiet down again. On occasions the air chambers in our boats would contract on cooling off, making a noise like the boom of a distant gun, every little sound being magnified by the utter stillness of the night.

There were other times when it was not so quiet. Hundreds of birds, geese, ducks and mud-hens had been seen the last few days. Also there were occasional cranes and herons, over a thousand miles from their breeding place at the mouth of the Colorado. As dusk settled, we would see these birds abandon their feeding in the mud, and line up on the shore, or on an island, and go to sleep. Occasionally one of these birds would start up out of a sound sleep with an unearthly squawk. Possibly an otter had interrupted its dreams, or a fox had pounced on one as it slept. It may be that it was only a bad dream of these enemies that caused their fright, but whatever it was, that first call would start up the entire flock and they would circle in confusion like a stampeded herd of cattle, their discordant cries putting an end to the stillness of the night. Finally they would settle down in a new spot, and all would be quiet once more.

We saw a few birds that were strangers to us, — water birds which we imagined belonged to the salt water rather than the inland streams, making a little excursion, perhaps, away from their accustomed haunts. One type we saw on two occasions, much like a gull, but smaller, pure white as far as we could tell, soaring in graceful flight above the river.

Camp No. 26 was close to the beginning of a new canyon. The country had been changing in appearance

H

from rather flat plains to small bare hills, gradually increasing in height with smooth, rounded sides, and going up to a point, usually of a dirty clay colour, with little vegetation of any kind on them. The river for miles past had swept in long graceful curves, the hills being close to the river on the outside of the curve, leaving a big flat on the inside. This flat gradually sloped back to hills of an equal height to those opposite. Then the curve would reverse, and the same conditions would be met with again, but on opposite sides from the previous bend. After passing a creek the evening before, the hills became higher, and from our camp we could see the first place where they came close on both sides to the river. We felt now that our beautiful tree-covered canyons were behind us and from now on we would be hemmed in by the great eroded canyons of the Southwest. We were sorry to leave those others behind, and could easily understand why Major Powell had named this Desolation Canyon.

As the canyon deepened the cliffs were cut into fantastic shapes, as is usual in rocks unprotected by vegetation. There was a hard rock near the top in places, which overhung a softer formation. This would erode, giving a cornice-like effect to the cliffs. Others were surmounted by square towers and these were capped by a border of little squares, making the whole look much like a castle on the Rhine. For half a day we found no rapids, but pulled away on a good current. The walls gradually grew higher and were more rugged; a few trees cropped out on their sides. At noon our boats were lashed together and lunch was eaten as we drifted. We covered about three miles in this way, taking in the scenery as we passed. We saw a great stone arch, or natural bridge, high on a stupendous cliff to our right, and wondered if any one had ever climbed up to it. Our lunch was no more than finished when the first rapid was heard ahead of us. Quickly unlashing our boats, we prepared for strenuous work. Friday the 13th proved to be a lucky day; thirteen large rapids and thirteen small ones were placed behind us before we camped at Rock Creek — a splashing, laughing mountain stream, no doubt containing trout.

The following morning we found there was a little ranch house below us, but, though we called from our boats, no one came out. We wondered how any one could reach this out-of-the-way place, as a road would be almost an impossibility. Later we found a well-constructed trail on the right-hand side all the way through the canyon. We saw a great many cattle travelling this trail. Some were drinking at the river when we swept into view. Our boats filled them with alarm, and they scrambled for the hillsides, looking after us with frightened expressions as we left them to the rear.

We put in a full day at running rapids, one after another,

until fifteen large ones were passed, no count being kept of the smaller ones. Some of these rapids resembled dams from six to twelve feet high, with the water falling abruptly over a steep slope. Others were long and rough, with swift water in places. Above one of these we had landed, then found we could get a much better view from the opposite shore. Emery crossed and landed, I followed. We had been having heavy winds all day. When crossing here I was caught by a sudden gust of wind and carried to the head of the rapid. I heard Emery call, "Look out for the big rock!" then over I went. The wind and water together had turned my boat sideways, and try as I would I could not get it turned around. I saw the rock Emery referred to straight ahead of me. It was about fifteen feet square and about fourteen feet from the shore, with a powerful current shooting between the rock and the shore. It seemed as if I must strike the rock broadside, and I ceased my struggle, but held out an oar with both hands, hoping to break the blow. But it never came. The water struck this rock with great force, then rebounded, and actually kept me from even touching the rock with the oar, but it caught the boat and shot it through the narrow channel, bow first, as neatly as it could possibly be done, then turned the boat around again as I scrambled to regain my hold on both oars. No other rocks threatened, however, and besides filling the cockpit with water, no damage was done.

Emery had no desire to follow my passage and crossed back to the other side. Shooting over the upper end of the rapid, his boat ran up on a rounded rock, the stern sticking high in the air; it paused a moment, the current slowly turning it around as if on a pivot, and the boat slid off; then down he came lurching and plunging, but with no more difficulty. Many times in such places as these we saw the advantage of our flat-bottomed boats over one with a keel, for these would surely be upset when running up on such a rock.

CHAPTER X

THE appearance of Desolation Canyon had changed entirely in the lower end. Instead of a straight canyon, without a break, we were surrounded by mountain peaks nearly 2500 feet high, with many side canyons between them and with little level parks at the end of the canyons beside the river. The tops were pine-covered; cedars clung to the rocky slopes. Some of these peaks were not unlike the formations of the Grand Canyon, as seen from the inner plateau, and the red colouring was once more found in the rocks.

These peaks were gradually dropping down in height; and at one open section, with alfalfa and hay fields on gently sloping hillsides, we found a small ranch, the buildings being set back from the river. We concluded to call and found three men, the rancher and two young cowboys, at work in a blacksmith shop. Emery had forgotten to remove his life-preserver, and the men looked at him with some astonishment, as he was still soaking wet from the splashing waves of the last rapid.

When I joined him he was explaining that no one had been drowned, and that we were merely making an excursion down the river. Mr. McPherson, the rancher, we learned, owned all the cattle seen up the river. The little cabin at our last camp was a sort of headquarters for his cowboys. The cattle were just being driven from the mountains before the snows came, and were to be wintered here in the canyons. Some of these cattle were much above the usual grade of range cattle, being thoroughbreds, although most of them ran loose on the range. This ranch had recently lost a valuable bull which had been killed by a bear up in the mountains — not unlike similar conflicts in more civilized sections of the country. McPherson camped on this bear's trail for several days and nights before he finally hung his pelt on a tree. He was a large cinnamon-coloured grizzly. Four other bears had been killed this same year, in these mountains.

McPherson's home had burned down a short time before our visit, and his family had removed to Green River, Utah. A number of tents were erected, neatly boarded up, and we were informed that one of these was reserved for company, so we need not think of going any farther that day. These men, while absolutely fearless in the saddle, over these rough mountain trails, had "no use for the river" they told us; in fact, we found this was the usual attitude of the cattle men wherever we met them. McPherson's respect for the river was not without reason, as his father, with two others, had been drowned while making a crossing in a light boat near this point, some years before. Some accident occurred, possibly the breaking of a rowlock, and they were carried into a rapid. McPherson's men found it necessary to cross their cattle back and forth, but always took the wise precaution to have on some life-preservers. These cork preservers hung in the blacksmith shop, where they could easily be reached at a moment's notice.

Desolation Canyon, with a slight breaking down of the walls for a short distance only, gave place to Gray Canyon below the McPherson Ranch. A good-sized mountain stream, part of which irrigated the ranch above, found its way through this division. We had been told that more rapids lay ahead of us in Gray Canyon, but they were not so numerous in our next day's travel. What we did find were usually large, but we ran them all without difficulty. About noon we met five men in a boat, rowing up the stream in a long, still stretch. They told us they were working on a dam, a mile or two below. They followed us down to see us make the passage through the rapid which lay above their camp. The rapid was long and rocky, having a seventeen-foot fall in a half mile. We picked our channel by standing up in the boat before entering the rapid and were soon at the bottom with no worse mishap than bumping a rock or two rather lightly. We had bailed out and were tying our boats, when the men came panting down the hill up which they had climbed to see us make this plunge. A number of men were at work here, but this being Sunday, most of them had gone to Green River, Utah, twenty-one miles distant.

Among the little crowd who came down to see us resume our rowing was a lady and a little girl who lived in a rock building, near the other buildings erected for the working-men. Emery showed the child a picture of his four-year-old daughter, Edith, with her mother — a picture he always carried in a note-book. Then he had her get in the boat with him, and we made a photograph of them. They were very good friends before we left.

In a few hours we emerged from the low-walled canyon into a level country. A large butte, perhaps 700 feet high, stood out by itself, a mile from the main cliffs. This was Gunnison Butte, an old landmark near the Gunnison trail. We were anxious to reach Blake or Green River, Utah, not many miles below, that evening; but we failed to make it. There were several rapids, some of them quite large, and we had run them all when we came to a low dam that obstructed our passage. While looking it over, seeing how best to make a portage, a young man whom we had just seen remarked:

"Well, boys, you had better tie up and I will help you in the morning."

It was 5.30 then, and we were still six miles from Green River, so we took his advice and camped. On seeing our sleeping bags, tightly strapped and making rather a small roll, he remarked:

"Well, you fellows are not Mormons; I can tell by the size of your beds!"

Our new friend gave the name of Wolverton. There was another man named Wilson who owned a ranch just below the dam. Both of these men were much interested in our experiences. Wolverton had considerable knowledge of the river and of boats; very little persuasion would have been necessary to have had him for a companion on the balance of our journey. But we had made up our minds to make it alone, now, as it looked feasible. Both Wilson and Wolverton knew the country below Green River, Utah, having made surveys through much of the surrounding territory. Wolverton said we must surely see his father, who lived down the river and who was an enthusiast on motor boats. A few minutes' work the next morning sufficed to get our boats over the dam. The dam was constructed of loose rock and piles, chinked with brush and covered with sloping planks, — just a small dam to raise the water for irrigation purposes. Much of the water ran through the canal; in places the planks were dry, in others some water ran over. The boats, being unloaded, were pulled up on these planks, then slid into the water

Copyright by Kolb Bros.

PAT LYNCH: THE CANYON HERMIT.

below. Wilson had a large water wheel for irrigation purposes, the first of several such wheels which we were to see this day. These wheels, twenty feet or more in height, — with slender metal buckets each holding several gallons of water, fastened at intervals on either side, — were placed in a swift current, anchored on the shore to stout piles, or erected over mill-races cut in the banks. There they revolved, the buckets filling and emptying automatically, the water running off in troughs above the level of the river back to the fertile soil. Some of these wheels had ingenious floating arrangements whereby they accommodated themselves to the different stages of a rising or falling river. We took a few pictures of Wilson's place before leaving. He informed us that he had telephoned to certain people in Green River who would help us in various ways. Two hours' rowing, past many pretty little ranches, brought us to the railroad bridge, a grateful sight to us. A pumping plant stood beside the bridge under charge of Captain Yokey, one of Wilson's friends. Yokey owned a large motor boat, which was tied up to the shore. Our boats were left in his charge while we went up to the town, a mile distant. Another of Wilson's friends met us, and secured a dark room for us, so that we could do a little developing and we prepared for work on the following day.

That night a newspaper reporter hunted us out, anxious for a story. We gave him what we had, making light of our previous difficulties, which were exciting enough at times; but owing to the comparatively small size of the stream, we seldom thought our lives were in any great danger. The papers made the most of these things, and the stories that came out had little semblance to our original statements. We have since learned that no matter how much one minimizes such things, they are seldom published as reported.

We put in a busy day unpacking new films and plates, developing all films from the smaller cameras and sending these home. A new stock of provisions had to be purchased, enough for one month at least, for there was no chance of securing supplies until we reached our canyon home, about 425 miles below.

We had a valuable addition to our cargo in two metal boxes that had been shipped here, as it was not possible to get them before leaving Wyoming. These cases or trunks were sent from England, and were water-tight, if not waterproof, there being a slight difference. Well constructed, with rubber gaskets and heavy clamps, every possible precaution had been taken, it seemed, to exclude the water and still render them easy of access. They were about thirty inches long, fifteen wide, and twelve high, just the thing for our photographic material. Up to this time everything had to be kept under the decks when in bad water. These boxes were placed in the open section in front of us, and were thoroughly fastened

to the ribs to prevent loss, ready to be opened or closed
in a moment, quite a convenience when pictures had to
be taken hurriedly.

The following day we went over the boats, caulking
a few leaks. The bottoms of the boats were considerably
the worse for wear, owing to our difficulties in the first
canyons. We got some thin oak strips and nailed them
on the bottom to help protect them, when portaging.
Sliding the boats on the scouring sand and rough-sur-
faced rock was hard on the half-inch boards on the bottom
of the boats. This work was all completed that day, and
everything was ready for the next plunge.

In passing the station, we noticed the elevation above
sea-level was placed at 4085 feet, and remembered that
Green River, Wyoming, was 6080 feet, showing that our
descent in the past 425 miles had been close to 2000 feet.
We had not found it necessary to line or portage any
rapids since leaving Lodore Canyon; we were hopeful
that our good luck would continue.

Nothing was to be feared from what remained of the
Green River, 120 miles or more, for motor boats made the
journey to its junction with the Grand, and we were
told even ascended the Grand for some distance. Below
this junction was the Colorado River, a different stream
from the one we were still to navigate.

Before leaving, we ate a final hearty breakfast at the
boarding-house where we had been taking our meals.

A number of young men, clerks in some of the business houses here, were among the boarders. The landlady, a whole-souled German woman and an excellent cook, was greatly worried over their small appetites, thinking it was a reflection on her table. She remarked that she hoped we had good appetites, and I am sure she had no complaint to make so far as we were concerned. We had never stinted ourselves when on the river, but the change and the rest seemed to give us an abnormal appetite that could not be satisfied, and we would simply quit eating because we were ashamed to eat more. Less than half an hour after one of these big meals, I was surprised to see my brother in a restaurant with a sheepish grin on his face, and with a good-sized lunch before him.

CHAPTER XI

Thursday, October the 19th. We embarked again with two of our new-found friends on board as passengers for a short ride, their intention being to hunt as they walked back. They left us at a ranch beside the San Rafæl River, a small stream entering from the west. They left some mail with us to be delivered to Mr. Wolverton, whose son we had met above. About 20 miles below Green River we reached his home. Judging by a number of boats — both motor and row boats — tied to his landing, Mr. Wolverton was an enthusiastic river-man. After glancing over his mail, he asked how we had come and was interested when he learned that we were making a boating trip. He was decidedly interested when he saw the boats and learned that we were going to our home in the Grand Canyon. His first impression was that we were merely making a little pleasure trip on the quiet water.

Going carefully over the boats, he remarked that they met with his approval with one exception. They seemed to be a little bit short for the heavy rapids of the Colorado, he thought. He agreed that our experience in the upper rapids had been good training, but said there was no comparison in the rapids. We would have a river ten times as great as in Lodore to contend with; and in numerous places, for short distances, the descent was as abrupt as anything we had seen on the Green. Wolverton was personally acquainted with a number of the men who had made the river trip, and, with the one exception of Major Powell's expeditions, had met all the parties who had successfully navigated its waters. This not only included Galloway's and Stone's respective expeditions, which had made the entire trip, but included two other expeditions which began at Green River, Utah, and had gone through the canyons of the Colorado.[1] These were the Brown-Stanton expedition, which made a railroad survey through the canyons of the Colorado; and another commonly known as the Russell-Monnette expedition, two of the party making the complete trip, arriving at Needles after a voyage filled with adventure and many narrow escapes. Mr. Wolverton remarked that every one knew of those who had navigated the entire series of canyons, but that few people knew of those who

---

[1] Brown-Stanton. May 25, 1889.

Russell-Monnette. Sept. 20, 1907.

For a more complete record of these expeditions, as well as others who attempted the passage of the canyons below this point, see appendix.

had been unsuccessful. He knew of seven parties that had failed to get through Cataract Canyon's forty-one miles of rapids, with their boats, most of them never being heard of again.

These unsuccessful parties were often miners or prospectors who wished to get into the comparatively flat country which began about fifty miles below the Junction of the Green and the Grand rivers. Here lay Glen Canyon, with 150 miles of quiet water. Nothing need be feared in this, or in the 120 miles of good boating from Green River, Utah, to the junction. Between these two points, however, lay Cataract Canyon, beginning at the junction of the two rivers. Judging by its unsavory record, Cataract Canyon was something to be feared.

Among these parties who had made short trips on the river was one composed of two men. Phil Foote was a gambler, stage robber, and bad man in general. He had broken out of jail in Salt Lake City and, accompanied by another of similar character, stole a boat at Green River, Utah, and proceeded down the river. Soon after entering Cataract Canyon, they lost their boat and provisions. Finding a tent which had been washed down the river, they tore it into strips and constructed a raft out of driftwood, tying the logs together with the strips of canvas. Days of hardship followed, and starvation stared them in the face; until finally Foote's partner gave up, and said he would drown himself. With an oath Foote

I

drew his revolver, saying he had enough of such cowardice and would save him the trouble. His companion then begged for his life, saying he would stick to the end, and they finally got through to the Hite ranch, which lay a short distance below. They were taken care of here, and terminated their voyage a short distance beyond, going out over land. Foote was afterwards shot and killed while holding up a stage in Nevada.

The Hite ranch also proved to be a place of refuge for others, the sole survivors of two other parties who were wrecked, one person escaping on each occasion. Hite's ranch, and Lee's Ferry, 140 miles below Hite, had mail service. We had left instructions at the post-office to forward our mail to one or the other of these points. These were also the only places on our 425-mile run to Bright Angel Trail where we could expect to see any people, so we were informed. We were about to descend into what is, possibly, the least inhabited portion of the United States of America.

A party of civil engineers working here, joined us that evening at Wolverton's home. A young man in the party asked us if we would consent to carry a letter through with us and mail it at our destination. He thought it would be an interesting souvenir for the person to whom it was addressed. We agreed to do our best, but would not guarantee delivery. The next morning two letters were given us to mail, and were accepted

Copyright by Kolb Bros.

SKELETON FOUND IN THE GRAND CANYON.

with this one reservation. Before leaving Mr. Wolverton showed us his motor boat with much pardonable pride. On this boat he sometimes took small parties down to the beginning of the Colorado River, and up the Grand, a round trip of three hundred miles or more. The boat had never been taken down the Colorado for the simple reason that the rapids began almost immediately below the junction.

Wolverton, while he had never been through the rapids in a boat, had followed the river on foot for several miles and was thoroughly familiar with their nature. On parting he remarked,

"Well, boys, you are going to tackle a mighty hard proposition, but I'm sure you can make it if you are only careful. But look out and go easy."

Wolverton was no novice, speaking from much experience in bad water, and we were greatly impressed by what he had to say.

Five uneventful days were spent in Labyrinth and Stillwater canyons, through which the Green peacefully completed its rather violent descent. In the upper end we usually found rough water in the canyons and quiet water in the open sections. Here at least were two canyons, varying from 300 feet at their beginning to 1300 feet in depth, both without a rapid. The first of these was Labyrinth Canyon, so named from its elaborately winding course as well as its wonderful intricate system of dry, lateral canyons, and its reproduction in rock of architectural forms, castles, arches, and grottos; even animals and people were represented in every varying form.

Our Sunday camp was beside what might be called a serpentine curve or series of loops in the river. This was at the centre of what is known as the Double Bow Knot, three rounded loops, very symmetrical in form, with an almost circular formation of flat-topped rock, a mile or more in diameter in the centre of each loop. A narrow neck of rock connects these formations to the main mesa, all being on the same level, about 700 feet above the river. The upper half of the rock walls was sheer; below was a steep boulder-covered slope. The centre formation is the largest and most perfect, being nearly two miles in diameter and almost round; so much so, that a very few minutes are necessary to climb over the narrow neck which connects this formation to the mesa. It took 45 minutes of hard rowing on a good current to take us around this one loop. The neck is being rapidly eroded, two hundred feet having disappeared from the top, and at some distant day will doubtless disappear entirely, making a short cut for the river, and will leave a rounded island of rock standing seven hundred feet above the river. A bird's-eye view of the three loops would compare well in shape to the little mechanical contrivance known as the "eye" in the combination of "hook and eye." All women and many men will get a clear idea of the shape of the Double Bow Knot from this comparison.

We recorded an interesting experiment with the thermometer at this camp, showing a great variety of temperatures, unbelievable almost to one who knows nothing of conditions in these semi-arid plateaus. A little ice had formed the night before. Under a clear sky the next day at noon, our thermometer recorded 54 degrees in the shade, but ran up to 102 degrees in the sun. At the same time the water in the river was 52 degrees Far. The effect of being deluged in ice-cold waves, then running into deep sunless canyons with a cold wind sweeping down from the snow on top, can be easier imagined than described. This is what we could expect to meet later.

The colouring of the rocks varied greatly in many localities, a light red predominating. In some places the red rock was capped by a gray, flint-like limestone; in others this had disappeared, but underneath the red were regular strata of various-coloured rocks, pink, brown, light yellow, even blue and green being found in two or three sections.

The forms of erosion were as varied as the rock itself, each different-coloured rock stratum presenting a different surface. In one place the surface was broken into rounded forms like the backs of a herd of elephants. In others we saw reproductions of images, carved by the drifting sands — a Diana, with uplifted arm, as large as the

Goddess of Liberty; a Billiken on a throne with a hundred worshippers bowed around. Covered with nature-made ruins and magnificent rock structures, as this section is, it is not entirely without utility. It is a grazing country. Great numbers of contented cattle, white-faced, with red and white, or black and white patches of colour on their well-filled hides, were found in the open spaces between the sheer-walled cliffs. Dusty, well-beaten trails led down through these wide canyons, trails which undoubtedly gained the top of the level, rocky plateau a few miles back from the river. As is usual in a cattle country at the end of the summer season, the bunch-grass, close to the water supply — which in this case happened to the river — was nibbled close to the roots. The cattle only came here to drink, then travelled many miles, no doubt, to the better grazing on the upper plateaus. The sage, always gray, was grayer still, with dust raised by many passing herds. There was a band of range horses too, those splendid wild-eyed animals with kingly bearing, and wind-blown tails and manes, lean like a race-horse, strong-muscled and tough-sinewed, pawing and neighing, half defiant and half afraid of the sight of men, the only thing alive to which they pay tribute.

It is a never ending source of wonder, to those unacquainted with the semi-arid country, how these animals can exist in a land which, to them, seems utterly

THE BUTTES OF THE CROSS.

Copyright by Kolb Bros.

destitute and barren. To many such, a meadow carpeted with blue grass or timothy is the only pasture on which grazing horses or grazing cattle can exist; the dried-out looking tufts of bunch-grass, scattered here and there or sheltered at the roots of the sage, mean nothing; the grama-grass hidden in the grease-wood is unnoticed or mistaken for a weed.

But if the land was bare of verdure, the rock saved it from being monotonous. Varied in colour, the red rock predominated — blood-red at mid-day, orange-tinted at sunset, with gauze-like purple shadows, and with the delicate blue outlines always found in the Western distances; such a land could never be called uninteresting.

The banks of the stream, here in the open, were always green. From an elevation they appeared like two emerald bands through a land of red, bordering a stream the tint of the aged pottery found along its shores. We were continually finding new trees and strange shrubs. Beside the cottonwoods and the willows there was an occasional wild-cherry tree; in the shrubs were the service-berry, and the squaw-berry, with sticky, acid-tasting fruit. The cacti were small, and excepting the prickly pear were confined nearly altogether to a small "pin-cushion" cactus, growing a little larger as we travelled south. And always in the mornings when out of the deep canyons the moist, pungent odour of the sage greeted our nostrils. It is inseparable from the West. There is no stuffy germ-laden air there, out in the sage; one is glad to live, simply to breathe it in and exhale and breathe again.

In Stillwater Canyon the walls ran up to 1300 feet in height, a narrow canyon, with precipitous sides. Occasionally we could see great columns of rock standing on top of the mesa. Late one evening we saw some small cliff dwellings several hundred feet above the river, and a few crude ladders leaning against the cliff below the dwellings. A suitable camp could not be made here, or we would have stopped to examine them. The shores were slippery with mud and quicksands, and there was no fire-wood in sight. From here to the end of the canyons we would have to depend almost entirely on the drift-piles for fire-wood.

A landing was finally made where a section of a cliff had toppled from above, affording a solid footing leading up to the higher bank. We judged from our maps that we were within a very few miles of the Colorado River. Here some footprints and signs of an old boat landing, apparently about a week old, were seen in the sand. This surprised us somewhat, as we had heard of no one coming down ahead of us.

CHAPTER XII

COULD WE SUCCEED ?

An hour or two at the oars the next morning sufficed to bring us to the junction of the Green and the Grand rivers. We tied up our boats, and prepared to climb out on top, as we had a desire to see the view from above. A mile back on the Green we had noticed a sort of canyon or slope breaking down on the west side, affording a chance to reach the top. Loading ourselves with a light lunch, a full canteen, and our smaller cameras, we returned to this point and proceeded to climb out. Powell's second expedition had climbed out at this same place; Wolverton had also mentioned the fact that he had been out; so we were quite sure of a successful attempt before we made the climb.

The walk close to the river, over rocks and along narrow ledges, was hard work; the climb out was even more so. The contour maps which we carried credited these walls with 1300 feet height. If we had any doubt concerning the accuracy of this, it disappeared before we finally reached the top. What we saw, however, was worth all the discomfort we had undergone. Close to the top, three branches of dry, rock-bottomed gullies, carved from a gritty, homogeneous sandstone, spread out from the slope we had been climbing. These were less precipitous. Taking the extreme left-hand gully, we found the climb to the top much easier. At the very end we found an irregular hole a few feet in diameter, not a cave, but an opening left between some immense rocks, touching at the top, seemingly rolled together.

Gazing down through this opening, we were amazed to find that we were directly above the Colorado itself. It was so confusing at first that we had to climb to the very top to see which river it was, I contending that it was the Green, until satisfied that I was mistaken. The view from the top was overwhelming, and words can hardly describe what we saw, or how we were affected by it.

We found ourselves on top of an irregular plateau of solid rock, with no earth or vegetation save a few little bushes and some very small cedars in cracks in the rocks. Branching canyons, three or four hundred feet in depth, and great fissures ran down in this rock at intervals. Some were dark and crooked, and the bottom could not be seen. Between these cracks, the rock rounded like elephants' backs sloping steeply on either side. Some could be crossed, some could not. Others resembled a "maze," the puzzle being how to get from one point to another a few

Copyright by Kolb Bros.

"ROCKS OVERHANGING THE COLORADO'S GORGE."
NOTE FIGURE.

Copyright by Kolb Bros.

"THE LAND OF STANDING ROCKS WAS LIKE A MAZE."

feet away. The rock was a sandstone and presented a rough surface affording a good hold, so there was little danger of slipping. We usually sat down and "inched" our way to the edge of the cracks, jumping across to little ledges when possible, always helping each other.

The rock at the very edge of the main canyon overhung, in places 75 to 100 feet, and the great mass of gigantic boulders — sections of shattered cliffs — on the steep slope near the river gave evidence of a continual breaking away of these immense rocks.

To the north, across the canyon up which we had climbed, were a great number of smooth formations, from one hundred to four hundred feet high, rounded on top in domes, reminding one of Bagdad and tales from the Arabian Nights. "The Land of Standing Rocks," the Utes call it. The rock on which we stood was light gray or nearly white; the river walls at the base for a thousand feet above the river were dark red or chocolate-brown; while the tops of the formations above this level were a beautiful light red tint.

But there were other wonders. On the south side of the Colorado's gorge, miles away, were great spires, pointing heavenward, singly and in groups, looking like a city of churches. Beyond the spires were the Blue Mountains, to the east the hazy LaSalle range, and nearest of all on the west just north of the Colorado lay the snow-covered peaks of the Henry Mountains. Directly below us was the Colorado River, muddy, swirling, and forbidding. A mile away boomed a rapid, beyond that was another, then the river was lost to view.

Standing on the brink of all this desolation, it is small wonder if we recalled the accounts of the disasters which had overtaken so many others in the canyon below us. Many who had escaped the water had climbed out on to this death trap, as it had proven to be for them, some to perish of thirst and starvation, a few to stagger into the ranch below the canyon, a week or more after they had escaped from the water. Small wonder that some of these had lost their reason. We could only conjecture at the fate of the party whose wrecked boat had been found by the Stone expedition, a few miles below this place, with their tracks still fresh in the sand. No trace of them was ever found.

For the first time it began to dawn on us that we might have tackled a job beyond our power to complete. Most of the parties which had safely completed the trip were composed of several men, adding much to the safety of the expedition, as a whole. Others had boats much lighter than ours, a great help in many respects. Speaking for myself, I was just a little faint-hearted, and not a little overawed as we prepared to return to the boats.

While returning, we saw evidences of ancient Indians — some broken arrow-heads, and pottery also, and a small cliff ruin under a shelving rock.

Copyright by Kolb Bros.

THIRTEEN HUNDRED FEET ABOVE THE GREEN RIVER. NOTE FIGURE.

What could an Indian find here to interest him!
We had found neither bird, nor rabbit; not even a lizard
in the Land of Standing Rocks. Perhaps they were sun
worshippers, and wanted an unobstructed view of the
eastern sky. That at least could be had, in unrivalled
grandeur, here above the Rio Colorado.

The shadows were beginning to lengthen when we
finally reached our boats at the junction. Camp was
made under a large weeping willow tree, the only tree
of its kind we remembered having seen on the journey.

While Emery prepared a hasty meal I made a few
arrangements for embarking on the Colorado River the
next morning. We were prepared to bid farewell to
the Green River — the stream that had served us so
well. In spite of our trials, even in the upper canyons,
we had found much enjoyment in our passage through its
strange and beautiful surroundings.

From a scenic point of view the canyons of the Green
River, with their wonderful rock formations and stupendous gorges, are second only to those of the Colorado itself.
It is strange they are so little known, when one considers
the comparative ease with which these canyons on the
lower end can be reached. Some day perhaps, surfeited
globe-trotters, after having tired of commonplace scenery
and foreign lands, will learn what a wonderful region
this is, here on the lower end of the Green River.

Then no doubt, Wolverton, or others with similar

outfits, will find a steady stream of sight-seers anxious to take the motor boat ride down to this point, and up to Moab, Utah, a little Mormon town on the Grand River. A short ride by automobile from Moab to the D. & R. G. railway would complete a most wonderful journey; then the transcontinental journey could be resumed.

So I mused, as I contrived an arrangement of iron hooks and oak sticks to hold on a hatch cover, from which all the thumb screws had been lost. More than likely my dream of a line of sight-seeing motor boats will be long deferred; or they may even meet the fate of Brown's and Stanton's plans for a railroad down these gorges.

As a reminder of the fate which overtakes so many of our feeble plans, we found a record of Stanton's survey on a fallen boulder, an inscription reading "A 81 + 50, Sta.   D.C.C. & P.R.R.," the abbreviations standing for Denver, Colorado Canyons, and Pacific Railroad. It is possible that the hands that chiselled the inscription belonged to one of the three men who were afterwards drowned in Marble Canyon.

Emery — being very practical — interrupted my revery and plans for future sight-seers by announcing supper. The meal was limited in variety, but generous in quantity, and consisted of a dried-beef stew, fried potatoes, and cocoa. A satisfied interior soon dispelled all our previous apprehensiveness. We decided not to run our rapids before we came to them.

The water still gave indications of being higher than the low-water mark, although it was falling fast on the Green River. Each morning, for three days previous to our arrival at the junction, we would find the water about six inches lower than the stage of the evening before. Strange to say, we gained on the water with each day's rowing, until we had almost overtaken the stage of water we had lost during the night. More than likely we would have all the water we needed under the new conditions which were before us.

Beginning with the Colorado River, we made our journals much more complete in some ways, giving all the large rapids a number and describing many of them in detail. This was done, not only for our own satisfaction, but for the purpose of comparison with others who had gone through, for many of these rapids have histories.

It was often a question, when on the Green River, where to draw the line when counting a rapid; this was less difficult when on the Colorado. While the descent was about the same as in some of the rapids above, the increased volume of water made them look and act decidedly different. We drew the line, when counting a rapid, at a descent having a decided agitation of the water, hidden rocks, or swift descent and with an eddy or whirlpool below. Major Powell considered that many of these drops in the next canyon were above the ordinary rapid, hence the name, Cataract Canyon.

At one of the camps below Green River, Utah, my boat had been christened the *Defiance*, by painting the name on the bow. After leaving the Green we usually referred to the boats by their respective names, Emery being in the *Edith*, I in the *Defiance*.

Copyright by Kolb Bros.

THE JUNCTION OF THE TWO RIVERS. THE GRAND RIVER IS ON THE RIGHT. NOTE BOATS.

CHAPTER XIII

A COMPANION VOYAGER

THURSDAY morning, October the 26th, found Emery feeling very poorly, but insisting on going ahead with our day's work, so Camp No. 34 was soon behind us. We were embarked on a new stream, flowing west-south-west, with a body of water ten times the size of that which we had found in the upper canyons of the Green. Our sixteen-foot boats looked quite small when compared with the united currents of the Green and the Grand rivers. The Colorado River must have been about 350 feet wide here just below the junction, with a three-mile current, and possibly twenty-five feet deep, although this is only a guess. The Grand River appeared to be the higher of the two streams, and had a decidedly red colour, as though a recent storm was being carried down its gorges; while the colour of the Green was more of a coffee colour — coffee with a little cream in it.

A fourth of a mile below the junction the two currents began to mix, with a great ado about it, with small whirlpools and swift eddies, and sudden outbursts from beneath, as though a strangled current was struggling to escape from the weight which overpowered it. The boats were twisted this way and that, and hard rowing was necessary to carry us down to the steadied current, and to the first rapid, which we could hear when yet far above it.

Soon we were running rapids again, and getting a lot of sport out of it. There were some rocks, but there was water enough so that these could be avoided. If one channel did not suit us, we took another, and although we were drenched in every rapid, and the cockpit was half filled each time, it was not cold enough to cause us any great discomfort, and we bailed out at the end of each rapid, then hurried on to tackle the next. Each of these rapids was from a fourth to a third of a mile in length. The average was at least one big rapid to the mile. When No. 5 was reached we paused a little longer, and looked it over more carefully than we had the others. It had a short, quick descent, then a long line of white-topped waves, with a big whirlpool on the right. There were numerous rocks which would take careful work to avoid. The waves were big, — big enough for a motion picture, — so Emery remained on shore with both the motion-picture camera and the 8×10 plate camera in position, ready to take the picture, while I ran my boat.

At the head of this rapid we saw footprints in the sand, but not made with the same shoe as that which we had noticed above the junction. We had also seen signs of a camp, and some fishes' heads above this point, and what we took to be a dog's track along the shore.

At the head of the next rapid we saw them again, but on the opposite side of the river, and could see where a boat had been pulled up on the sand. This next rapid was almost as bad as the one above it, but with a longer descent, instead of one abrupt drop. The following rapid was so close that we continued along the shore to look it over at the same time, saving a stop between the two rapids. The shores were strewn with a litter of gigantic boulders — fallen sections of the overhanging cliffs. We found more of this in Cataract Canyon than in any of the canyons above. This was partly responsible for the violence of the rapids, although the descent of the river would make rough water even if there were no boulders. Working back along the shore, we were suddenly electrified into quick action by seeing the *Edith* come floating down the river, close to the shore and almost in the rapid. Emery was a short distance ahead and ran for the *Defiance;* I caught up a long pole and got on a projecting rock, hoping I might steer her in. She passed me, and was soon in the midst of the rapid before Emery had launched the boat. Three gigantic boulders extended above the water about fifty feet from shore, with a very crooked channel between. Down toward these boulders came the *Edith*, plunging like a thing possessed. How it was done I could never tell, but she passed through the crooked channel without once touching, and continued over the rapid. Meanwhile Emery had run the other side and had gained on the *Edith*, but only caught her when close to the next rapid; so he turned her loose and came to the shore for me.

Emery had not been feeling his best and I advised him to remain on shore while I took the boat. As we made the change we again observed the boat, bounding through the next rapid, whirling on the tops of the waves as though in the hands of a superhuman juggler. I managed to overtake her in a whirlpool below the rapid, and came to shore for her captain. He was nearly exhausted with his efforts; still he insisted on continuing. A few miles below we saw some ducks, and shot at them with a revolver. But the ducks flew disdainfully away, and landed in the pool below.

By 4.30 P.M. we were twelve miles below the junction, a very good day's run considering the kind of water we were travelling on, and the amount of time we spent on the shore. We had just run our twelfth rapid, and were turning the boats around, when we saw a man back from the shore working over a pile of boxes which he had covered with a piece of canvas. A boat was tied to the water's edge. We called to him, and he answered, but did not seem nearly as much interested in seeing companion travellers as we were, and proceeded with his

work. We landed, and, to save time, introduced ourselves, as there seemed to be a certain aloofness in his
manner. He gave the name of Smith — with some hesi-
tation, we thought.

Smith was about medium size, but looked tough and
wiry; he had a sandy complexion, with light hair and
mustache. He had lost one eye, the other was that
light gray colour that is usually associated with indomi-
table nerve. He had a shrewd, rather humorous expression, and gave one the impression of being very capable.
Dressed in a neat whipcord suit, wearing light shoes and
a carefully tied tie, recently shaved — a luxury we
had denied ourselves, all this time — he was certainly
an interesting character to meet in this out-of-the-way
place. We should judge he was a little over forty years
old; but whether prospector, trapper, or explorer it was
hard to say. Some coyote skins, drying on a rock, would
give one the impression that he was the second, with a
touch of the latter thrown in. These coyotes were
responsible for the tracks we had seen, and had mistaken for dog tracks, but of all the canyons we had
seen he was in the last place where we would expect to
find a trapper. The coyotes evidently reached the
river gorge through side canyons on the left, where we
had seen signs of ancient trails. Apart from that there
was no sign of animal life. With the last of the wooded
canyons, the signs of beaver had disappeared. There

were a few otter tracks, but they are wily fellows, and are seldom trapped. While there are laws against the trapping of beaver, they seldom prevent the trappers from taking them when they get the chance; they are only a little more wary of strangers; the thought occurred to us that this trapper may have secured some beaver in the open sections above, and mistrusted us for this reason.

It was too late to go any farther that evening, so we camped a hundred yards below him, close to where our boats were pulled out. At this place there was a long, wide flat in the canyon, with plenty of driftwood, so we saw no reason why we should quarrel with our neighbour. Smith accepted our invitation to supper, stating that he had just eaten before we arrived, but enjoyed some pineapple which we had kept for some special occasion, and which was served for dessert.

Over the table we became better acquainted, and, after learning what we were doing, he recounted his experiences. He told us he had left Green River, Utah, a month before, and had been trapping as he came along. He knew there was a canyon, and some rapids below, but had no idea they were so bad, and thought they were about ended. No one had warned him, for he had told no one what he intended doing. He had bought an old water-logged boat that had been built by Galloway, and seeing the uselessness of trying to run the rapids with it,

Copyright by Kolb Bros.

LOOKING WEST INTO CATARACT CANYON.

CHARLES SMITH AND HIS BOAT.

had worked it down along the shores by holding it with
a light chain.   Once he had been pulled into the river,
twice the boat had been upset, and he was just about
dried out from the last spill when we arrived.   He had
heard us shooting at the ducks, so rather expected company — this in brief was his amazing story.

We were surprised when we examined the boat closely.
It had been well made, but was so old and rotten that it
seemed ready to fall to pieces.   In places, the nail heads
had pulled through the boards.   It was entirely open
on top — a great risk in such water.   His boxes were tied
in to prevent loss.   These boxes were now piled on the
shore, with a large canvas thrown over them.   This
canvas, fastened at the top and sloping to the ground,
served him for a tent; his bed was underneath.   A pair
of high-topped boots, placed bottom up over two sticks,
stuck in the sand beside the camp-fire, explained the different tracks we had seen above.

Smith evidently was not much alarmed over his
situation.   About the only thing that seemed to bother
him was the fact that his smoking tobacco had been wet
several times.   That evening we got out our guide-book
— Dellenbaugh's "A Canyon Voyage" — and tried to
give him an idea of what was ahead.   The walls ahead
grew higher, and closer together; sometimes there was a
shore on one side, sometimes on the other, at one or two
places there was no shore on either side, and the rapids

continued to get worse, — so we gathered from Dellen-baugh's experience. Above this point there were several places where one could climb out, — we had even seen signs of ancient trails in two side canyons, — below here few such places existed.

Smith listened to all this attentively, then smiled and said "I guess there will be some way through." After a short visit he returned to his camp. We noticed that he slept on his gun, — to keep it dry, no doubt, for it looked like rain.

Morning found us very sorry that we had not erected our tent, for it rained nearly all night, but when once in our beds it was a question which was preferable; to get out in the rain and put up our tent, or remain in our comfortable beds. We remained where we were. As we prepared to leave, we offered Smith a chance to accompany us through Cataract Canyon, telling him that we would help him with his boat until the quiet water of Glen Canyon was reached. He declined the opportunity, saying that he would rather travel slowly and do what trapping he could. He welcomed a chance to take a ride on the *Defiance*, however. We took him over two small rapids, and gave him an insight into our method of avoiding the dangers. He was very enthusiastic about it. On reaching the next rapid we all concluded it would be very unwise to carry any passengers, for it was violent water, so he got out on the shore.

Smith had once seen some moving pictures of Japanese shooting rapids, but he said they were nothing compared to these, remarking that a bronco could hardly buck any harder. The next rapid was just as bad, Rapid No. 14 for Cataract Canyon, and Smith helped us secure a motion picture. Then he prepared to return to his camp. Just before leaving he explained rather apologetically, that ranchers, or others, were usually very unfriendly to a stranger coming into their section of the country. He had heard us shooting at the ducks and he imagined we belonged in some of the side canyons or on the top. This explained his puzzling attitude at our first meeting. If he had any beaver skins in his pack this would make him even more suspicious of strangers. We wished him nothing but the best of luck, and were good friends when we parted. His decision to make the trip alone, poorly equipped as he was, seemed like suicide to us. He promised to write to us if he got out, and with a final wave of the hand we left him on the shore.

The rapid just passed was possibly the scene of the disaster discovered by the Stone expedition. They found a clumsy boat close to the shore, jammed in a mass of rocks, smashed and abandoned. There were tracks of three people in the sand, one track being a boy's. A coat was left on the shore. The tracks disappeared up a box canyon. Mr. Stone corresponded with the only settlements in all that region, few in number, and far distant; but nothing was ever heard of them. Two other parties have left Green River, Utah, within a year of this find and disappeared in like manner. This seemed to be the usual result of these attempts. In nearly every case they have started in boats that are entirely unfitted for rough water, and, seemingly without any knowledge of the real danger ahead, try to follow where others, properly equipped, have gone through.

What a day of excitement that was! We always thought we needed a certain amount of thrills to make life sufficiently interesting for us. In a few hours' time, in the central portion of Cataract Canyon, we experienced nearly enough thrills to last us a lifetime. In one or two of the upper canyons we thought we were running rapids. Now we were learning what rapids really were. No sooner were we through one than another presented itself. At each of them we climbed along the boulder-strewn shores — the lower slopes growing steeper, the walls above towering higher — clear to the end of the rapid. Looking upstream we could pick out the submerged rocks hidden in the muddy water, and looking like an innocent wave from above. Twice we had picked out channels in sharp drops, after carefully observing their actions and deciding they were free from obstructions, when suddenly the waves would part for an instant and disclose a hidden rock — in one case as sharp as a hound's tooth — sure disaster if we ever struck it. As soon as we had decided on a channel we would lose no time in getting back to our boats and running it, for we could feel our courage oozing from our finger tips with each second's delay. Time and again we got through just by a scratch. Success bred confidence; I distinctly remember feeling that water alone would not upset the boat; that it would take a collision with a rock to do it. And each time we got through. Twice I almost had reason to reverse my impression of the power of water. First the stern rose up in front of me, as if squaring off at the tops of the cliffs, then descended, until it seemed to be trying to plumb the depths of the river. The waves, rolling over me, almost knocked me out of the boat, I lost my hold on the oars and grabbed the sides of the boat; then, regaining the oars, I finished the run by pulling with the bow headed downstream, for the boat had "swapped ends" in the interval, and was heavy with about three barrels of water in the cockpit. I bailed out with a grocery box, kept under the seat for that purpose. It had been growing quite cold, and Emery's indisposition — or what was really acute indigestion — had weakened him for the past two days, but he pluckily declined to stop. I was soaked with my last immersion and chilled with the wind, so concluded there was no use having him go through the same experience and I ran his boat while he made a picture. We were both ready to camp then, but there was no suitable place and we had to push on to the next rapid. On looking it over we almost gave up our intention of running it. It was about a fourth of a mile long; a mass of submerged rocks extended entirely across the river; the entire rapid seemed impossible. We finally concluded it might be run by shooting up, stern first, on a sloping rock near the shore, then return as the current recoiled and ran back, dividing on either side of the rock. The only clear channel was one about twelve feet wide, between this rock and the shore. A projecting shore above prevented a direct entrance to this channel.

We threw logs in and watched their action. In each case they paused when within five or six feet of the top of the slope, then returned with the current, whirled back to the side and shot through close to the shore. We planned to go through as close together as possible. Emery was ready first, I held back in a protecting pool, waiting for him to get out of the way. He got his position, facing stern downstream, gave the slightest shove forward, and the released boat whizzed down for fifty feet and ran up on the rock. She paused a moment, as the water prepared to return. He gave two quick pulls, shooting back again, slightly to the right, until he struck the narrow channel, then reversed his course and went through stern first exactly as we had planned it. The square stern, buoyed up by the air-chamber, lifted the boat out of the resulting wave as he struck the bottom of

Copyright by Kolb Bros.

RAPID NO. 22 IN CATARACT CANYON.

the descent. This much of the rapid had only taken a few seconds.

I followed at once, but was not so fortunate. The *Defiance* was carried to the left side, where some water dropped over the side of the rock, instead of reversing. I pulled frantically, seeing visions, meanwhile, of the boat and myself being toppled off the side of the rock, into the boulders and waves below. My rowing had no effect whatever, but the boat was grabbed by the returning wave and shot, as if from a catapult, back and around to the right, through the sloping narrow channel, — my returning course describing a half circle. Instead of rising, the pointed bow cut down into the waves until the water was on my shoulders. Emery turned his head for an instant to see what success I was having, and his boat was thrown on to a rock close to the shore. I passed him and landed, just before going into the next rapid. I then went back and helped him off the rock, and he continued his course over the leaping waves. He broke a rowlock before he landed, and had to use the substitute we had hung beside it.

We found a good spot for a camp just above the next rapid. Our tent was stretched in front of a large boulder. A large pile of driftwood gave us all the fuel needed, and we soon had a big fire going and our wet clothes steaming on the line.

CHAPTER XIV

A PATIENT AMID THE CATARACTS

An hour or so after making our camp, we began to doubt the wisdom of our choice of a location, for a downpour of rain threatened to send a stream of water under the tent. The stream was easily turned aside, while a door and numerous boards found in the drift pile, made a very good floor for the tent and lifted our sleeping bags off the wet sand. We had little trouble in this section to find sufficient driftwood for fires. The pile at this camp was enormous, and had evidently been gathering for years. Some of it, we could be sure, was recent, for a large pumpkin was found deposited in the drift pile twenty-five feet above the low-water stage on which we were travelling. This pumpkin, of course, could only have come down on the flood that had preceded us

What a mixture of curios some of those drift piles were, and what a great stretch of country they represented! The rivers, unsatisfied with washing away the fertile soil of the upper country, had levied a greedy toll on the homes along their banks, as well. Almost everything that would float, belonging to a home, could be found in some of them. There were pieces of furniture and toilet articles, children's toys and harness, several smashed boats had been seen, and bloated cattle as well. A short distance above this camp we had found two cans of white paint, carefully placed on top of a big rock above the high-water mark, by some previous voyager.[1] The boats were beginning to show the effect of hard usage, so we concluded to take the paint along. At another point, this same day, we found a corked bottle containing a faded note, undated, requesting the finder to write to a certain lady in Delta, Colorado. A note in my journal, beneath a record of this find, reads : "Aha ! A romance at last !" Judging by the appearance of the note it might have been thrown in many years before. Delta, we knew, was on the Gunnison River, a tributary of the Grand River. The bottle must have travelled over two hundred miles to reach this spot.

A letter which I sent out later brought a prompt answer, with the information that this bottle and four others with similar notes were set adrift by the writer and four of her schoolmates, nearly two years before. An agreement was made that the one first receiving an answer was to treat the others to a dinner. Our find was the second, so this young lady was a guest instead of the host.

[1] Left by the Stone expedition.]

Emery took but little interest in our camp arrangements this evening, and went to bed as soon as it was possible for him to do so. He said little, but he was very weak, and I could tell from his drawn face that he was suffering, and knew that it was nothing but nervous energy that kept him at his work — that, and a promise which he had made to build a fire, within a stated time now less than two weeks away, in Bright Angel Creek Canyon, nearly three hundred miles below this camp, a signal to his wife and baby that he would be home the next day. I was worried about his condition and I feared a fever or pneumonia. For two or three days he had not been himself. It was one thing to battle with the river when well and strong; it would be decidedly different if one of us became seriously ill.

For the first time in all our experiences together, where determination and skill seemed necessary to success, I had taken the lead during the past two days, feeling that my greater weight and strength, perhaps, would help me pull out of danger where he might fail. In two or three rapids I felt sure he did not have the strength to pull away from certain places that would smash the boats. After running the *Defiance* through these rapids I suggested to him that he would take a picture while I brought the *Edith* down. He would stay near the *Defiance*, ready to aid in case of emergency. After being once through a rapid I found it quite a simple matter to run the second boat, and the knowledge that he would save me in case of an upset greatly lessened any danger that might have existed. He was too nervous to sleep, and asked me to take a last look at the boats before going to bed. They were pulled well up on the shore and securely tied, I found, so that it would take a flood to tear them loose. The rain, which had stopped for a while, began again as I rolled into the blankets; the fire, fed with great cotton-wood logs, threw ghostly shadows on the cliffs which towered above us, and sputtered in the rain but refused to be drowned; while the roar of rapids, Nos. 22 and 23 combined, thundered and reverberated from wall to wall, and finally lulled us to sleep.

The rain continued all night, but the weather cleared in the morning. Emery felt much the same as he had the day before, so we kept the same camp that day. We took some pictures, and made a few test developments, hanging the dark-room, or tent, inside the other tent for want of a better place to tie to.

Sunday, October the 29th, we remained at the same place, and by evening were both greatly benefited by the rest. On Monday morning we packed up again, leaving only the moving-picture camera out, and pictured each other, alternately, as the boats made the plunge over the steep descent in rapid No. 23. Both boats disappeared from sight on two or three occasions in this rapid and emerged nearly filled with water.

L

The section just passed is credited with the greatest descent on the rivers, a fall of 75 feet in ¾ of a mile. This includes the three rapids: Nos. 21, 22, and 23.

Proceeding on our way the canyon narrowed, going up almost sheer to a height of 2500 feet or over. Segregated spires, with castle-like tops, stood out from the upper walls. The rapids, or cataracts, compared well with those passed above, connected in some instances by swift-rushing water instead of the quiet pools which were usually found between the rapids. We ran ten rapids this day, but several of these which were counted as one were a series of two or three rapids, which might be one in high water. All had a shore on one side or the other, but caution was imperative when crossing in the swift water between the rapids. A mishap here meant destruction. We figured that we had travelled about ten miles for this day's run.

The menacing walls continued to go higher with the next day's travel, until they reached a height of 2700 feet. The left wall was so sheer that it almost seemed to overhang. The little vegetation which we had found on the lower slope gradually disappeared as the walls grew steeper, but a few scattered shrubs, sagebrush, and an occasional juniper grew on the rocky sides, or in one or two side canyons which entered from the south. These side canyons had the appearance of running back for considerable distances, but we did not ex-

Copyright by Kolb Bros.

CAMP IN THE HEART OF CATARACT CANYON.

plore any of them and could tell very little about them from the river.

After our noon lunch this day, in order to keep our minds from dwelling too much on the rather depressing surroundings, we proposed having a little sport. On two or three occasions we had made motion pictures from the deck of the boats as we rowed in the quiet water; here we proposed taking a picture from the boats as we went over the rapids. The two boats were fastened stern to stern, so that the rowing would be done from the first boat. My brother sat on the bow behind with the motion-picture camera in front of him, holding it down with his chin, his legs clinging to the sides of the boat, with his left hand clutching at the hatch cover, and with his right hand free to turn the crank. In this way we passed over two small rapids. After that one experience we never tried it in a large rapid. As Smith had said a few days before the boat bucked like a broncho, and Emery had a great deal of difficulty to stay with the boat, to say nothing of taking a picture. Once or twice he was nearly unseated but pluckily hung on and kept turning away at the crank when it looked as if he and the camera would be dumped into the river.

At one point in the lower end of Cataract Canyon we saw the name and date A. G. Turner, '07. Below this, close to the end of the canyon, were some ruins of cliff dwellings, and a ladder made by white men, placed against the walls below the ruins.

On reaching a very deep, narrow canyon entering from the south, locally known as Dark Canyon, we knew that we were nearing the end of the rapids in Cataract Canyon. Dark Canyon extends a great distance back into the country, heading in the mountains we had seen to the south, when we climbed out at the junction of the Green and the Grand. Pine cones and other growths entirely foreign to the growth of the desert region were found near its mouth. A flood had recently filled the bottom of this narrow canyon to a depth of several feet, but the water had settled down again and left a little stream of clear water running through the boulders. The rapid at the end of this canyon was one of the worst of the entire series, and had been the scene of more than one fatality, we had been told. It had a very difficult approach and swung against the right wall, then the water was turned abruptly to the left by a great pile of fallen boulders. The cresting waves looked more like breakers of the ocean than anything we had seen on the river.

We each had a good scare as we ran this rapid. Emery was completely hidden from my view, he was nearly strangled and blinded by the waves for a few seconds while struggling in the maelstrom; the *Edith* was dropped directly on top of a rock in the middle of this rapid, then lifted on the next wave. I also had a thrilling experience but avoided the rock. In the lower part of the rapid a rowlock pulled apart; and to prevent the boat from turning sideways in the rapid, I threw up my knee, holding the oar against it for a lever until I was in quieter water, and could get the other rowlock in position.

Separated from my brother in this instance, I had an opportunity to see the man and water conflict, with a perspective much as it would have appeared to a spectator happening on the scene. I was out of the heat of the battle. The excitement and indifference to danger that comes with a hand-to-hand grapple was gone. I heard the roar of the rapid; a roar so often heard that we forgot it was there. I saw the gloom of the great gorge, and the towering, sinister shafts of rock, weakened with cracks, waiting for the moment that would send them crashing to the bottom. I saw the mad, wild water hurled at the curving wall. Jagged rocks, like the bared fangs of some dream-monster, appeared now and then in the leaping, tumbling waves. Then down toward the turmoil — dwarfed to nothingness by the magnitude of the walls — sped the tiny shell-like boat, running smoothly like a racing machine! There was no rowing. The oar-blades were tipped high to avoid loss in the first comber; then the boat was buried in the foam, and staggered through on the other side. It was buffeted here and there, now covered with a ton of water, now topping a ten-foot wave. Like a skilled boxer — quick of eye, and ready to seize any temporary advantage — the oarsman shot in his oars for two quick strokes, to straighten the boat with the current or dodge a threatening boulder; then covered by lifting his oars and ducking his head as a brown flood rolled over him. Time and again the manoeuvre was repeated: now here, now there. One would think the chances were about one to a hundred that he would get through. But by some sort of a system, undoubtedly aided, many times, by good luck, the man and his boat won to land.

After running a small rapid, we came to another, in the centre of which was an island, — the last rapid in Cataract Canyon. While not as bad as the one at Dark Canyon it was rather difficult, and at this point we found no shore on either side. The south side was rendered impassable by great boulders, much higher than the river level, which were scattered through the channel. The opposite channel began much like the rapid at Dark Canyon, sweeping under the wall until turned by a bend and many fallen rocks below the end of the island, then crossed with a line of cresting waves to the opposite side, where it was joined by the other stream, and the left wall was swept clean in like manner. We ran it by letting our boats drop into the stream, but pulled away from the wall and kept close to the island, then when its end was reached crossed the ridge of waves and pulled for the right-hand shore. In such rapids as this we often found the line of waves in the swift-rushing centre to be several feet higher than the water along the shore.

Then our thoughts reverted to Smith. What would he do when he came to this rapid ? The only escape was a narrow sloping ledge on the right side, beginning close to the water some distance above the rapid, reaching a height of sixty or seventy feet above the water at the lower end, while a descent could be made to the river some distance below here. It would be possible for him to climb over this with his provisions, but the idea of taking his boat up there was entirely out of the question, and, poorly equipped as he was, an attempt to run it would surely end in disaster. The breaking of an oar, the loss of a rowlock, or the slightest knock of his rotten boat against a rock, and Smith's fate would be similar to those others whose bones lay buried in the sands.

In the next four miles we had no more rapids, but had some fine travelling on a very swift river. It was getting dusk, but we pulled away, for just ahead of us was the end of Cataract Canyon. We camped by a large side canyon on the left named Mille Crag Bend, with a great number of jagged pinnacles gathered in a group at the top of the walls, which had dropped down to a height of about 1300 feet. We felt just a little proud of our achievement, and believed we had established a record for Cataract Canyon, having run all rapids in four days' travelling, and come through in safety.

We had one rapid to run the next morning at the beginning of Narrow Canyon, the only rapid in this nine-mile long canyon. The walls here at the beginning were twelve or thirteen hundred feet high, and tapered to the end, where they rise about four hundred feet above the Dirty Devil River. Narrow Canyon contains the longest straight stretch of river which we remembered having seen. When five miles from its mouth we could look through and see the snow-capped peak of Mt. Ellsworth beyond. This peak is one of the five that composes the Henry Mountains, which lay to the north of the river.

Three hours' rowing brought us to the end. We paused a few minutes to make a picture or two of the Dirty Devil River, — or the Frémont River as it is now recorded on the maps. This stream, flowing from the north, was the exact opposite of the Bright Angel Creek, that beautiful stream we knew so well, two hundred and fifty miles below this point. The Dirty Devil was muddy and alkaline, while warm springs containing sulphur and other minerals added to its unpalatable taste. After tasting it we could well understand the feeling of the Jack Sumner, whose remark, after a similar trial, suggested its name to Major Powell.

A short distance below this we saw a tent, and found it occupied by an old-timer named Kimball. Among other things he told us that he had a partner, named Turner, who had made the trip through the canyons

Copyright by Kolb Bros.

LOWER CATARACT CANYON. BOATS TANDEM.

BEGINNING OF A NATURAL BRIDGE. GLEN CANYON.

above, and arrived at this point in safety. This was the man whose name we had seen on the walls in Cataract Canyon. Less than two miles more brought us to the Hite ranch, and post-office. John Hite gave us a cordial reception. He had known of our coming from the newspapers; besides, he had some mail for us. We spent the balance of the day in writing letters, and listening to Hite's interesting experiences of his many years of residence in this secluded spot. Hite's home had been a haven for the sole survivor of two expeditions which had met with disaster in Cataract. In each case they were on the verge of starvation. Hite kept a record of all known parties who had attempted the passage through the canyons above. Less than half of these parties, excepting Galloway's several successful trips, succeeded in getting through Cataract Canyon without wrecking boats or losing lives.

After passing the Frémont River the walls on the right or north side dropped down, leaving low, barren sandstone hills rolling away from the river, with a fringe of willows and shrubs beside the water, and with the usual sage-brush, prickly pear, cactus and bunch-grass on the higher ground. We had seen one broken-down log cabin, but this ranch was the only extensive piece of ground that was cultivated. Judging by the size of his stacks of alfalfa, Hite had evidently had a good season. The banks of the south side of the river were about two hundred feet high, composed of a conglomerate mass of clay and gravel. This spot has long been a ferry crossing, known far and wide as Dandy Crossing, the only outlet across the river for the towns of southeastern Utah, along the San Juan River. The entire 150 miles of Glen Canyon had once been the scene of extensive placer operations. The boom finally died, a few claims only proving profitable.

One of these claims was held by Bert Loper, one of the three miners who had gone down the river in 1908. Loper never finished, as his boat — a steel boat, by the way — was punctured in a rapid above Dark Canyon but was soon repaired. His cameras and plates being lost, he sent from Hite out for new ones. His companions — Chas. Russell, and E. R. Monette — were to wait for him at Lee's Ferry, after having prospected through Glen Canyon. Some mistake was made about the delivery of the cameras and, as Hite post-office only had weekly communication with the railroad, a month elapsed before he finally secured them. Lee's Ferry had been discontinued as a post-office at that time, and, although he tried to get a letter in to them, it was never delivered. His disappointment can be imagined better than described, when he reached Lee's Ferry and found his companions had left just a few days previous. They naturally thought if he were coming at all he would have been there long before that, and they gave him up, not knowing the cause of the delay. They left a letter, however, saying they would only go to the Bright Angel Trail, and the trip could be completed together on the following year.

Loper spent many hard days working his boat, with his load of provisions, back against the current, and located a few miles below the Hite ranch.

CHAPTER XV

WE passed Loper's claim after resuming our journey the next day. His workings were a one-man proposition and very ingenious. We found a tunnel in the gravel a hundred feet above the river, and some distance back from the river bank. A track of light rails ran from the river bank to these workings; the gravel and sand was loaded into a car, and hauled or pushed to the bank, then dumped into a chute, which sent it down to the river's edge.

Loper was not at his work however, neither did we find him at his ranch, a mile down the river. He had a neat little place, with fruit trees and a garden, a horse or two, and some poultry. After resuming our rowing, when about a mile down the river, some one called to us from the shore, and Loper himself came running down to meet us. John Hite had requested us to stop and see his brother, Cass Hite, who owned a ranch and placer working nearly opposite where Loper had halted us; so

Loper crossed with us, as he was anxious to know of our passage through the canyons.

We found, in Cass Hite, an interesting "old-timer," one who had followed the crowd of miners and pioneers, in the West, since the discovery of gold on the coast. He was the discoverer of the White Canyon Natural Bridges, of Southern Utah, located between this point and the San Juan River, and had been the first to open the ferry at Dandy Crossing. Hite had prospected Navajo Mountain, southwest of this point, in the early sixties, about the time of the Navajos' trouble with the United States army, under the leadership of Kit Carson, who dislodged them from their strongholds in the mountains after many others had failed. Hite's life was saved on more than one occasion by warnings from a friendly chief, or head man of the Western Navajos, known as Hoskaninni, who regarded him as a brother, and bestowed on him the name, Hosteen pes'laki, meaning "Silver man." He is still known by this name, and refers to his pretty ranch as Tick a Bo, a Ute word for "friendly." Hite proudly quoted a poem written by Cy Warman about the theme of the Indian's regard for his white friend. Warman had followed the crowd in to this spot at the time of the boom, looking for local colour — human local colour, not the glitter in the sands. It was at John Hite's home where Warman had composed the one time popular song, "Sweet Marie." It would be safe to say that he brought his inspiration with him, for this was decidedly a man's country. We were told that it had only been visited by one woman in the past twelve years. Hite insisted on our remaining until the following morning, and we concluded that the rest would do us good. He loaded us up with watermelons, and with raisins, which he was curing at that time. We spent a pleasant afternoon under a shaded arbour, listening to his reminiscences, and munching at the raisins.

That evening Loper told us his story of their canyon expedition. He felt a little bitter about some newspaper reports that had been published concerning this expedition, these reports giving the impression that his nerve had failed him, and that for this reason he had not continued on the journey. We mollified his feelings somewhat, when we told him that his companions were not responsible for these reports; but rather, that short telegraphic reports, sent out from the Grand Canyon, had been misconstrued by the papers; and that this accounted for the stories which had appeared. His companions had remained at the Grand Canyon for two days following their arrival at Bright Angel Trail. They gave Loper credit, to our certain knowledge, of being the only one of the party who knew how to handle the boats in rough water when they began the trip, and had stated that he ran all the boats through certain rapids until they caught the knack. They could not know of his reasons for the delay, and at that time had no knowledge of his arrival at Lee's Ferry, after they had gone. Naturally they were very much puzzled over his non-appearance.

It got quite cold that night, and we were glad to have the shelter of Hite's hospitable roof. In our trip down the river to this point we had seemed to keep even with the first cold weather. In all places where it was open, we would usually find a little ice accompanied by frost in the mornings, or if no ice had frozen the grass would be wet with dew. In the canyons there was little or no ice, and the air was quite dry. Naturally we preferred the canyons if we had a choice of camps.

Loper looked as though he would like to accompany us as we pulled away the next morning, after having landed him on the south side of the stream. We, at least, had full confidence in his nerve to tackle the lower Colorado, after his record in Cataract Canyon. The five scattered peaks of the Henry Mountains were now to the north-northwest of us, rugged and snow-capped, supreme in their majesty above this desolate region.

Signs of an ancient Indian race were plentiful in this section. There were several small cliff dwellings, walled up in ledges in the rocks, a hundred feet or so above a low flat which banked the river. At another place there were hundreds of carvings on a similar wall which over-hung a little. Drawings of mountain-sheep were plentiful; there was one representing a human figure with a bow and arrow, and with a sheep standing on the arrow — their way of telling that he got the sheep, no doubt. There were masked figures engaged in a dance, not unlike some of the Hopi dances of to-day, as they picture them. There were geometrical figures, and designs of many varieties. A small rock building half covered with sand and the accumulations of many years stood at the base of the cliff; and quantities of broken pottery were scattered about the ruin. Farther down the river a pathway was worn into the sandstone where countless bare and moccasined feet had toiled, and climbed over the sloping wall to the mesa above. The ruins in this section were not extensive, like those found in the tributary canyons of the San Juan River, for instance, not a very great distance from here. Possibly this people stopped here as they travelled back and forth, trading with their cousins to the north; or the dwellings may have been built by the scattered members of the tribe, when their strongholds were assailed by the more warlike tribes that crowded in on them from all sides.

What a story these cliffs could tell! What a romance they could narrate of various tribes, as distinct from each other as the nations of Europe, crowding each other; and at the last of this inoffensive race, coming from the far south, it may be; driven from pillar to post, making their last stand in this desert land; to perish of pestilence, or to be almost exterminated by the blood-

Copyright by Kolb Bros.

PICTOGRAPHS IN GLEN CANYON.

thirsty tribes that surrounded them — then again, when the tide changed, and a new type of invader travelled from the east, pushing ever to the west, conquering all before them! But like the sphinx, the cliffs are silent and voiceless as the hillocks and sand-dunes along the Nile, that other desert stream, with a history no more ancient and momentous than this.

That night we camped opposite the ruins of a dredge, sunk in the low water at the edge of the river. This dredge had once represented the outlay of a great deal of money. It is conceded by nearly all experts that the sands of these rivers contain gold, but it is of such a fine grain — what is known as flour gold — and the expense of saving it is so great, that it has not paid when operated on such a large scale. A few placers in Glen Canyon have paid individual operators, some of these claims being in gravel deposits from six hundred to eight hundred feet above the present level of the river.

On the following day we again entered deep canyon; sheer for several hundred feet, creamy white above, with a dark red colour in the lower sandstone walls. That afternoon we passed a small muddy stream flowing from the north, in a narrow, rock-walled canyon. This was the Escalante River, a stream rising far to the north, named for one of the Spanish priests who had travelled this country, both to the north and the south of this point, as early as the year 1776, about the time when

M

the New England colonists were in the midst of their struggle with the mother country.

Just below the Escalante River, the canyon turned almost directly south, continuing in this general direction for several miles. A glimpse or two was had of the top of a tree-covered snow-capped peak directly ahead of us, or a little to the southwest. This could be none other than Navajo Mountain, a peak we could see from the Grand Canyon, and had often talked of climbing, but debated if we could spare the time, now that we were close to it.

In all this run through Glen Canyon we had a good current, but only one place resembling a rapid. Here, below the Escalante, it was very quiet, and hard pulling was necessary to make any headway. We were anxious to reach the San Juan River that evening, but the days were growing short, and we were still many miles away when it began to grow dusk; so we kept a lookout for a suitable camp. The same conditions that had bothered us on one or two previous occasions were found here; slippery, muddy banks, and quicksand, together with an absence of firewood. We had learned before this to expect these conditions where the water was not swift. The slower stream had a chance to deposit its silt, and if the high water had been very quiet, we could expect to find it soft, or boggy. In the canyons containing swift water and rapids we seldom found mud, but found a clean, firm sand, instead. Here in Glen Canyon we had plenty of mud, for the river had been falling the last few days. Time and again we inspected seemingly favourable places, only to be disappointed. The willows and dense shrubbery came down close to the river; the mud was black, deep, and sticky; all driftwood had gone out on the last flood. Meanwhile a glorious full moon had risen, spreading a soft, weird light over the canyon walls and the river; so that we now had a light much better than the dusk of half an hour previous, our course being almost due south. Finally, becoming discouraged, we decided to pull for the San Juan River, feeling sure that we would find a sand-bar there. It was late when we reached it, and instead of a sand-bar we found a delta of bottomless mud. We had drifted past the point where the rivers joined, before noticing that the stream turned directly to the west, with canyon walls two or three hundred feet high, and no moonlight entered there. Instead, it was black as a dungeon. From down in that darkness there came a muffled roar, reverberating against the walls, and sounding decidedly like a rapid. There was not a minute to lose. We pulled, and pulled hard — for the stream was now quite swift close to the right shore, and a sheer bank of earth about ten feet high made it difficult to land. Jumping into the mud at the edge of the water, we tied the boats to some bushes, then tore down the bank and climbed out on a dry, sandy point of land. At the end or sharp turn of the sheer wall we found a fair camp, with driftwood enough for that night. Emery, weak from his former illness and the long day's run, went to bed as soon as we had eaten a light supper. I looked after the cooking that evening, making some baking-powder bread, — otherwise known as a flapjack, — along with other arrangements for the next day; but I fear my efforts as a cook always resulted rather poorly.

We had breakfast at an early hour the next morning, and were ready for the boats at 7.15, the earliest start to our record. Our rapid of the night before proved to be a false alarm, being nothing more than the breaking of swift water as it swept the banks of rocks at the turn. It was quite different from what we had pictured in our minds.

We had long looked forward to this day. Navajo Mountain, with bare, jagged sides and tree-covered dome, was located just a few miles below this camp. It was a sandstone mountain peak, towering 7000 feet above the river, the steep slope beginning some five or six miles back from the stream. The base on which it rested was of sandstone, rounded and gullied into curious forms, a warm red and orange colour predominating. The north side, facing the river, was steep of slope, covered with the fragments of crumbled cliffs and with soft cream-tinted pinnacles rising from its slope. The south side, we had reason to believe, was tree-covered from top to bottom; the north side held only a few scattered cedar and piñon. We had often seen the hazy blue dome from the Grand Canyon, one hundred and twenty miles away, and while it was fifty miles farther by the river, we felt as if we were entered on the home stretch; as if we were in a country with which we were somewhat familiar.

The Colorado and the San Juan rivers form the northern boundary of the Navajo Indian Reservation, comprising a tract of land as large as many Eastern states, extending over a hundred miles, both east and west from this point. Embodied in this reservation, and directly opposite our camp, was a small section of rugged land set aside for some Utes, who had friendly dealings, and who had intermarried with the Navajo. But if we expected to find the Navajo, or Utes on the shore, ready to greet us, we were doomed to disappointment.

We explored a few side canyons this morning, hoping to find a spot where some of Major Powell's party — particularly those men who were afterwards killed by the Indians — had chiselled their names, which record we were told was to be found near the San Juan, but on which side we were not sure. While in one of these canyons, or what was really nothing more than a crooked overhanging slit in the rocks, containing a small stream, Emery found himself in some soft quicksand, plunged instantly above his knees, and sinking rapidly. He would have had a difficult time in getting out of this quicksand without help, for a smooth rock wall was on one side, the other bank of the stream was sheer above him for a few feet, and there was nothing solid which he could reach. We had seen a great deal of quicksand before this, but nothing of this treacherous nature. Usually we could walk quickly over these sands, without any danger of being held in them, or if caught — while lifting on a boat for instance — had no difficulty in getting out. When once out of this canyon we gave up our search for the carved record.

But it was not the hope of shortening our homeward run, or the prospect of meeting Indians on the shores, or of finding historical records, even, that caused us to make this early start. It was the knowledge that the wonderful Rainbow Natural Bridge, recently discovered, and only visited by three parties of whites, lay hidden in one of the side canyons that ran from the north slope of Navajo Mountain. No one had gone into it from the river, but we were told it could be done. We hoped to find this bridge.

The current was swift, and we travelled fast, in spite of a stiff wind which blew up the stream, getting a very good view of the mountain from the river a few miles below our camp, and another view of the extreme top, a short distance below this place, not over six miles from the San Juan. We had directions describing the canyon in which the bridge was located, our informant surmising that it was thirty miles below the San Juan. We thought it must be less than that, for the river was very direct at this place, and a person travelling over the extremely rough country which surrounded this side of the mountain slope would naturally have to travel much farther, so we began to look for it about twelve miles below camp. But mile after mile went by without any sign of the landmarks that would tell us we were at the "Bridge Canyon." Then the river, which had circled the northern side of the peak, turned directly away from it, and we knew that we had missed the bridge. At no point on the trip had we met with a disappointment to equal that; even the loss of our moving-picture film, after our spill in Lodore, was small when compared with it.

On looking back over the lay of the land, we felt sure that the bridge was at one of the two places, where we had seen the top of the mountain from the river. To go back against the current would take at least three days. Our provisions were limited in quantity and would not permit it; the canyon had deepened, and a second bench of sheer cliffs rose above the plateau, making it impossible to climb out: so we concluded to make the best of it, and pulled down the stream, trying to put as many miles as possible between ourselves and our great disappointment. This afternoon we passed from Utah into Arizona. For the remainder of the trip we would have Arizona on one side of the river at least. We had much the same difficulty this evening as we had had the night before in finding a camp. Judging by the evidence along the shore, the high water which came down the San Juan had been a torrent, much greater than the flood on the Colorado and its upper tributaries.

Copyright by Kolb Bros.

RAINBOW NATURAL BRIDGE BETWEEN THE COLORADO RIVER AND NAVAJO MOUNTAIN. HEIGHT THREE HUNDRED AND EIGHT FEET; SPAN TWO HUNDRED AND SEVENTY FEET. NOTE FIGURE ON TOP. PHOTO BY KOLB BROTHERS, SEPTEMBER, 1913.

CHAPTER XVI

A WARNING

WE camped that night at the Ute Ford, or the Crossing of the Fathers; a noted landmark of bygone days, when Escalante (in 1776) and others later followed the inter-tribal trails across these unfriendly lands. Later marauding Navajo used this trail, crossing the canyon to the north side, raiding the scattered Mormon settlements, bringing their stolen horses, and even sheep, down this canyon trail. Then they drove them across on a frozen river, and escaped with them to their mountain fastness. The Mormons finally tired of these predatory visits, and shut off all further loss from that source by blasting off a great ledge at the north end of the trail. This ruined the trail beyond all hope of repair, and there is no travel at present over the old Ute Crossing. The fording of the river on horseback was effected by dropping down to the river through a narrow side canyon, and crossing to the centre on a shoal, then following a centre shoal down for quite a distance, and completing the crossing at a low point on the opposite side. This was only possible at the very lowest stage of water.

The morning following our arrival here, we walked about a mile up the gravelly slope on the south side, to see if we could locate the pass by which the trail dropped down over these 3000-foot walls. The canyon had changed in appearance after leaving the mountain, and now we had a canyon; smaller, but not unlike the Grand Canyon in appearance, with an inner plateau, and a narrow canyon at the river, while the walls on top were several miles apart, and towering peaks or buttes rose from the plateau, reaching a height almost equal to the walls themselves. The upper walls were cream-tinted or white sandstone, the lower formation was a warm red sandstone. We could not discover the pass without a long walk to the base of the upper cliffs, so returned to the boats.

About this time we heard shots, seeming to come from some point down the river, and on the north side. Later a dull hollow sound was heard like pounding on a great bass drum. We could not imagine what it was, but knew that it must be a great distance away. We had noticed instances before this, where these smooth, narrow canyons had a great magnifying effect on noises. In the section above the San Juan, where the upper walls overhung a little, a loud call would roll along for minutes before it finally died. A shot from a revolver sounded as if the cliffs were falling.

Our run this morning was delightful. The current was the best on which we had travelled. The channel swung from side to side, in great half circles, with most of the water thrown against the outside bank, or wall, with a five- or six-mile an hour current close to the wall. We took advantage of all this current, hugging the wall, with the stern almost touching, and with the bow pointed out so we would not run into the walls or scrape our oars. Then, when it seemed as if our necks were about to be permanently dislocated, from looking over one shoulder, the river would reverse its curve, the channel would cross to the other side, and we would give that side of our necks a rest. Once in a great while I would bump a rock, and would look around sheepishly, to see if my brother had seen me do it. I usually found him with a big grin on his face, if he happened to be ahead of me.

We rowed about twenty miles down the river before we learned what had caused the noises heard in the morning. On rounding a turn we saw the strange spectacle of fifteen or twenty men at work on the half-constructed hull of a flat-bottomed steamboat, over sixty feet in length. This boat was on the bank quite a distance above the water, with the perpendicular walls of a crooked side canyon rising above it. It was a strange sight, here in this out-of-the-way corner of the world. Some men with heavy sledges were under the boat, driving large spikes into the planking. This was the noise we had heard that morning.

The blasting, we learned later, was at some coal mines, several miles up this little canyon, which bore the name of Warm Creek Canyon. A road led down through the canyon, making it possible to haul the lumber for the boat, clear to the river's edge. The nearest railroad was close to two hundred miles from this place, quite a haul considering the ruggedness of the country. The material for the boat had been shipped from San Francisco, all cut, ready to put together. The vessel was to be used to carry coal down the river, to a dredge that had recently been installed at Lee's Ferry.

The dinner gong had just sounded when we landed, and we were taken along with the crowd. There were some old acquaintances in this group of men, we found, from Flagstaff, Arizona. These men had received a Flagstaff paper which had published a short note we had sent from Green River, Utah. They had added a comment that no doubt this would be the last message we would have an opportunity to send out. Very cheering for Emery's wife, no doubt. Fortunately she shared our enthusiasm, and if she felt any apprehension her few letters failed to show it.

We resumed our rowing at once after dinner, for we wished to reach Lee's Ferry, twenty-five miles distant, that evening. We had a good current, and soon left our friends behind us. We pulled with a will, and mile after mile was covered in record time, for our heavy boats.

The walls continued to get higher as we neared our goal, going up sheer close to the river. We judged the greatest of these walls to be about eleven hundred feet high. After four hours of steady pulling we began to weary, for ours were no light loads to propel; but we were spurred to renewed effort by hearing the sounds of an engine in the distance. On rounding a turn we saw the end of Glen Canyon ahead of us, marked by a breaking down of the walls, and a chaotic mixture of dikes of rock, and slides of brilliantly coloured shales, broken and tilted in every direction. Just below this, close to a ferry, we saw the dredge on the right side of the river. We were quite close to the dredge before we were seen. Some men paused at their work to watch us as we neared them, one man calling to those behind him, "There come the brothers!"

A whistle blew announcing the end of their day's labour, and of ours as well, as it happened. There was some cheering and waving of hats. One who seemed to be the foreman asked us to tie up to a float which served as a landing for three motor boats, and a number of skiffs. A loudly beaten triangle of steel announced that the evening meal was ready at a stone building not far from the dredge. We were soon seated at a long table with a lot of others as hungry as we, partaking of a well-cooked and substantial meal. We made arrangements to take a few meals here, as we wished to overhaul our outfits before resuming our journey.

The meal ended, we inquired for the post-office, and were directed to a ranch building across the Paria River, a small stream which entered from the north, not unlike the Frémont River in size and appearance. Picking our way in the darkness, on boulders and planks which served as a crossing, we soon reached the building, set back from the river in the centre of the ranch. A man named Johnson, with his family, had charge of the ranch and post-office as well. Mail is brought by carrier from the south, a cross-country trip of 160 miles, through the Hopi and Navajo Indian Reservations.

Johnson informed us that an old-time friend named Dave Rust had waited here three or four days, hoping to see us arrive, but business matters had forced him to leave just the day before. We were very sorry to have missed him. Rust lived in the little Mormon town of Kanab, Utah, eighty miles north of the Grand Canyon opposite our home. In addition to being a cattle man and rancher, he had superintended the construction of a cable crossing, or tramway, over the Colorado River, beside the mouth of Bright Angel Creek, not many miles from our home. He also maintains a cozy camp at this place, for the accommodation of tourists and hunting parties, which he conducts up Bright Angel Creek and into the Kaibab Forest. It was while returning from such a hunting trip that we first met Rust. Many are the trips we have taken with him since then, Emery, with

PLACER DREDGE AT LEES FERRY.

his wife and the baby, even, making the "crossing" and the eighty-mile horseback ride to his home in Kanab, while I had continued on through to Salt Lake City. Rust had been the first to tell us of Galloway and his boating methods; and had given us a practical demonstration on the river. Naturally there was no one we would have been more pleased to see at that place, than Rust.

In our mail we found a letter from him, stating, among other things, that he had camped the night before on the plateau, a few hundred feet above a certain big rapid, well known through this section as the Soap Creek Rapid. This locality is credited with being the scene of the first fatality which overtook the Brown-Stanton expedition; Brown being upset and drowned in the next rapid which followed, after having portaged the Soap Creek Rapid. Rust wrote also that there was a shore along the rapid, so there would be no difficulty in making the portage; and concluded by saying that he had a very impressive dream about us that night, the second of its kind since we had started on our journey.

We understood from this that he had certain misgivings about this rapid, and took his dream to be a sort of a warning. Rust should have known us better. With all the perversity of human nature that letter made me want to run that rapid if it were possible. Why not run the rapid, and get a moving picture as it was being done. Then we could show Rust how well we had learned our lesson! So I thought as we returned to the buildings near the dredge, but said nothing of what was in my mind to Emery, making the mental reservation that I would see the rapid first and decide afterwards.

The foreman of the placer mines called us into his office that evening, and suggested that it might be a good plan to go over our boats thoroughly before we left, and offered us the privilege of using their workshop, with all its conveniences, for any needed repairs. He also let us have a room in one of the buildings for our photographic work.

This foreman mourned the loss of a friend who had recently been drowned at the ferry. It seemed that the floods which had preceded us, especially that part which came down the San Juan River, had been something tremendous, rising 45 feet at the ferry, where the river was 400 feet wide; and rising much higher in the narrow portions of Glen Canyon. Great masses of driftwood had floated down, looking almost like a continuous raft. When the river had subsided somewhat, an attempt was made to cross with the ferry. The foreman and his friend, with two others, and a team of horses hitched to a wagon, were on the ferry. When in midstream, it overturned in the swollen current. Three of the men escaped, the other man and the horses were drowned.

A careful search had been made for the body to a

point a few miles down the river, then the canyon closed in and they could go no farther. The body was never recovered. It is seldom that the Colorado River gives up its dead. The heavy sands collect in the clothes, and a body sinks much quicker than in ordinary water. Any object lodged on the bottom is soon covered with a sand-bar. The foreman knew this, of course; yet he wished us to keep a lookout for the body, which might, by some chance, have caught on the shore, when the water receded. This was as little as any one would do, and we gave him our promise to keep a careful watch.

N

CHAPTER XVII

A NIGHT OF THRILLS

WE declined the offer of a roof that night, preferring to sleep in the open here, for the evening was quite warm. We went to work the next morning when the whistle sounded at the dredge. Beyond caulking a few leaks in the boats, little was done with them. The tin receptacles holding our photographic plates and films were carefully coated with a covering of melted paraffine; for almost anything might happen, in the one hundred miles of rapid water that separated us from our home.

Lee's Ferry was an interesting place, both for its old and its new associations. This had long been the home of John D. Lee, well known for the part he took in the Mountain Meadow Massacre, and for which he afterwards paid the death penalty. Here Lee had lived for many years, making few visits to the small settlements to the north, but on one of these visits he was captured. There were six or seven other buildings near the large stone building where we took our meals, so arranged that they made a short street, the upper row being built against a cliff of rock and shale, the other row being placed halfway between this row and the river. These buildings were all of rock, of which there was no lack, plastered with adobe, or mud. One, we were told, had been Lee's stronghold. It was a square building, with a few very small windows, and with loopholes in the sides. At the time of our visit it was occupied by two men; one, a young Englishman, recently arrived from South Africa — a remittance-man, in search of novelty — the other a grizzled forty-niner. Much could be written about this interesting group of men, and their alluring employment. There were some who had followed this work through all the camps of the West — to Colorado, to California, and to distant Alaska as well, they had journeyed; but it is doubtful if, in all their wanderings, they had seen any camp more strangely located than this, hemmed in with canyon walls. To us, their dredge and the steamboat up the river seemed as if they had been taken from the pages of some romance, or bit of fiction, and placed before us for our entertainment.

There were other men as well, just as interesting in their way as the "old-timers," the sons of some of the owners of this proposition, — clean-cut young fellows, — working side by side with the veterans, as enthusiastic as if on their college campus.

One feature about the dredge interested us greatly. This was a tube, or sucker, held suspended by a derrick above a float, and operated by compressed air. This tube was dropped into the sand at the bottom of the river, and would eat its way into it, bringing up rocks the size of one's fist, along with the gravel and sand. In a few hours a hole, ten or fifteen feet in depth and ten feet in diameter, would be excavated. Then the tube was raised, the float was moved, and the work started again. The coarse sand and gravel, carried by a stream of water, was returned to the river, after passing over the riffles; the screenings which remained passed over square metal plates — looking like sheets of tin — covered with quicksilver. These plates were cleaned with a rubber window-cleaner, and the entire residue was saved in a heavy metal pot, ready for the chemist.

One day only was needed for our work, and by evening we were ready for the next plunge. We might have enjoyed a longer stay with these men, but stronger than this desire was our anxiety to reach our home, separated from us by a hundred miles of river, no extended part of the distance being entirely free from rapids. We had written to the Grand Canyon, bidding them look for our signal fire in Bright Angel Creek Canyon, in from seven to ten days, and planned to leave on the following morning. Nothing held us now except the hope that the mail, which was due that evening, might bring us a letter, although that was doubtful, for we were nearly a week ahead of our schedule as laid out at Green River, Utah.

As we had anticipated, there was no mail for us, so we turned to inspect the mail carrier. He was a splendid specimen of the Navajo Indian, — a wrestler of note among his people, we were told, — large and muscular, and with a peculiar springy, slouchy walk that gave one the impression of great reserve strength. He had ridden that day from Tuba, an agency on their reservation, about seventy miles distant. This was the first sign of an Indian that we had seen in this section, although we had been travelling along the northern boundary of their reservation since leaving the mouth of the San Juan. These Indians have no use for the river, being children of the desert, rather than of the water. Beyond an occasional crossing and swimming their horses at easy fords, they make no attempt at its navigation, even in the quiet water of Glen Canyon.

Some of the men showed this Indian our boats, and told him of our journey. He smiled, and shrugged his massive shoulders as much as to say, he "would believe it when he saw it." He had an opportunity to see us start, at least, on the following morning.

Before leaving, we climbed a 300-foot mound on the left bank of the Paria River, directly opposite the Lee ranch. This mound is known as Lee's Lookout. Whether used by Lee or not, it had certainly served that purpose at some time. A circular wall of rock was built on top of the mound, and commanded an excellent view of all the approaches to the junction of the rivers. This spot is of particular interest to the geologist, for a great fault, indicated by the Vermilion Cliffs, marks the division between Glen Canyon and Marble Canyon. This line of cliffs extends to the south for many miles across the Painted Desert, and north into Utah for even a greater distance, varying in height from two hundred feet at the southern end to as many thousand feet in some places to the north. Looking to the west, we could see that here was another of those sloping uplifts of rock, with the river cutting down, increasing the depth of the canyon with every mile.

We had now descended about 2900 feet since leaving Green River City, Wyoming, not a very great fall for the distance travelled if an average is taken, but a considerable portion of the distance was on quiet water, as we have noted, with a fall of a foot or two to the mile, and with alternate sections only containing bad water. We were still at an elevation of 3170 feet above the sea-level, and in the 283 miles of canyon ahead of us — Marble Canyon and the Grand Canyon combined — the river descends 2330 feet, almost a continuous series of rapids from this point to the end of the Grand Canyon.

After a hasty survey from our vantage point, we returned to the river and prepared to embark. As we left the dredge, the work was closed down for a few minutes, and the entire crowd of men, about forty in number, stood on an elevation to watch us run the first rapid. The Indian had crossed to the south side of the river to feed his horse and caught a glimpse of us as we went past him. Running pell-mell down to his boat, he crossed the river and joined the group on the bank. About this time we were in the grip of the first rapid, a long splashy one, with no danger whatever, but large enough to keep us busy until we had passed from view.

A few miles below this, after running a pair of small rapids, we reached a larger one, known as the Badger Creek Rapid, with a twenty-foot drop in the first 250 feet, succeeded by a hundred yards of violent water. Emery had a little difficulty in this rapid, when his boat touched a rock which turned the boat sideways in the current, and he was nearly overturned in the heavy waves which followed. As it was, we were both drenched.

About the middle of the afternoon, twelve miles below Lee's Ferry, we reached the Soap Creek Rapid of which we had heard so much. The rapid had a fall of twenty-five feet, and was a quarter of a mile long. Most of the fall occurred in the first fifty yards. The river had narrowed down until it was less than two hundred feet wide at the beginning of the descent. Many rocks were scattered all through the upper end, especially at the first drop. On the very brink or edge of the first fall, there was a submerged rock in the centre of the channel, making an eight-foot fall over the rock. A violent current, deflected from the left shore, shot into this centre and added to the confusion. Twelve-foot waves, from the conflicting currents, played leap-frog, jumping over or through each other alternately. Clearly there was no channel on that side. On the right or north side of the stream it looked more feasible, as the water shot down a sloping chute over a hundred feet before meeting with an obstruction. This came in the shape of two rocks, one about thirty feet below the other. To run the rapid this first rock would have to be passed before any attempt could be made to pull away from the second rock, which was quite close to the shore. Once past that there was a clear channel to the end of the rapid, if the centre, which contained many rocks, was avoided. Below the rapid was the usual whirlpool, then a smaller rapid, running under the left wall. This second rapid was the one that had been so fatal for Brown. The Soap Creek rapid in many ways was not as bad as some we had gone over in Cataract Canyon, but there were so many complications that we hesitated a long time before coming to a decision that we would make an attempt with one boat, depending on our good luck which had brought us through so many times, as much as we depended on our handling of the boat.

It was planned that I should make the first attempt, while Emery remained with the motion-picture camera just below the rock that we most feared, with the agree-

ment that he was to get a picture of the upset if one
occurred, then run to the lower end of the rapid with a
rope and a life-preserver.

After adjusting life-preservers I returned to my boat
and was soon on the smooth water above the rapid, holding my boat to prevent her from being swept over the
rock in the centre, jockeying for the proper position before
I would allow her to be carried into the current. Once
in, it seemed but an instant until I was past the first
rock, and almost on top of the second. I was pulling
with every ounce of strength, and was almost clear of
the rock when the stern touched it gently. I had no
idea the boat would overturn, but thought she would
swing around the rock, heading bow first into the stream,
as had been done before on several occasions. Instead
of this she was thrown on her side with the bottom of the
boat held against the rock while I found myself thrown
out of the boat, but hanging to the gunwale. Then the
boat swung around and instantly turned upright while I
scrambled back into the cockpit. Looking over my
shoulder, when I had things well in hand again, I saw my
brother was still at the camera, white as a sheet, but
turning at the crank as if our entire safety depended on it.
After I landed the water-filled boat, however, he confessed
to me that he had no idea whether he had caught the upset
or not, as he may have resumed the work when he saw
that I was safe.

Then we went to work to find out what damage was done. First we found that the case, which was supposed to be waterproof, had a half-inch of water inside, but fortunately none of our films were wet. Some plates which we had just exposed and which were still in the holders were soaked. The cameras also had suffered. We hurriedly wiped off the surplus water and piled these things on the shore, then emptied the boat of a few barrels of water.

This one experience, I suppose, should have been enough for me with that rapid, but I foolishly insisted on making another trial at it with the *Edith*, for I felt sure I could make it if I only had another chance, and the fact that Emery had the empty boat at the end of the rapid and could rescue me if an upset occurred greatly lessened the danger. The idea of making a portage, with the loss of nearly a day, did not appeal to me.

Emery agreed to this reluctantly, and advised waiting until morning, for it was growing dusk, but with the remark " I will sleep better with both boats tied at the lower end of the rapid," I returned to the *Edith*. To make a long story short I missed my channel, and was carried over the rock in the centre of the stream. The *Edith* had bravely mounted the first wave, and was climbing the second comber, standing almost on end, it seemed to me, when the wave crested over the stern, while the current shooting it from the side struck the submerged bow and she fell back in the water upside down. It was all done so quickly, I hardly knew what had occurred, but found myself in the water, whirling this way and that, holding to the right oar with a death-grip. I wondered if the strings would hold, and felt a great relief when the oar stopped slipping down, — as the blade reached the ring. It was the work of a second to climb the oar, and I found I was under the cockpit. Securing a firm hold on the gunwale, which had helped us so often, I got on the outside of the boat, thinking I might climb on top. About that time one of the largest waves broke over me, knocking me on the side of the head as if with a solid object, nearly tearing me from the boat. After that I kept as close to the boat as possible, paddling with my feet to keep them clear of rocks. Then the suction of the boat caught them and dragged them under, and for the rest of the rapid I had all I could do to hang to the boat. As the rapid dwindled I began to look for Emery, but was unable to see him, for it was now growing quite dark, but I could see a fire on shore that he had built. I tried to call but was strangled with the breaking waves; my voice was drowned in the roar of the rapid. One of the life-preservers was torn loose and floated ahead of me. Finally I got an answer, and could see that Emery had launched his boat. As he drew near I told him to save the life-preserver, which he did, then hurriedly pulled for me. I remarked with a forced laugh, to reassure him,

"Gee, Emery, this water's cold."

He failed to join in my levity, however, and said with feeling, "Thank the good Lord you are here!" and down in my heart I echoed his prayer of thanks.

Somehow I had lost all desire to successfully navigate the Soap Creek Rapid.

But our troubles were not entirely over. Emery had pulled me in after a futile attempt or two, with a hold sometimes used by wrestlers, linking his arm in mine, leaning forward, and pulling me in over his back. I was so numbed by the cold that I could do little to help him, after what, I suppose, was about a quarter of an hour's struggle in the water; although it seemed much longer than that to me.

We then caught the *Edith* and attempted to turn her over, but before this could be done we were dragged into the next rapid. Emery caught up the oars, while I could do nothing but hold to the upturned boat, half filled with water, striving to drag us against the wall on the left side of the stream. It was no small task to handle the two boats in this way, but Emery made it; then, when he thought we were sure of a landing, the *Edith* dragged us into the river again. Two more small rapids were run as we peered through the darkness for a landing. Finally we reached the shore over a mile below the Soap Creek Rapid. We were on the opposite side of the stream from that where we had unloaded the

THE SOAP CREEK RAPID; A LITTLE ABOVE LOWEST STAGE. PHOTO PUBLISHED BY PERMISSION OF JULIUS F. STONE.

Defiance. This material would have to stay where it was that night.

While bailing the water from the *Edith* we noticed a peculiar odour, and thought for a while that it might be the body of the man who was drowned at the ferry, but later we found it came from a green cottonwood log that had become water-soaked, and was embedded in the sand, close to our landing. It was Emery's turn to do the greater part of the camp work that night, while I was content to hug the fire, wrapped in blankets, waiting for the coffee to boil.

CHAPTER XVIII

MARBLE HALLS AND MARBLE WALLS

THERE was little of the spectacular in our work the next day as we slowly and laboriously dragged an empty boat upstream against the swift-running current, taking advantage of many little eddies, but finding much of the shore swept clean. I had ample opportunity to ponder on the wisdom of my attempt to save time by running the Soap Creek Rapid instead of making a portage, while we carried our loads over the immense boulders that banked the stream, down to a swift piece of water, past which we could not well bring the boats; or while we developed the wet plates from the ruined plate-holders. It was with no little surprise that we found all the plates, except a few which were not uniformly wet and developed unevenly, could be saved. It took a day and a half to complete all this work.

Marble Canyon was now beginning to narrow up, with a steep, boulder-covered slope on either side, three or four hundred feet high; with a sheer wall of dark red limestone of equal height directly above that. There was also a plateau of red sandstone and distant walls topped with light-coloured rock, the same formations with which we were familiar in the Grand Canyon. The inner gorge had narrowed from a thousand feet or more down to four hundred feet, the slope at the river was growing steeper and gradually disappearing, and each mile of travel had added a hundred feet or more to the height of the walls. Soon after resuming our journey that afternoon, the slope disappeared altogether, and the sheer walls came down close to the water. There were few places where one could climb out, had we desired to do so. This hard limestone wall, which Major Powell had named the marble wall, had a disconcerting way of weathering very smooth and sheer, with a few ledges and fewer breaks.

We made a short run that day, going over a few rapids, stopping an hour to make some pictures where an immense rock had fallen from the cliff above into the middle of the river bed, leaving a forty-foot channel on one side, and scarcely any on the other. Below this we found a rapid so much like the Soap Creek Rapid in appearance that a portage seemed advisable. It was evening when we got the *Edith* to the lower end of this rapid after almost losing her, as we lined her down, and she was wedged under a sloping rock that overhung the rapid. We had two ropes, one at either end, attached to the boat in this case. Emery stood below the rock ready to pull her in when once past the rock. There was a sickening crackling of wood as the deck of the boat wedged under and down to the level of the water, and at Emery's call I released the boat, throwing the rope into the river, and hurried to help him. He was almost dragged into the water as the boat swung around, fortunately striking against a sand-bank, instead of the many rocks that lined the shore. We were working with a stream different from the Green River, we found, and the *Defiance* was taken from the water the next day and slowly worked, one end at a time, over the rocks, up to a level sand-bank, twenty-five or thirty feet above the river. Then we put rollers under her, and worked her down past the rapid. This work was little to our liking, for the boats, now pretty well water-soaked, weighed considerably more than their original five hundred pounds' weight.

A few successful plunges soon brought back our former confidence, and we continued to run all other rapids that presented themselves. This afternoon we passed the first rapid we remembered having seen, where we could not land at its head before running it. A slightly higher stage of water, however, would have made many such rapids. Just below this point we found the body of a bighorn mountain-sheep floating in an eddy. It was impossible to tell just how he came to his death. There was no sign of any great fall that we could see. He had

Copyright by Kolb Bros.

ARCH IN MARBLE CANYON. NOTE FIGURE ON RIGHT.

Copyright by Kolb Bros.

"IT WAS TOO GOOD A CAMP TO MISS."

a splendid pair of horns, which we would have liked to have had at home, but which we did not care to amputate and carry with us.

On this day's travel, we passed a number of places where the marble — which had suggested this canyon's name to Major Powell — appeared. The exposed parts were checked, or seamed, and apparently would have little commercial value. We passed a shallow cave or two this day, then found another cave or hole, running back about fifteen feet in the wall, so suitable for a camp that we could not refuse the temptation to stop, although we had made but a very short run this day. The high water had entered it, depositing successive layers of sand on the bottom, rising in steps, one above the other, making convenient shelves for maps and journals, pots and pans; while little shovelling was necessary to make the lower level of sand fit our sleeping bags. A number of small springs, bubbling from the walls near by, gave us the first clear water that we had found for some time, and a pile of driftwood caught in the rocks, directly in front of our cave, added to its desirability for a camp. Firewood was beginning to be the first consideration in choosing a camp, for in many places the high water had swept the shores clean, and spots which might otherwise have made splendid camps were rendered most undesirable for this reason.

So Camp Number 47 was made in this little cave, with

o

a violent rapid directly beneath us, making a din that might be anything but reassuring, were we not pretty well accustomed to it by this time. The next day, Sunday, November the 12th, was passed in the same spot. The air turned decidedly cold this day, a hard wind swept up the river, the sky above was overcast, and we had little doubt that snow was falling on the Kaibab Plateau, which we could not see, but which we knew rose to the height of 5500 feet above us, but a few miles to the northwest of this camp. The sheer walls directly above the river dropped down considerably at this point, and a break or two permitted us to climb up as high as we cared to go on the red sandstone wall, which had lost its level character, and now rose in a steep slope over a thousand feet above us. These walls, with no growth but the tussocks of bunch-grass, the prickly pear cactus, the mescal, and the yucca, were more destitute of growth than any we had seen, excepting the upper end of Desolation Canyon, even the upper walls lacking the growth of piñon pine and juniper which we usually associated with them. We were now directly below the Painted Desert, which lay to the left of the canyon, and no doubt a similar desert was on the right-hand side, in the form of a narrow plateau; but we had no means of knowing just how wide or narrow this was, before it raised again to the forest-covered Buckskin Mountains and the Kaibab Plateau.

The rapid below our camp was just as bad as its roar, we found, on running it the next day. Most of the descent was confined to a violent drop at the very beginning, but there was a lot of complicated water in the big waves that followed. Emery was thrown forward in his boat, when he reached the bottom of the chute, striking his mouth, and bruising his hands, as he dropped his oars and caught the bulkhead. An extra oar was wrenched from the boat and disappeared in the white water, or foam that was as nearly white as muddy water ever gets. I nearly upset, and broke the pin of a rowlock, the released oar being jerked from my hand, sending me scrambling for an extra oar, when the boat swept into a swift whirlpool. Emery caught my oar as it whirled past him; the other was found a half-mile below in an eddy.

Some of the rapids in the centre of Marble Canyon were not more than 75 feet wide, with a corresponding violence of water. The whirlpools in the wider channels below these rapids were the strongest we had seen, and had a most annoying way of holding the boats just when we thought we had evaded them. Sometimes there would be a whirlpool on either side, with a sharply defined line of division in the centre, along which it was next to impossible to go without being caught on one side or the other. These whirlpools were seldom regarded as serious, for our boats were too wide and heavy to be readily overturned in them, although we saved ourselves more than one upset by throwing our weight to the opposite side. A small boat would have upset. On two occasions we were caught in small whirlpools, where a point of rock projected from the shore, turning upstream, splitting a swift current and making a very rapid and difficult whirl, where the boats were nearly smashed against the walls. Below all such places were the familiar boils, or fountains, or shoots, as they are variously termed. These are the lower end of the whirlpools, emerging often from the quiet water below a rapid with nearly as much violence as they disappeared in the rapids above. These would often rise when least expected, breaking under the boats, the swift upshoot of water giving them such a rap that we sometimes thought we had struck a rock. If one happened to be in the centre of a boil when it broke, it would send them sailing down the stream many times faster than the regular current was travelling, rowing the boat having about as little effect on determining its course as if it was loaded on a flat-car. The other boat, at times just a few feet away, might be caught in the whirlpools that formed at the edge of the fountains, often opening up suddenly under one side of the boat, causing it to dip until the water poured over the edge, holding it to that one spot in spite of every effort to row away.

Then we would strike peaceful water again, a mile or

Copyright by Kolb Bros.

WALLS OF MARBLE CANYON.

two perhaps, so quiet that a thin covering of clear water spread over the top of the silt-laden pool beneath, reflecting the tinted walls and the turquoise sky beneath its limpid surface. Gems of sunlight sparkled on its bosom and scintillated in the ripples left behind by the oars. When seated with our backs to the strongest light, and when glancing along the top of such a pool instead of into it, the mirror-like surface gave way to a peculiar purplish tone which seemed to cover the pool, so that one would forget it was roily water, and saw only the iridescent beauty of a mountain stream.

The wonderful marble walls — better known to the miners as the blue limestone walls — now rose from the water's edge to a height of eight or nine hundred feet, the surface of its light blue-gray rock being stained to a dark red, or a light red as the case might be, by the iron from the sandstone walls above. There were a thousand feet of these sandstone layers, red in all its varying hues, capped by the four-hundred foot cross-bedded sandstone wall, breaking sheer, ranging in tone from a soft buff to a golden yellow, with a bloom, or glow, as though illuminated from within. As we proceeded, another layer could be seen above this, the same limestone and with the same fossils — an examination of the rock-slides told us — as the topmost formation at the Grand Canyon. This was not unlike the cross-bedded sandstone in colour, but lacked its warmth and richness of tint.

A close examination of the rocks revealed many colours, that figured but little in the grand colour scheme of the canyon as a whole — the detailed ornamentation of the magnificent rock structure. A fracture of wall would show the true colour of the rock, beneath the stain; lime crystals studded its surface, like gems glinting in the sunlight; beautifully tinted jasper, resembling the petrified wood found in another part of Arizona, was embedded in the marble wall, — usually at the point of contact with another formation, — polished by the sands of the turbid river.

All this told us that we were coming into our own. Four of the seven notable divisions of rock strata found in the Grand Canyon were now represented in Marble Canyon, and soon the green shale, which underlies the blue limestone, began to crop out by the river as the walls grew higher and the stream cut deeper.

One turn of the canyon revealed a break where Stanton hid his provisions in a cave — after a second fatality in which two more of this ill-fated expedition lost their lives — and climbed out on top. Afterwards he re-outfitted with heavier boats and tackled the stream again.

Just below this break the scene changed as we made a sharp turn to the left. Vasey's Paradise — named by Major Powell after Dr. Geo. W. Vasey, botanist of the United States Department of Agriculture — was disclosed to view. Beautiful streams gushed from rounded holes, fifty yards above the river. The rock walls reminded one of an ivy-covered castle of old England, guarded by a moat uncrossed by any drawbridge. It was trellised with vines, maidenhair ferns, and water-moss making a vivid green background for the golden yellow and burnished copper leaves which still clung to some small cottonwood trees — the only trees we had seen in Marble Canyon.

In our haste to push on, we left the brass motion-picture tripod head on an island, from which we pictured this lovely spot. A rapid was put behind us before we noticed our loss, and there was no going back then.

Another turn revealed a Gothic arch, or grotto, carved at the bend of the wall by the high water, with an overhang of more than a hundred feet, and a height nearly as great, for the flood waters ran above the hundred-foot stage in this narrow walled section. Then came a gloomy, prison-like formation, with a "Bridge of Sighs" two hundred feet above a gulch, connecting the dungeon to the perpendicular wall beyond; and with a hundred cave-like openings in its sheer sides like small windows, admitting a little daylight into its dark interior. The sullen boom of a rapid around the turn sounded like the march of an army coming up the gorge, so we climbed back into our boats after a vain attempt to climb up to some of the caves, and advanced to meet our foe. This rapid — the tenth for the day — while it was clear of rocks, had an abrupt drop, with powerful waves which did all sorts of things to us and to our boats; breaking a rowlock and the four pieces of line which held it, and flooding us both with a ton of water. We went into camp a short distance below this, in a narrow box canyon running back a hundred yards from the river, a gloomy, cathedral-like interior, with sheer walls rising several hundred feet on three sides of us, and with the top of the south wall 2500 feet above us in plain sight of our camp, the one camp in Marble Canyon where our sleep was undisturbed by the roar of a rapid. But instead of the roar of a rapid, a howling wind swept down from the Painted Desert above, piling the mingled desert sands and river sands about our beds, scattering our camp material over the bottom of the narrow gorge.

Soon after this camp — the fourth and the last in Marble Canyon — was left behind us, the walls began to widen out, especially on the north-northwest, and by noon we had passed from the narrow, direct canyon, into one with slopes and plateaus breaking the sheer walls, the wall on the left or southeast side being much the lower of the two, and more nearly perpendicular, rising to a height of 3200 feet, while the northwest side lifted up to the Kaibab Plateau, one point — miles back from the river — rising 6000 feet above us.

We halted at noon beside the Nancoweep Valley, a wide tributary heading many miles back in the plateau on the right, with a ramified series of canyons running into it, and with great expanses of sage-covered flats between. Deer tracks were found on these flats, deer which came down from the forest of the Buckskin Mountains. This was the point selected by Major Powell for the construction of a trail when he returned from his voyage of exploration to study the geology of this section. The trail, although neglected for many years, is still used by prospectors from Kanab, Utah, who make a yearly trip into the canyons to do some work on a mineral ledge a few miles below here.

What a glorious, exhilarating run we had that day! From here to the end of Marble Canyon the rapids were almost continuous, with few violent drops and seldom broken by the usual quiet pools. It was the finest kind of water for fast travelling, and we made the most of it. The only previous run we had made that could in any way compare with it was in Whirlpool and Split Mountain canyons, when the high water was on. As we travelled, occasional glimpses were had of familiar places on Greenland Point — that thirty-mile peninsula of the Kaibab Plateau extending between Marble Canyon and the Grand Canyon — where we had gone deer-hunting, or on photographic expeditions with Rust.

Another valley from the right was passed, then a peak rose before us close to the river, with its flat top rising to a height equal to the south wall. This was Chuar

Butte. Once more we were in a narrow canyon, narrowed by this peak, but a canyon just the same. Soon we were below a wall we once had photographed from the mouth of the Little Colorado; then the stream itself came in view and we were soon anchored beside it. This was the beginning of the Grand Canyon.

Copyright by Kolb Bros.

APPROACHING THE GRAND CANYON. NOTE BOAT.

CHAPTER XIX

SIGNALLING OUR CANYON HOME

How long we had waited for this view! How many memories it recalled — and how different it seemed to our previous visit there! Then, the high water was on, and the turquoise-tinted mineral water of the Colorado Chiquito was backed up by the turbid flood waters of the Rio Colorado, forty feet or more above the present level. Now it was a rapid stream, throwing itself with wild abandon over the rocks and into the Colorado. There was the same deserted stone hut, built by a French prospector, many years before, and a plough that he had packed in over a thirty-mile trail — the most difficult one in all this rugged region! There was the little grass-plot where we pastured the burro, while we made a fifteen-mile walk up the bed of this narrow canyon! What a hard, hot journey it had been! A year and a half ago we sat on that rock, and talked of the day when we should come through here in boats! Even then we talked of building a raft, and of loading the burro on it for a spin on the flood waters. Lucky for us and for the burro that we didn't! We understand the temper of these waters now.

Cape Desolation, a point of the Painted Desert on the west side of the Little Colorado, was almost directly above us, 3200 feet high. Chuar Butte, equally as high and with walls just as nearly perpendicular, extended on into the Grand Canyon on the right side, making the narrowest canyon of this depth that we had seen. The Navajo reservation terminated at the Little Colorado, although nothing but the maps indicated that we had passed from the land of the Red man to that of the White. Both were equally desolate, and equally wonderful. With the entrance of the new stream the canyon changes its southwest trend and turns directly west, and continues to hold to this general direction until the northwest corner of Arizona is reached.

But we must be on again! Soon familiar segregated peaks in the Grand Canyon began to appear. There was Wotan's Throne on the right, and the "Copper Mine Mesa" on the left. Three or four miles below the junction a four-hundred foot perpendicular wall rose above us. The burro, on our previous visit, was almost shoved off that cliff when the pack caught on a rock, and was only saved by strenuous pulling on the neck-rope and pack harness. Soon we passed some tunnels on both sides of the river where the Mormon miners had tapped a copper ledge. At 4.15 P.M. we were at the end of the Tanner Trail, the outlet of the Little Colorado Trail to the rim above. It had taken seven hours of toil to cover the same ground we now sped over in an hour and a quarter. Major Powell, in 1872, found here the remnant of a very small hut built of mesquite logs, but whether the remains of an Indian's or white man's shelter cannot be stated. The trail, without doubt, was used by the Indians before the white man invaded this region.

The canyon had changed again from one which was very narrow to one much more complex, greater, and grander. The walls on top were many miles apart; Comanche Point, to our left, was over 4000 feet above us; Desert View, Moran Point, and other points on the south rim were even higher. On the right we could see an arch near Cape Final on Greenland Point, over 5000 feet up, that we had photographed, from the top, a few years before. Pagoda-shaped temples — the formation so typical of the Grand Canyon — clustered on all sides. The upper walls were similar in tint to those in Marble Canyon, but here at the river was a new formation; the algonkian, composed of thousands of brilliantly coloured bands of rock, standing at an angle — the one irregularity to the uniform layers of rock — a remnant of thousands of feet of rock which once covered this region, then was planed away before the other deposits were placed. All about us, close to the river, was a deep, soft sand formed by the disintegration of the rocks above, as brilliantly coloured as the rocks from which they came. What had been a very narrow stream above here spread out over a thousand feet wide, ran with a good current, and seemed to be anything but a shallow stream at that.

We had travelled far that day but still sped on, — with a few rapids which did not retard, but rather helped us on our way, and with a good current between these rapids, — only stopping to camp when a three-hundred foot wall rose sheer from the river's edge, bringing to an end our basin-like river bottom, where one could walk out on either side. It was not necessary to hunt for driftwood this evening, for a thicket of mesquite — the best of all wood for a camp-fire — grew out of the sand-dunes, and some half-covered dead logs were unearthed from the drifted sand, and soon reduced to glowing coals.

Meanwhile, we were enjoying one of those remarkable Arizona desert sunsets. Ominous clouds had been gathering in the afternoon, rising from the southwest, drifting across the canyon, and piling up against the north wall. A few fleecy clouds in the west partially obscured the sun until it neared the horizon, then a shaft of sunlight broke through once more, telegraphing its approach long before it reached us, the rays being visibly hurled through space like a javelin, or a lightning bolt, striking peak after peak so that one almost imagined they would hear the thunder roll. A yellow flame covered the western sky, to be succeeded in a few minutes by a crimson glow. The sharply defined colours of the different layers of rock had merged and softened, as the sun dropped from sight; purple shadows crept into the cavernous depths, while shafts of gold shot to the very tiptop of the peaks, or threw their shadows like silhouettes on the wall beyond. Then the scene shifted again, and it was all blood-red, reflecting from the sky and staining the rocks below, so that distant wall and sky merged, with little to show where the one ended and the other began. That beautiful haze, which tints, but does not obscure, enshrouded the temples and spires, changing from heliotrope to lavender, from lavender to deepest purple; there was a departing flare of flame like the collapse of a burning building; a few clouds in the zenith, torn by the winds so that they resembled the craters of the moon, were tinted for an instant around the crater's rims; the clouds faded to a dove-like gray; they darkened; the gray disappeared; the purple crept from the canyon into the arched dome overhead; the day was ended, twilight passed, and darkness settled over all.

We sat silently by the fire for a few minutes, then rose and resumed our evening's work. This camp was at a point that could be seen from the Grand View hotel, fourteen miles from our home. We talked of building a signal fire on the promontory above the camp, knowing that the news would be telephoned to our home if the fire was seen. But we gave up the plan. Although less than twenty miles from Bright Angel Trail, we were not safely through by any means. Two boats had been wrecked or lost in different rapids less than six miles from this camp. The forty-foot fall in the Hance or Red Canyon Rapid was three miles below us; the Sockdologer, the Grapevine, and other rapids nearly as large followed those; we might be no more fortunate than the others, and a delay after once giving a signal would cause more anxiety than no signal at all we thought, and the fire was not built.

Particular attention was paid to the loading of the boats the next morning. The moving-picture film was tucked in the toes of our sleeping bags, and the protecting bags were carefully laced. We were not going to take any chances in this next plunge — the much-talked-of entrance to the granite gorge. A half-hour's run and a dash through one violent rapid landed us at the end of the Hance Trail — unused for tourist travel for several years — with a few torn and tattered tents back in the side canyon down which the trail wound its way. We half hoped that we would find some of the prospectors who make this section their winter home either at the Tanner or the Hance Trail, but there was no sign of recent visitors at either place, unless it was the numerous burro tracks in the sand. These tracks were doubtless made by some of the many wild burros that roam all over the lower plateaus in the upper end of the Grand Canyon.

After a careful inspection of the Hance Rapid we were glad the signal fire was not built. It was a nasty rapid. While reading over our notes one evening we were amused to find that we had catalogued different rapids with an equal amount of fall as "good," "bad," or "nasty," the difference depending nearly altogether on the rocks in the rapids. The "good rapids" were nothing but a descent of "big water," with great waves, — for which we cared little, but rather enjoyed if it was not too cold, — and with no danger from rocks; the "bad rapids" contained rocks, and twisting channels, but with half a chance of getting through. A nasty rapid was filled with rocks, many of them so concealed in the foam that it was often next to impossible to tell if rocks were there or not, and in which there was little chance of running through without smashing a boat. The Hance Rapid was such a one.

Such a complication of twisted channels and protruding rocks we had not seen unless it was at Hell's Half Mile. It meant a portage — nothing less — the second since leaving that other rapid in Lodore. So we went to work, carrying our duffle across deep, soft sand-dunes, down to the middle of the rapid, where it quieted for a hundred yards before it made the final

P

plunge. The gathering dusk of evening found all material and one boat at this spot, with the other one at the head of the rapid, to be portaged the next day. But we did not portage this boat. A good night's rest, and the safeguard of a boat at the bottom of the plunge made it look much less dangerous, and five minutes after breakfast was finished, this boat was beside its mate, and we had a reel of film which we hoped would show just how we successfully ran this difficult rapid. While going over the second section, on the opposite side of the river, Emery was thrown out of his boat for an instant when the *Edith* touched a rock in a twenty-five mile an hour current, similar to my first upset in the Soap Creek Rapid — the old story: out again; in again; on again — landing in safety at the end of the rapid not one whit the worse for the spill.

This rapid marks the place where the granite, or igneous rock, intrudes, rising at a sharp angle, sloping upward down the stream, reaching the height of 1300 feet about one mile below. It marks the end of the large deposit of algonkian. The granite, when it attains its highest point, is covered with a 200-foot layer of sedimentary rock called the tonto sandstone. The top of this formation is exposed by a plateau from a quarter of a mile to three miles in width, on either side of the granite gorge; the same walls which were found in Marble Canyon rise above this. The temples

Copyright by Kolb Bros.

IN THE GRANITE GORGE BELOW THE SOCKDOLOGER RAPID. EXTREME HEIGHT OF WALL ABOUT FIVE THOUSAND FEET.

which are scattered through the canyon — equal in height, in many cases, to the walls—have their foundation on this plateau. These peaks contain the same stratified rock with a uniform thickness whether in peak or wall, with little displacement and little sign of violent uplift, nearly all this canyon being the work of erosion: 5000 feet from the rim to the river; the edges of six great layers of sedimentary rock laid bare and with a narrow 1300-foot gorge through the igneous rock below — the Grand Canyon of Arizona.

The granite gorge seemed to us to be the one place of all others that we had seen on this trip that would cause one to hesitate a long time before entering, if nothing definite was known of its nature. Another person might have felt the same way of the canyons we had passed, Lodore or Marble Canyon, for instance. A great deal depends on the nerves and digestion, no doubt; and the same person would look at it in a different light at different times, as we found from our own experiences. Our digestions were in excellent condition just at that time, and we were nerved up by the thought that we were going "to the plate for a home run" if possible, yet the granite gorge had a decidedly sinister look. The walls, while not sheer, were nearly so; they might be climbed in many places to the top of the granite; but the tonto sandstone wall nearly always overhangs this, breaks sheer, and seldom affords an outlet to the plateaus above, except where lateral canyons cut through. The rocks are very dark, with dikes of quartz, and with twisting seams of red and black granite, the great body of rock being made up of decomposed micaceous schists and gneiss, a treacherous material to climb. The entrance to this gorge is made on a quiet pool with no shore on either side after once well in.

But several parties had been through since Major Powell made his initial trip, so we did not hesitate, but pushed on with the current. Now we could truly say that we were going home. The Hance Rapid was behind us; Bright Angel Creek was about twelve miles away. Soon we were in the deepest part of the gorge. Great dikes and uplifts of jagged rocks towered above us; and up, up, up, lifted the other walls above that. Bissell Point, on the very top, could plainly be seen from our quiet pool.

Then came a series of rapids quite different from the Hance Rapid, and many others found above. Those others were usually caused in part by the detritus or deposit from side canyons, which dammed the stream, and what might be a swift stream, with a continuous drop, was transformed to a succession of mill-ponds and cataracts, or rapids. In nearly every case, in low water such as we were travelling on, the deposit made a shore on which we could land and inspect the rapid from below. The swift water invariably makes a narrow channel if it has no obstruction in its way; it is the quiet stream that makes a wide channel. But the rapids we found this day were nearly all different. They were seldom caused by great deposits of rock, but appeared to be formed by a dike or ledge of hard rock rising from the softer rock — the same intrusion being sometimes found on both sides of the stream — forming a dam the full width of the channel, over which the water made a swift descent, with a long line of interference waves below. But for a cold wind which swept up the stream, this style of rapid was more to our fancy. These were "good rapids," the "best" we had seen. There were few rocks to avoid. Some of the rapids were violent, but careful handling took us past every danger. There was little chance to make a portage at several of these places had we desired to do so. We gave them but a glance from the decks of the boats, then dropped into them. In one instance I saw the *Edith* literally shoot through a wave bow first, both ends of the boat being visible, while her captain was buried in the foam.

We had learned to discriminate by its noise, long before we could see a rapid, whether it was filled with rocks, or was merely a descent of big water. The latter, often just as impressive as the former, had a sullen, steady boom; the rocky rapids had the same sound, punctuated by another sound, like the crack of regiments of musketry. All were greatly magnified in sound by the narrow, echoing walls. We became so accustomed to this noise that we almost forgot it was there, and it was only after the long, quiet stretches that the noise was noticed. In a few instances only we noticed the shattering vibration of air that is associated with waterfalls. Still there is noise enough in many rapids so that their boom can be heard several miles away from the top of the canyons.

Guided by these sounds, and aided by our method of holding the boat in mid-stream, while making a reconnoissance, we were quite well aware of what we were likely to find before we anchored above a rapid. We were never fearful of being drawn into a cataract without having a chance to land somewhere. The water is strangely quiet, to a comparatively close distance above nearly all rapids. We usually tied up anywhere from fifty feet to a hundred yards above a drop, before inspecting it. If it was a "big-water" rapid, we usually looked it over standing on the seat in the boats, then continued. By signals with the hands, the one first over would guide the other, if any hidden rocks or dangerous channel threatened. While we did not think much about it, we usually noted the places where one might climb out on the plateau. Little could be told about the upper walls from the river.

A chilling wind swept up the river, penetrating our soaked garments. But we paid little attention to this, only pulling the harder, not only to keep the circulation

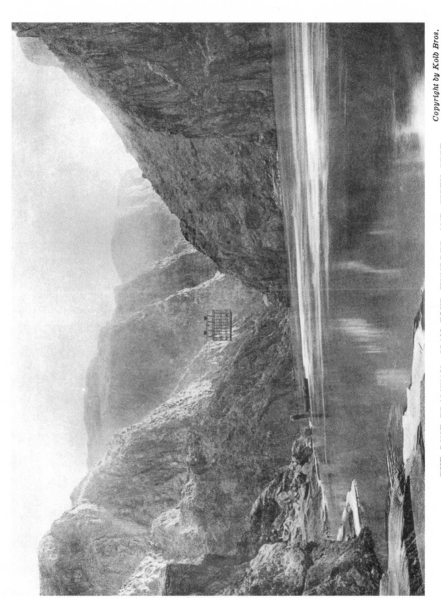

THE RUST TRAMWAY. SPAN FOUR HUNDRED AND FIFTY FEET.

Copyright by Kolb Bros.

going, but every pull of the oars put us that much nearer home. We never paused in our rowing until we anchored at 4.30 P.M. under Rust's tramway, close to the mouth of Bright Angel Creek. According to the United States Geological Survey there is a descent of 178 feet from the head of the Hance Rapid to the end of Bright Angel Trail, one mile below the creek. We would have a very moderate descent in that mile. The run from the Hance Rapid had been made in less than five hours.

Our boats were tied in the shadow of the cage hanging from a cable sixty feet above. It stretched across a quiet pool, 450 feet across — for the river is dammed by débris from the creek below, and fills the channel from wall to wall. Hurriedly we made our way up to Rust's camp, — closed for the winter; for heavy snows would cover the North Rim in a few days or a few weeks at the farthest, filling the trails with heavy drifts and driving the cougar into the canyon where dogs and horses cannot follow. But the latch-string was out for us, we knew, had we cared to use the tents. Our signal fire was built a mile above the camp, at a spot that was plainly visible on a clear day from our home on the other side, six miles away as the crow flies. We had often looked at this spot, with a telescope, from the veranda of our studio, watching the hunting and sight-seeing parties ride up the bed of the stream. We rather feared the drifting clouds and mists would hide the fire from view, but now and then a rift appeared, and we knew if they were looking they could see its light. Camp No. 51 was made close to Bright Angel Creek, that evening, Thursday, October the 16th, two months and eight days from the time we had embarked on our journey.

Three or four hours were spent in packing our material the next morning, so it could be stored in a miners' tunnel, near the end of the trail. We would pack little of this out, as we intended to resume our river work in a week or ten days. A five-minute run took us over the rapid below Bright Angel Creek, and down to a bend in the river, just above the Cameron or Bright Angel Trail. Two men — guides from the hotel — called to us as our boats swept into view. We made a quick dash over the vicious little drop below the bend, — easy for our boats, but dangerous enough for lighter craft on account of a difficult whirlpool, — and were soon on shore greeting old friends. Up on the plateau, 1300 feet above, a trail party of tourists and guides called down their welcome. The stores were put in the miners' tunnel as we had planned, and the boats were taken above the high-water mark; placed in dry dock one might say.

The guides had good news for us and bad news too. Emery's wife had been ill with appendicitis nearly all the time we were on our journey. We had received letters from her at every post-office excepting Lee's Ferry, but never a hint that all was not well. She knew it would break up the trip. _ Pretty good nerve, we thought!

Ragged and weary, but happy; a little lean and over-trained, but feeling entirely "fit,"—we commenced our seven-mile climb up the trail, every turn of which seemed like an old friend. When 1300 feet above the river, our little workshop beside a stream on the plateau — only used at intervals when no water can be had on top, and closed for three months past — gave us our first cheerless greeting. Although little more than a hundred feet from the trail, we did not stop to inspect it. Cameron's Indian Garden Camp was also closed for the day, and we were disappointed in a hope that we could telephone to our home, 3200 feet above. But the tents, under rows of waving cottonwoods, and surrounded by beds of bloom-ing roses and glorious chrysanthemums, gave us a more cheerful welcome than our little building below. We only stopped to quench our thirst in the bubbling spring, then began the four-mile climb that would put us on top of the towering cliff. Soon we overtook the party we had seen on the plateau. Some of the tourists kindly offered us their mules, but mules were too slow for us, and they were soon far below us. Calls, faint at first, but growing louder as we advanced, came floating down from above. On nearing the top our younger brother Ernest, who had come on from Pittsburg to look after our business, came running down the trail to greet us. One member of a troupe of moving-picture actors, in cowboy garb, remarked that we "didn't look like moving-picture explorers"; then little Edith emerged from our studio just below the head of Bright Angel Trail and came skipping down toward us, but stopped suddenly when near us, and said smilingly:

"Is that my Daddy with all those whiskers?"

Copyright by Kolb Bros.

BRIGHT ANGEL CREEK AND CANYON.

CHAPTER XX

ONE MONTH LATER

NATURALLY we were very impatient to know just what success we had met with in our photographic work. Some of the motion pictures had been printed and returned to us. My brother, who meanwhile had taken his family to Los Angeles, sent very encouraging reports regarding some of the films.

Among the Canyon visitors who came down to inspect the results of our trip were Thomas Moran, the famous artist, with his daughter, Miss Ruth, whose interest was more than casual. Thomas Moran's name, more than any other, with the possible exception of Major Powell's, is to be associated with the Grand Canyon. It was his painting which hangs in the capital at Washington that first acquainted the American public with the wonders of the Canyon. This painting was the result of a journey he made with Major Powell, from Salt Lake City to the north side of the Canyon, thirty-eight years before. In addition he had made most of the cuts that illustrated Major Powell's government report; making his sketches on wood from photographs this expedition had taken with the old-fashioned wet plates that had to be coated and developed on the spot — wonderful photographs, which for beauty, softness, and detail are not excelled, and are scarcely equalled by more modern plates and photographic results. The only great advantage of the dry plates was the fact that they could catch the action of the water with an instantaneous exposure, where the wet plates had to have a long exposure and lost that action.

Thomas Moran could pick up almost any picture that we made, and tell us at once just what section it came from and its identifying characteristics. His daughter, Miss Ruth, was just as much interested in our trip and its results. She was anxious to know when we would go on again and planned on making the trail trip down to the plateau to see us take the plunge over the first rough rapid. She was just a little anxious to see an upset, and asked if we could not promise that one would occur.

A month passed before my brother returned from Los Angeles. His wife, who had remained there, was in good health again, and insisted on his finishing the trip at once. We were just as anxious to have it finished, but were not very enthusiastic about this last part on account of some very cold weather we had been having. On the other hand, we feared if the trip was not finished then it might never be completed. So we consoled ourselves with the thought that it was some warmer at the bottom than it was on top, and prepared to make the final plunge — 350 miles to Needles, with a 1600-foot descent in the 185 miles that remained of the Grand Canyon.

A foot of snow had fallen two nights before we planned on leaving. The thermometer had dropped to zero, and a little below on one occasion, during the nights for a week past. Close to the top the trail was filled with drifts. The walls were white with snow down to the plateau, 3200 feet below; something unusual, as it seldom descends as snow lower than two thousand feet, but turns to rain. But a week of cold, cloudy weather, accompanied by hard winds, had driven all warmth from the canyon, allowing this snow to descend lower than usual. Under such conditions the damp cold in the canyon, while not registered on the thermometer as low as that on top, is more penetrating. Very little sun reaches the bottom of the inner gorge in December and January. It is usually a few degrees colder than the inner plateau above it, which is open, and does get some sun. These were the conditions when we returned to our boats December the 19th, 1911, and found a thin covering of ice on small pools near the river.

Our party was enlarged by the addition of two men who were anxious for some river experience. One was our younger brother, Ernest. We agreed to take him as far as the Bass Trail, twenty-five miles below, where he could get out on top and return to our home. The other was a young man named Bert Lauzon, who wanted to make the entire trip, and we were glad to have him. Lauzon, although but 24 years old, had been a quartz miner and mining engineer for some years. Coming from the mountains of Colorado, he had travelled over most of the Western states, and a considerable part of Mexico, in his expeditions. There was no question in our minds about Lauzon. He was the man we needed.

To offset the weight of an extra man for each boat, our supplies were cut to the minimum, arrangements having been made with W. W. Bass — the proprietor of the Bass Camps and of the Mystic Springs Trail — to have some provisions packed in over his trail. What provisions we took ourselves were packed down on two mules, and anything we could spare from our boats was packed out on the same animals. As we were about ready to leave a friendly miner said: "You can't hook fish in the Colorado in the winter, they won't bite nohow. You'd better take a couple of sticks of my giant-powder along. That will help you get 'em, and it may keep you from starving." Under the circumstances it seemed like a wise precaution and we took his giant-powder, as he had suggested.

The river had fallen two feet below the stage on which we quit a month before. A scale of foot-marks on a rock wall rising from the river showed that the water

Copyright by Kolb Bros.

ROUGH WATER IN HERMIT CREEK RAPID. HEIGHT OF DISTANT WAVE ABOUT FIFTEEN FEET.

was twenty-seven feet deep at that spot. No measurement was made in the middle of the river channel. The current here between two small rapids flows at five and three-fourths miles per hour. The width of the stream is close to 250 feet. The high-water mark here is forty-five feet above the low-water stage, then the river spreads to five hundred feet in width, running with a swiftness and strength of current and whirlpool that is tremendous. The highest authentic measurement in a narrow channel, of which we know, is one made by Julius F. Stone in Marble Canyon. He recorded one spot where the high-water mark was 115 feet above the low-water mark. These figures might look large at first, but if they are compared with some of the floods on the Ohio River, for instance, and that stream were boxed in a two hundred foot channel the difference would not be great, we imagine.

One of the young men who greeted us when we landed came down with a companion to see us embark. On the plateau 1300 feet above, looking like small insects against the sky-line, was a trail party, equally interested. They did not stand on the point usually visited by such parties but had gone to a point about a mile to the west, where they had a good view of a short, rough rapid. The little rapid below the trail, while it was no place that one would care to swim in, had no comparison with this other rapid in violence. We had promised the party that we would run this rapid that afternoon, so we spent little time in packing systematically, but hurriedly threw the stuff in and embarked. Less than an hour later we had made the two-mile run and the dash through the short rapid, to the entire satisfaction of all concerned.

We camped a short distance below the rapid, just opposite a grave of a man whose skeleton had been found halfway up the granite, five years before. Judging by his clothes and hob-nailed shoes he was a prospector. He was lying in a natural position, with his head resting on a rock. An overcoat was buttoned tightly about him. No large bones were broken, but he might have had a fall and been injured internally. More likely he became sick and died. The small bones of the hands and feet had been taken away by field-mice, and no doubt the turkey-buzzards had stripped the flesh. His pockets contained Los Angeles newspapers of 1900; he was found in 1906. The pockets also contained a pipe and a pocket-knife, but nothing by which he could be identified. The coroner's jury — of which my brother was a member — buried him where he was found, covering the body with rocks, for there was no earth.

Such finds are not unusual in this rugged country. These prospectors seldom say where they are going, no track is kept of their movements, and unless something about their clothes tells who they are, their identity is seldom established. The proximity of this grave made us wonder how many more such unburied bodies there were along this river. We thought too of our friend Smith, back in Cataract Canyon, and wondered if we would hear from him again.

Our helpers got a lot of experience in motion-picture making the next day, while we ran our boats through a number of good, strong rapids, well known locally as the Salt Creek Rapid, Granite Falls or Monument Rapid, the Hermit, the Bouchere, and others. This was all new to the boys, and provided some thrilling entertainment for them. When a difficult passage was safely made Bert would wave his hat and yell "Hoo" in a deep, long call that would carry above the roar of the rapids, then he and Ernest would follow along the shore with their cameras, as these rapids all had a shore on one side or the other. The sun shone on the river this day, and we congratulated ourselves on having made the most of our opportunities.

In our first rapid the next morning, we had to carry our passengers whether we wanted to or not. There was no shore on either side. In such plunges they would lie down on the deck of the boat behind the oarsman, holding to the raised bulkhead, ducking their heads when an oncoming wave prepared to break over them. Then they would shake themselves as a water-spaniel does, and Bert with a grin would say,

Q

"Young fellows, business is picking up !"

Ernest agreed, too, that he had never seen anything in Pittsburg that quite equalled it. If the rapid was not bad, they sat upright on the deck, but this made the boats top-heavy, and as much of the oarsman's work depended on swinging his weight from side to side, it was important that no mistake should be made about this distribution of weight. Often the bottom of a boat would show above the water as it listed to one side. At such a time a person sitting on the raised deck might get thrown overboard.

Before starting on this last trip we had thought it would be only right to give our younger brother a ride in a rapid that would be sure to give him a good ducking, as his experience was going to be short. But the water and the wind, especially in the shadows, was so very cold that we gave this plan up, and avoided the waves as much as possible. He got a ducking this morning, however, in a place where we least expected it. It was not a rapid, just smooth, very swift water, while close to the right shore there was one submerged rock with a foot of water shooting over it, in such a way that it made a "reverse whirl" as they are called in Alaska — water rolling back upstream, and from all sides as well, to fill the vacuum just below the rock. This one was about twelve feet across; the water disappeared as though it was being poured down a manhole.

The least care, or caution, would have taken me clear of this place; but the smooth water was so deceptive, and was so much stronger than I had judged it to be, that I found myself caught sideways to the current, hemmed in with waves on all sides of the boat, knocked back and forth, and resisted in all my efforts to pull clear. The boat was gradually filling with the splashing water. Ernest was lying on the deck, hanging on like grim death, slipping off, first on one side, then on the other, and wondering what was going to happen. So was I. To be held up in the middle of a swift stream was a new experience, and I was not proud of it. The others passed as soon as they saw what had happened, and were waiting in an eddy below. Perhaps we were there only one minute, but it seemed like five. I helped Ernest into the cockpit. About that time the boat filled with splashing water and sunk low, the stream poured over the rock and into the boat, and she upset instantly.

Ernest had on two life-preservers, and came up about thirty feet below, swimming very well considering that he was weighted with heavy clothes and high-topped shoes. The boys pulled him in before he was carried against a threatening wall. Meanwhile, I held to the boat, which was forced out as soon as she was overturned, and climbed on top, or rather on the bottom. I was trying to make the best of things and was giving a cheer when some one said,

"There goes your hatch cover and you've lost the motion-picture camera."

Perhaps I had. My cheering ceased. The camera had been hurriedly shoved down in the hatch a few minutes before.

On being towed to shore, however, we found the camera had not fallen out. It had been shoved to the side less than one inch, but that little bit had saved it. It was filled with water, though, and all the pictures were on the unfinished roll in the camera, and were ruined. We had been in the ice-cold water long enough to lose that glow which comes after a quick immersion and were chilled through; but what bothered me more than anything else was the fact that I had been caught in such a trap after successfully running the bad rapids above. We made a short run after that so as to get out of sight of the deceptive place, then proceeded to dry out. The ruined film came in handy for kindling our camp-fire.

We were now in the narrowest part of the upper portion of the Grand Canyon, the distance from rim to rim at one point being close to six miles. The width at Bright Angel varied from eight to fourteen miles. The peaks rising from the plateau, often as high as the canyon walls, and with flat tops a mile or more in width, made the canyon even narrower, so that at times we were in canyons close to a mile in depth, and little over four miles across at the tops.

In this section of the granite there were few places where one could climb out. Nearly all the lateral canyons ended quite a distance above the river, then fell sheer; the lower parts of the walls were quite often smooth-surfaced, where they were polished by the sands in the stream. The black granite in such cases resembled huge deposits of anthracite coal. Sections of the granite often projected out of the water as islands, with the softer rock washed away, the granite being curiously carved by whirling rocks and the emery-like sands. Holes three and four feet deep were worn by small whirling rocks, and grooves were worn at one place by growing willows working back and forth in the water, the sand, strange to say, having less effect on the limbs than it had on the hard rocks.

About noon of the day following this upset we reached the end of the Bass Trail and another cable crossing, about sixty feet above the water. Three men were waiting for us, and gave a call when we rowed in sight of their camp. One was Lauzon's brother, another was Cecil Dodd, a cowboy who looked after Bass' stock, and the breaking of his horses, the third was John Norberg, an "old timer" and an old friend as well, engaged at that time in working some asbestos and copper claims.

The granite was broken down at this point, and another small deposit of algonkian was found here. There were intrusions, faults, and displacements both in these formations and in the layers above. These fractures exposed mineral seams and deposits of copper and asbestos on both sides of the river, some of which Bass had opened up and located, waiting for the day when there would be better transportation facilities than his burros afforded.

This was not our first visit to this section. On other occasions we had descended by the Mystic Spring (or Bass) Trail, on the south side, crossed on the tramway, and were taken by Bass over some of his many trails, on the north side. We had visited the asbestos claims, where the edge of a blanket formation of the rock known as serpentine, containing the asbestos, lay exposed to view, twisting around the head of narrow canyons, and under beetling cliffs. We went halfway up the north rim trail, through Shinumo and White canyons, our objective point on these trips being a narrow box canyon which contained a large boulder, rolled from the walls above, and wedged in the flume-like gorge far above our heads. This trail continues up to the top, going over the narrow neck which connects Powell's Plateau — a segregated section of thickly wooded surface several miles in extent — with the main extent of the Kaibab Plateau.

Ernest, though slightly affected with tonsillitis, was loath to leave us here. It was zero weather on top, we were told, and it looked it. The walls and peaks were

Copyright by Kolb Bros.

TYPE OF RAPID IN THE GRANITE, NEAR BASS TRAIL.

white with snow. He would not have an easy trip. The drifted snow was only broken by the one party that we found at the river, and quite likely it would be very late when he arrived at the ranch. John went up with him a few miles to get a horse for the ride home the next day. Ernest took with him a few hurriedly written letters and the exposed plates. The film we were going to save was lost in the upset.

On inspecting the provisions which were packed in here we found the grocers had shipped the order short, omitting, besides other necessities, some canned baked beans, on which we depended a great deal. This meant one of two things. We would have to make a quicker run than we had planned on, or would have to get out of the canyon at one of the two places where such an exit could easily be made.

The M. P. as our motion-picture camera was called — and which was re-christened but not abbreviated by Bert, as "The Member of Parliament" — had to be cleaned before we could proceed. It took all this day, and much of the next, to get the moisture and sand out of the delicate mechanism, and have it running smoothly again. After it was once more in good condition Emery announced that he wanted to work out a few scenes of an uncompleted "movie-drama." The action was snappy. The plot was brief, but harmonized well with the setting, and the "props." Dodd, who was a big Texan, was cast for the role of horse thief and bad man in general. Bert's brother, Morris Lauzon, was the deputy sheriff, and had a star cut from the top of a tomato can to prove it. John was to be a prospector. He would need little rehearsing for this part. In addition, he had not been out where he could have the services of a barber for six months past, which was all the better. John had a kind, quiet, easy-going way that made friends for him on sight. He was not consulted about the part he was to play, but we counted on his good nature and he was cast for the part. Emery, who was cast for the part of a mining engineer, arrived on the scene in his boat, after rounding the bend above the camp, tied up and climbed out over the cliffs to view the surrounding country.

The hidden desperado, knowing that he was being hunted, stole the boat with its contents, and made his escape. The returning engineer arrived just in time to see his boat in the middle of the stream, and a levelled rifle halted him until the boat was hidden around the bend. At that moment the officer joined him, and a hurried consultation was held. Then the other boat, which had been separated from its companion, pulled into sight, and I was hailed by the men on shore. They came aboard and we gave chase. Could anything be better? The thief naturally thought he was safe, as he had not seen the second boat! After going over a few rapids, he saw a fire up in the cliffs, on the opposite side of the river. He landed, and climbed up to the camp where John was at work. John shared his camp fare with him, and directed him to a hidden trail. The pursuers, on finding the abandoned boat, quietly followed the trail, and surprised Dodd in John's camp. He was disarmed and sent across the river in the tramway, accompanied by the deputy, and was punished as he richly deserved to be.

This was the scenario. Bert handled the camera. Emery was the playwright, director, and producer. All rights reserved.

Everything worked beautifully. The film did not get balled up in the cogs, as sometimes happened. The light was good. Belasco himself could not have improved on the stage-setting. The trail led over the wildest, and most picturesque places imaginable. Dodd made a splendid desperado, and acted as if he had done nothing but steal horses and dodge the officers all his life. A pile of driftwood fifty feet high and with a tunnel underneath made a splendid hiding place for him while the first boat was being tied. Being a cowpuncher, it may be that he did not handle the oars as well as an experienced riverman, but any rapid could be used for an insert. The deputy, though youthful, was determined and never lost sight of the trail. The engineer acted his part well and registered surprise and anger, when he found how he had been tricked. John, who had returned, humoured us, and dug nuggets of gold out of limestone rocks, where no one would have thought of looking for them. The fact that the tramway scene was made before any of the others did not matter. We could play our last act first if we wanted to. All we had to do was to cut the film and fasten it on to the end. Emery was justly proud of his first efforts as a producer. We were sorry this film had not been sent out with Ernest.

This thrilling drama will not be released in the near future. One day later we found that a drop of water had worked into the lens cell at the last upset. This fogged the lens. We focussed with a scale and had overlooked the lens when cleaning the camera. Nothing but a very faint outline showed on the film. We had all the film we needed for a week after this, for kindling our fires.

CHAPTER XXI

WHAT CHRISTMAS EVE BROUGHT

IN recording our various mishaps and upsets in these pages, it may seem to the reader as if I have given undue prominence to the part I took in them. If so, it has not been from choice, but because they happened in that way. No doubt a great deal of my trouble was due to carelessness. After I had learned to row my boat fairly well I sometimes took chances that proved to be anything but advisable, depending a good deal on luck, and luck was not always with me. My brother was less hasty in making his decisions, and was more careful in his movements, with the result that his boat had few marks of any kind, and he had been more fortunate than I with the rapids.

It is my duty to record another adventure at this point, in which we all three shared, each in a different manner. This time I am going to give my brother's record of the happenings that overtook us about four o'clock in the afternoon of December the 24th, less than three hours after we left our friends at the Bass Trail with "best wishes for a Merry Christmas," and had received instructions from John "to keep our feet dry."

My brother's account follows :

"The fourth rapid below the Bass Trail was bad, but after looking it over we decided it could be run. We had taken chances in rapids that looked worse and came through unharmed; if we were successful here, it would be over in a few minutes, and forgotten an hour later. So we each made the attempt."

"Lauzon had gone near the lower end of the rapid, taking the left shore, for a sixty-foot wall with a sloping bench on top rose sheer out of the water on the right. The only shore on the right was close to the head of the rapid, a small deposit or bank of earth and rock. The inner gorge here was about nine hundred feet deep."

"Ellsworth went first, taking the left-hand side. I picked out a course on the right as being the least dangerous; but I was scarcely started when I found myself on a nest of jagged rocks, with violent water all about me, and with other rocks, some of them submerged, below me. I climbed out on the rocks and held the boat."

"If the others could land below the rapid and climb back, they might get a rope to me and pull me off the rocks far enough to give me a new start, but they could not pull the boat in to shore through the rough water. A person thinks quickly under such circumstances, and

I had it all figured out as soon as I was on the rocks. The greatest trouble would be to hold the boat if she broke loose."

"Then I saw that the *Defiance* was in trouble. She was caught in a reverse whirl in the very middle of the pounding rapid, bouncing back and forth like a great rubber ball. Finally she filled with the splashing water, sank low, and the water pouring over the rock caught the edge of the twelve-hundred pound boat and turned her over as if she were a toy; my brother was holding to the gunwale when she turned. Still she was held in the whirl, jumping as violently as ever, then turned upright again and was forced out. Ellsworth had disappeared, but came up nearly a hundred feet below, struggling to keep on top but going down with every breaking wave. When the quieter water was reached, he did not seem to have strength enough to swim out, but floated, motionless, in a standing position, his head kept up by the life-preservers. The next rapid was not over fifty yards below. If he was to be saved it must be done instantly."

"I pried the boat loose, jumped in as she swung clear, and pulled with all my might, headed toward the centre of the river. I was almost clear when I was drawn over a dip, bow first, and struck a glancing blow against another rock I had never seen. There was a crash, and the boards broke like egg-shells. It was all done in a few moments. The *Edith* was a wreck, I did not know how bad. My brother had disappeared. Lauzon was frantically climbing over some large boulders, trying to reach the head of the next rapid, where the boat was held in an eddy. My boat was not upset, but the waves were surging through a great hole in her side. She was drawn into an eddy, close to the base of the wall, where I could tie up and climb out. It seemed folly to try the lower end with my filled boat. Climbing to the top of the rock, I could see half a mile down the canyon, but my brother was nowhere to be seen and I had no idea that he had escaped. I was returning to my wrecked boat when Bert waved his arms, and pointed to the head of the rapid. Going back once more, I saw him directly below me at the base of the sheer rock, in an opening where the wall receded. He had crawled out twenty feet above the next rapid. Returning to my wrecked boat, I was soon beside him. He was exhausted with his struggle in the icy waves; his outer garments were frozen. I soon procured blankets from my bed, removed the wet clothes, and wrapped him up. Lauzon, true to our expectations of what he would do when the test came, swam out and rescued the *Defiance* before she was carried over the next rapid. He was inexperienced at the oars and had less than two hours practice after he had joined us. It was a tense moment when he started across, above the rapid. But he made it! Landing with a big grin, he exclaimed, 'Young fellows, business is picking up !' then added, 'And we're losing lots of good pictures !'"

"These experiences were our Christmas presents that year. They were not done up in small packages."

"We repaired the boat on Christmas day. Three smashed side ribs were replaced with mesquite, which we found growing on the walls. The hole was patched with boards from the loose bottom. This was painted; canvas was tacked over that and painted also, and a sheet of tin or galvanized iron went over it all. This completed the repair and the *Edith* was as seaworthy as before."

This is Emery's account of the "Christmas Rapid."

I will add that the freezing temperature of the water and the struggle for breath in the breaking waves left me exhausted and at the mercy of the river. An eddy drew me out of the centre of the stream when I had given up all hope of any escape from the next rapid. I had seen my brother on the rock below the head of the rapid and knew there was no hope from him. As I was being drawn back into the current, close to the end of the sheer wall on the right, my feet struck bottom on some débris washed down from the cliff. I made three efforts to stand but fell each time, and finally crawled out on my hands and knees. I had the peculiar sensation of seeing a rain-storm descending before my eyes, although I knew no such thing existed; every fibre in my body ached and continued to do so for days afterward; and the moment I would close my eyes to sleep I would see mountainous waves about me and would feel myself being whirled head over heels just as I was in that rapid; but this rapid, strange to say, while exceedingly rough and swift, did not contain any waves that we would have considered large up to this time. In other words, it depended on the circumstances whether it was bad or not. When standing on the shore, picking a channel, it appeared to be a moderately bad rapid, in which a person, aided with life-preservers, should have little difficulty in keeping on top, at least half the time. After my battle, in which, as far as personal effort went, I had lost, and after my providential escape, that one rapid appeared to be the largest of the entire series.

It is difficult to describe the rapids with the foot-rule standard, and give an idea of their power. One unfamiliar with "white water" usually associates a twelve-foot descent or a ten-foot wave with a similar wave on the ocean. There is no comparison. The waters of the ocean rise and fall, the waves travel, the water itself, except in breakers, is comparatively still. In bad rapids the water is whirled through at the rate of ten or twelve miles an hour, in some cases much swifter; the surface is broken by streams shooting up from every submerged rock; the weight of the river is behind it, and the waves, instead of tumbling forward, quite as often break upstream. Such waves, less than six feet high, are often

Copyright by Kolb Bros.

THE BREAK IN THE "EDITH."

Copyright by Kolb Bros.

MERRY CHRISTMAS! THE REPAIR WAS MADE WITH BILGE BOARDS, CANVAS, PAINT, AND TIN.

dangers to be shunned. After being overturned in them we learned their tremendous power, a power we would never have associated with any water, before such an experience, short of a waterfall.

There is a certain amount of danger in the canyons, — plenty of it. Still, in most cases, with care and forethought, much of it can be avoided. We think we are safe in saying that half of the parties who have attempted a passage through these canyons have met with fatalities. Most of these have occurred in Cataract Canyon, not because it is any worse than other sections, — certainly no worse than the Grand Canyon, — but because it is easily entered from the quiet, alluring water of the lower Green River. Without a doubt each successful expedition is responsible in a way for others' attempts. In nearly every instance the unfortunate ones have underestimated the danger, and have attempted the passage with inadequate boats, such as Smith had for instance, undecked and without air chambers. Both of these are imperative for safety.

We had the benefit of the experiences of others. In addition, our years of work in the canyons had robbed them of their imaginary dangers, and — while we trust that we are not entirely without imagination — much of their weirdness and glamour with which they are inseparable to the idealist and the impressionist. Each of these upsets could have been avoided by a portage had we

R

desired to make one, but success in other rapids made us a little reckless and ready to take a chance.

Beyond getting our flour wet on the outside, we suffered very little loss to our cargo. We placed the two flour sacks beside the fires each evening, until the wet flour dried to a crust. We continued to use out of the centre of the sacks as though nothing had ever happened.

Bert and I each had a little cough the next morning, but it disappeared by noon. Beyond that, we suffered no great inconvenience from our enforced bath. Sleeping in the open, with plenty of healthful exercise, kept us physically fit.

The cold air and the cold water did not seem to bother the others, but I could not get comfortably warm during this cold snap. Added to this, it took me some time to get over my scare, and I could see all kinds of danger, in rapids, where Emery could see none. I insisted on untying the photographic cases from the boats, and carrying them around a number of rapids before we ran them. It is hardly necessary to say that no upset occurred in these rapids.

Then came a cold day, with a raw wind sweeping up the river. A coating of ice covered the boats and the oars. We had turned directly to the north along the base of Powell's plateau, and were nearing the end of a second granite gorge, with violent rapids and jagged rocks. Emery made the remark that he had not had a swim for some time. In a half-hour we came to a rapid with two twelve-foot waves in the centre of the stream, with a projecting point above that would have to be passed, before we could pull out of the swift-running centre. Emery got his swim there. I was just behind and was more fortunate. I never saw anything more quickly done. Before the boat was fully overturned he swung an oar, so that it stuck out at an angle from the side of the boat, and used the oar for a step; an instant later he had cut the oar loose, and steered toward the shore. Bert threw him a rope from the shore, and he was pulled in. He was wearing a thin rubber coat fitting tightly about his wrists, tied about his neck, and belted at the waist. This protected him so thoroughly that he was only wet from the waist down.

If we were a little inclined to be proud of our record above Bright Angel we had forgotten all about it by this time. We were scarcely more than sixty miles from home and had experienced three upsets and a smashed boat, all in one week.

Just at the end of the second granite section we made our first portage since leaving Bright Angel. Bert and I worked on the boats, while Emery cooked the evening meal.

Hot rice soup, flavoured with a can of prepared meat, was easily and quickly prepared, and formed one of the usual dishes at these meals. It contained a lot of nutriment, and the rice took up but little space in the boats. Sometimes the meat was omitted, and raisins were substituted. Prepared baked beans were a staple dish, but were not in our supply on this last part of the trip. We often made "hot cakes" twice a day; an excuse for eating a great deal of butter and honey, or syrup. None of these things were luxuries. They were the best foodstuff we could carry. We seemed to crave sweet stuff, and used quantities of sugar. We could carry eggs, when packed in sawdust, without trouble but did not carry many. We had little meat; what we had was bacon, and prepared meats of the lunch variety. Cheese was our main substitute for meat. It was easily carried and kept well. Dried peaches or apricots were on the bill for nearly every meal, each day's allowance being cooked the evening before. We tried several condensed or emergency foods, but discarded them all but one, for various reasons. The exception was Erbeswurst, a patent dried soup preparation. Other prepared soups were carried also. I must not forget the morning cereal. It was Cream of Wheat, easily prepared; eaten — not served, perhaps devoured would be a better word — with sugar and condensed cream, as long as it lasted, then with butter. Any remainder from breakfast was fried for other meals. Each evening, we would make some baking-powder biscuit in a frying-pan. A Dutch oven is better, but had too much weight. The appellation for such bread is "flapjack" or "dough-god." When I did the baking they were fearfully and wonderfully made. Cocoa, which was nourishing, often took the place of coffee. In fact our systems craved just what was most needed to build up muscle and create heat. We found it was useless to try to catch fish after the weather became cold. The fish would not bite.

On the upper end of our journey we carried no tobacco, as it happened that Jimmy as well as ourselves were not tobacco users. There were no alcoholic stimulants. When Bert joined us, a small flask, for medicinal purposes only, was taken along. The whiskey was scarcely touched at this time. Bert enjoyed a pipe after his meals, but continued to keep good-natured even when his tobacco got wet, so tobacco was not absolutely necessary to him.

Uninteresting and unromantic these things may be, but they were most important to us. We were only sorry the supply was not larger. While we never stinted ourselves, or cut the allowance of food, the amount was growing smaller every day, and it was not a question any more whether we would go out or not, to get provisions, to "rustle" as Bert called it, but where we would go out. We might go up Cataract Creek or Ha Va Su Creek, as it is sometimes called. We had been to the mouth of this canyon on foot, so there would be no danger of missing it. The Ha Va Supai Indians, about two hundred in number, lived in this lateral canyon, about seven or eight miles from the river. An agent and a farmer lived with them, and might be able to sell us some provisions; if not, it would be fifty miles back to our home. The trail was much more direct than the river. The great drawback to this course was the fact that Ha Va Su Canyon, sheer-walled, deep, and narrow, contained a number of waterfalls, one of them about 175 feet high. The precipice over which it fell was nothing but a mineral deposit from the water, building higher every year. Formerly this was impassable, until some miners, after enlarging a sloping cave, had cut a winding stairway in it, which allowed a descent to be made to the bottom of the fall. A recent storm had remodelled all the falls in Cataract Creek Canyon, cutting out the travertine in some places, piling it up in others. A great mass of cottonwood trees were also mixed with the débris. The village, too, had been washed away and was then being rebuilt. We had been told that the tunnel was filled up, and as far as we knew no one had been to the river since the flood.

The other outlet was Diamond Creek Canyon, much farther down the river. We would decide when we got to Ha Va Su just what we would do.

Tapeets Creek, one mile below our camp, — a stream which has masqueraded under the title of Thunder

River, and about which there has been considerable speculation, — proved to be a stream a little smaller than Bright Angel Creek, flowing through a narrow slot in the rocks, and did not fall sheer into the river, as has been reported. Perhaps a small cascade known as Surprise Falls which we passed the next day has been confused with Tapeets Creek. This stream corkscrews down through a narrow crevice and falls about two hundred feet, close to the river's edge. We are told that the upper end of Tapeets Creek is similar to this, but on a much larger scale.

Just opposite this fall a big mountain-sheep jumped from under an overhanging ledge close to the water, and stared curiously at us, as though he wondered what strange things those were coming down with the current. It is doubtful if he ever saw a human being before. This sight sent us scrambling in our cases for cameras and firearms; and it was not the game laws, but a rusted trigger on the six-shooter instead, that saved the sheep. He finally took alarm and scampered away over the rocks, and we had no mutton stew that night.

We had one night of heavy rain, and morning revealed a little snow within three hundred feet of the river, while a heavy white blanket covered the upper cliffs. It continued to snow on top, and rained on us nearly all this day. Emery took this opportunity to get the drop of moisture out of the lens, and put the camera in such shape that we could proceed with our picture making. A short run was made after this work was completed.

The camp we were just leaving was about three miles above Kanab Canyon. The granite was behind us, disappearing with a steep descent much as it had emerged at the Hance Trail. There was also a small deposit of algonkian. This too had been passed, and we were back in the limestone and sandstone walls similar to the lower end of Marble Canyon. While the formations were the same, the canyon differed. The layers were thicker, the red sandstone and the marble walls were equally sheer; there was no plateau between. What plateau this canyon contained lay on top of the red sandstone. Few peaks rose above this. The canyon had completed its northern run and was turning back again to the west-southwest with a great sweep or circle. Less than an hour's work brought us to Kanab Canyon.

PULLING CLEAR OF A ROCK.   *Copyright by Kolb Bros.*

A SHOWER BATH.   *Copyright by Kolb Bros.*

CHAPTER XXII

SHORT OF PROVISIONS IN A SUNLESS GORGE

In the mud at Kanab Canyon we saw an old footprint of some person who had come down to the river through this narrow, gloomy gorge. It was here that Major Powell terminated his second voyage, on account of extreme high water. A picture they made showed their boats floated up in this side canyon. Our stage was much lower than this. F. S. Dellenbaugh, the author of "A Canyon Voyage," was a member of this second expedition. This book had been our guide down to this point; we could not have asked for a better one. Below here we had a general idea of the nature of the river, and had a set of the government maps, but we had neglected to provide ourselves with detailed information such as this volume gave us.

Evening of the following day found us at Cataract Creek Canyon, but with a stage of water in the river nearly fifty feet lower than that which we had seen a few years before. The narrow entrance of this great canyon gives no hint of what it is like a few miles above.

The Indian village is in the bottom of a 3000-foot canyon, half a mile wide and three miles long, covered with fertile fields, peach and apricot orchards. It even contained a few fig trees. Below the village the canyon narrowed to a hundred yards, with a level bottom, covered with a tangle of wild grape vines, cactus, and cottonwood trees. This section contained the two largest falls, and came to an end about four miles below the first fall. Then the canyon narrowed, deep and gloomy, until there was little room for anything but the powerful, rapidly descending stream. At the lower end it was often waist deep and fifteen or twenty feet wide. It was no easy task to go through this gorge. The stream had to be crossed several times. The canyon terminated in an extremely narrow gorge 2500 feet deep, dark and gloomy, one of the most impressive gorges we have ever seen. The main canyon was similar, with a few breaks on the sides, those breaks being ledges, or narrow sloping benches that would extend for miles, only to be brought to an abrupt end by side canyons. There are many mountain-sheep in this section, but we saw none either time. We could see many fresh tracks where they had followed these ledges around, and had gone up the narrow side canyon. It was cold in the main canyon, and no doubt the sheep could be found on the plateaus, which were more open, and would get sun when the sun shone. This plateau was 2500 feet above us. At the turn of the canyon we

Copyright by Kolb Bros.

GRAND CANYON AT MOUTH OF HA VA SU CANYON.   MEDIUM HIGH WATER.
NOTE FIGURE.   FRONTISPIECE SHOWS SAME PLACE IN LOW WATER.

could see the other walls 2000 feet above that. The
rapids in the section just passed had been widely separated and compared well with those of Marble Canyon,
not the worst we had seen, but far from being tame.
There was plenty of shore room at each of these rapids.

Cactus of different species was now a feature of the
scenery. The ocotilla or candlewood with long, lash-like
stalks springing from a common centre — that cactus,
which, when dried, needs only a lighted match to set it
afire — flourishes in the rocky ledges. A species of small
barrel-cactus about the size of a man's head, with fluted
sides, or symmetrical vertical rows of small thorned lumps
converging at the top of the "nigger-head," as they are
sometimes called, grows in great numbers in crevices on
the walls. The delicate "pin cushion" gathered in
clusters of myriad small spiny balls. The prickly pear,
here in Ha Va Su Canyon, were not the starved, shrivelled,
mineral-tinted cactus such as we found at the beginning
of our trip. Instead they were green and flourishing,
with large fleshy leaves joining on to each other until
they rise to a height of three feet or more and cover large
patches of ground to the utter exclusion of all other
growth. What a display of yellow and red these desert
plants put forth when they are in bloom! A previous
visit to Ha Va Su was made in the month of May when
every group of prickly pear was a riot of pure colour. All
this prolific growth is made possible by the extreme heat

of the summer months aided in the case of those plants and trees which flourish in the fertile soil of Ha Va Su by the sub-irrigation and the spray from the fall.

After making an inventory of our provisions we concluded not to try the tedious and uncertain trip up Cataract Creek. With care and good fortune we would have enough provisions to last us to Diamond Creek.

With our run the next day the inner gorge continued to deepen, the walls drew closer together, so that we now had a narrow gorge hemming us in with 3000-foot walls from which there was no escape. They were about a fourth of a mile apart at the top. A boat at the foot of one of these walls was merely an atom. The total depth of the canyon was close to 4500 feet. There is nothing on earth to which this gorge can be compared. Storm-clouds lowered into the chasm in the early morning. The sky was overcast and threatening. We were travelling directly west again, and no sunlight entered here, even when the sun shone. The walls had lost their brighter reds, and what colour they had was dark and sombre, a dirty brown and dark green predominating. The mythology of the ancients, with their Inferno and their River Styx, could hardly conjure anything more supernatural or impressive than this gloomy gorge.

There were a few bad rapids. One or two had no shore, others had an inclination to run under one wall, and had to be run very carefully. If we could not get down alongside of a rapid, we could usually climb out on the walls at the head of the rapid and look it over from that vantage point. The one who climbed out would signal directions to the others, who would run it at once, and continue on to the next rapid. They would have its course figured out when the last boat arrived.

One canyon entered from the left, level on the bottom, and about one hundred feet wide; it might be a means of outlet from this canyon, but it is doubtful, for the marble has a way of ending abruptly and dropping sheer, with a polished surface that is impossible to climb.

New Year's Eve was spent in this section. The camp was exceptionally good. A square-sided, oblong section of rock about fifty feet long had fallen forward from the base of the cliff. This left a cave-like opening which was closed at one end with our dark-room tent. High water had placed a sandy floor, now thoroughly dry, in the bottom. Under the circumstances we could hardly ask for anything better. Of driftwood there was none, and our camp-fires were made of mesquite which grew in ledges in the rocks; in one case gathered with a great deal of labour on the shore opposite our camp, and ferried across on our boats. If a suitable camp was found after 3.30 P.M., we kept it, rather than run the risk of not finding another until after dark.

Another day, January 1, 1912, brought us to the end of this gorge and into a wider and more open canyon, with the country above covered with volcanic peaks and cinder cones. Blow-holes had broken through the canyon walls close to the top of the gorge, pouring streams of lava down its sides, filling the bottom of the canyon with several hundred feet of lava. This condition extended down the canyon for twenty miles or more. Judging by the amount of lava the eruption must have continued for a great while. Could one imagine a more wonderful sight — the turbulent stream checked by the fire flood from above! What explosions and rending of rocks there must have been when the two elements met. The river would be backed up for a hundred miles! Each would be shoved on from behind! There was no escape! They must fight it out until one or the other conquered. But the fire could not keep up forever, and, though triumphant for a period, it finally succumbed, and the stream proceeded to cut down to the original level.

Two miles below the first lava flow we saw what we took to be smoke and hurried down wondering if we would find a prospector or a cattle rustler. We agreed, if it was the latter, to let them off if they would share with us. But the smoke turned out to be warm springs, one of them making quite a stream which fell twenty feet into the river. Here in the river was a cataract, called Lava Falls, so filled with jagged pieces of the black rock that a portage was advisable. The weather had not moderated any in the last week, and we were in the water a

LAVA FALLS: LAVA ON LEFT; WARM SPRINGS ON RIGHT.

Copyright by Kolb Bros.

great deal as we lifted and lined the boats over the rocks at the edge of the rapids. We would work in the water until numbed with the cold, then would go down to the warm springs and thaw out for a while. This was a little quicker than standing by the fire, but the relief was only temporary. This portage was finished the next morning.

Another portage was made this same day, and the wide canyon where Major Powell found some Indian gardens was passed in the afternoon. The Indians were not at home when the Major called. His party felt they were justified in helping themselves to some pumpkins or squash, for their supplies were very low, and they could not go out to a settlement — as we expected to do in a day or two — and replenish them.

We found the fish would not bite, just as our friend, the miner, had said, but we did succeed in landing a fourteen-pound salmon, in one of the deep pools not many miles from this point, and it was served up in steaks the next day. If our method of securing the salmon was unsportsmanlike, we excused ourselves for the methods used, just as Major Powell justified his appropriation of the Indians' squash. If that fish was ever needed, it was then, and it was a most welcome addition to our rapidly disappearing stock of provisions. We were only sorry we had not taken more "bait."

The next day we did see a camp-fire, and on climbing the shore, found a little old prospector, clad in tattered garments, sitting in a little dugout about five feet square, which he had shovelled out of the sand. He had roofed it with mesquite and an old blanket. A rapid, just below, made so much noise that he did not hear us until we were before his door. He looked at the rubber coats and the life-preservers, then said, with a matter-of-fact drawl, "Well, you fellows must have come by the river!" After talking awhile he asked :

"What do you call yourselves?" This question would identify him as an old-time Westerner if we did not already know it. At one time it was not considered discreet to ask any one in these parts what their name was, or where they were from. He gave us a great deal of information about the country, and said that Diamond Creek was about six miles below. He had come across from Diamond Creek by a trail over a thousand foot ridge, with a burro and a pack mule, a month before. He had just been out near the top on the opposite side, doing some assessment work on some copper claims, crossing the river on a raft, and stated that on a previous occasion he had been drawn over the rapid, but got out.

When he learned that we had come through Utah, he stated that he belonged near Vernal, and had once been upset in the upper canyons, about twenty years before. He proved to be the Snyder of whom we had heard at Linwood, and also from the Chews, who had given him a horse so he could get out over the mountains. Yet here he was, a thousand miles below, cheerful as a cricket, and sure that a few months at the most would bring him unlimited wealth. He asked us to "share his chuck" with him, but we could see nothing but a very little flour, and a little bacon, so pleaded haste and pushed on for Diamond Creek.

The mouth of this canyon did not look unlike others we had seen in this section, and one could easily pass it without knowing that it ran back with a gentle slope for twenty miles, and that a wagon road came down close to the river. It contained a small, clear stream. The original tourist camp in the Grand Canyon was located up this canyon. We packed all our plates and films, ready to take them out. The supplies left in the boats when we went out the next morning were:

5 pounds of flour, partly wet and crusted.

2 pounds mildewed Cream of Wheat.

3 or 4 cans (rusty) of dried beef.

Less than one pound of sugar.

We carried a lunch out with us. This was running a little too close for comfort.

The mouth of Diamond Creek Canyon was covered with a growth of large mesquite trees. Cattle trails wound through this thorny thicket down to the river's edge. The trees thinned out a short distance back, and the canyon widened as it receded from the river. A half mile back from the river was the old slab building that

s

had served as headquarters for the campers. Here the canyon divided, one containing the small stream heading in the high walls to the southeast; while the other branch ran directly south, heading near the railroad at the little flag-station of Peach Springs, twenty-three miles distant. It was flat-bottomed, growing wider and more valley-like with every mile, but not especially interesting to one who had seen the glory of all the canyons. Floods had spoiled what had once been a very passable stage road, dropping 4000 feet in twenty miles, down to the very depths of the Grand Canyon. Some cattle, driven down by the snows, were sunning themselves near the building. Our appearance filled them with alarm, and they "high tailed it" to use a cattle man's expression, scampering up the rocky slopes.

A deer's track was seen in a snow-drift away from the river. On the sloping walls in the more open sections of this valley grew the stubby-thorned chaparral. The hackberry and the first specimens of the palo verde were found in this vicinity. The mesquite trees seen at the mouth of the canyon were real trees — about the size of a large apple tree — not the small bushes we had seen at the Little Colorado. All the growth was changing as we neared the lower altitudes and the mouth of the Grand Canyon, being that of the hot desert, which had found this artery or avenue leading to the heart of the rocky plateaus and had pushed its way into this foreign land.

Even the animal life of the desert has followed this same road. Occasional Gila monsters, which are supposed to belong to the hot desert close to the Mexico line, have been found at Diamond Creek, and lizards of the Mojave Desert have been seen as far north as the foot of Bright Angel Trail.

But we saw little animal life at this time. There were occasional otters disporting themselves near our boats, in one instance unafraid, in another raising a gray-bearded head near our boat with a startled look in his eyes. Then he turned and began to swim on the surface until our laughter caused him to dive. Tracks of the civet-cat or the ring-tailed cat — that large-eyed and large-eared animal, somewhat like a raccoon and much resembling a weasel — were often seen along the shores. The gray fox, the wild-cat, and the coyote, all natives of this land, kept to the higher piñon-covered hills. The beaver seldom penetrates into the deep canyons because of the lack of vegetation, but is found in all sections in the open country from the headwaters to the delta in Mexico.

We went out by this canyon on January the 5th, and returned Sunday, January the 8th, bringing enough provisions to last us to the end of the big canyon. We imagined we would have no trouble getting what we needed in the open country below that. We sent some telegrams and received encouraging answers to them before returning. With us were two brothers, John and Will

Nelson, cattle men who had given us a cattle man's welcome when we arrived at Peach Springs. There was no store at Peach Springs, and they supplied us with the provisions that we brought back. They drove a wagon for about half the distance, then the roads became impassable, so they unhitched and packed their bedding and our provisions in to the river. The Nelsons were anxious to see us run a rapid or two.

We found the nights to be just as cold on top as they ever get in this section — a little below zero — although the midday sun was warm enough to melt the snow and make it slushy. I arrived at the river with my feet so swollen that I had difficulty in walking, a condition brought on by a previous freezing they had received, being wet continually by the icy water in my boat — which was leaking badly since we left Bright Angel — and the walk out through the slush. I was glad there was little walking to do when once at the river, and changed my shoes for arctics, which were more roomy and less painful.

On the upper part of our trip there were occasional days when Emery was not feeling his best, while I had been most fortunate and had little complaint to make; now things seemed to be reversed. Emery, and Bert too, were having the time of their lives, while I was "getting mine" in no small doses.[1]

---

[1] While Major Powell was making his second voyage of exploration, another party was toiling up these canyons towing their boats from the precipitous shores.

We had always imagined that the Grand Canyon lost its depth and impressiveness below Diamond Creek. We were to learn our mistake. The colour was missing, that was true, for the marble and sandstone walls were brown, dirty, or colourless, with few of the pleasing tones of the canyon found in the upper end. But it was still the Grand Canyon. We were in the granite again — granite just as deep as any we had seen above, it may have been a little deeper, and in most cases it was very sheer. There was very little plateau, the limestone and sandstone rose above that, just as they had above Kanab Canyon. The light-coloured walls could not be seen.

Many of the rapids of this lower section were just as

This party was under the leadership of Lieutenant Wheeler of the U. S. Army. The party was large, composed of twenty men, including a number of Mojave Indians, in the river expedition, while others were sent overland with supplies to the mouth of Diamond Creek. By almost superhuman effort they succeeded in getting their boats up the canyon as far as Diamond Creek. While there is no doubt that they reached this point, there were times when we could hardly believe it was possible when we saw the walls they would have to climb in this granite gorge. In some places there seemed to be no place less than five hundred feet above the river where they could secure a foothold. Their method was to carry a rope over these places, then pull the boats up through the rapids by main force. It would be just as easy to pull a heavy rowboat up the gorge of Niagara, as through some of these rapids. Their best plan, by far, would have been to haul their boats in at Diamond Creek and make the descent, as they did after reaching this point. The only advantage their method gave them was a knowledge of what they would meet with on the downstream run. Lieutenant Wheeler professed to disbelieve that Major Powell had descended below Diamond Creek, and called his voyage the completion of the exploration of the Colorado River. In a four days' run they succeeded in covering the same distance that had taken four weeks of endless toil, to bring their boats up to this point.

bad as any we had gone over; one or two have been considered worse by different parties. Two hours after leaving the Nelsons we were halted by a rapid that made us catch our breath. It was in two sections — the lower one so full of jagged rocks that it meant a wrecked boat. The upper part fell about twenty feet we should judge and was bad enough. It was a question if we could run this and keep from going over the lower part. If we made a portage, our boats would have to be taken three or four hundred feet up the side of the cliff. The rapid was too strong to line a boat down. We concluded to risk running the first part. Bert climbed to the head of the second section of the rapid, where a projecting point of granite narrowed the stream, and formed a quiet eddy just above the foaming plunge. If we could keep out of the centre and land here we would be safe. Our shoes were removed, our trousers were rolled to our knees and we removed our coats. If we had to swim there, we were going to be prepared. The life-preservers were well inflated, and tied; then we made the plunge, Emery taking the lead, I following close behind. Our plan was to keep as near the shore as possible. Once I thought it was all over when I saw the *Edith* pulled directly for a rock in spite of all Emery could do to pull away. Nothing but a rebounding wave saved him. I went through the same experience. Several times we were threatened with an upset, but we landed in safety. The portage was short and easy. Flat granite rocks were covered with a thin coat of ice. The boats were unloaded and slid across, then dropped below the projecting rock. The *Defiance* skidded less than two feet and struck a projecting knob of rock the size of a goose egg. It punctured the side close to the stern, fortunately above the water line, and the wood was not entirely broken away.

Two miles below this we found another bad one. This was lined while Bert got supper up in a little sloping canyon; about as uncomfortable a camp as we had found. Many of the rapids run the next day were violent. The river seemed to be trying to make up for lost time. We passed a canyon coming from the south containing two streams, one clear, and one muddy. The narrowest place we had seen on the river was a rapid run this day, not over forty feet wide. Evening brought us to a rapid with a lateral canyon coming in from each side, that on the right containing a muddy stream. The walls were sheer and jagged close to the rapid, with a break on the rugged slopes here and there. A sloping rock in the middle of the stream could be seen in the third section of the rapid. This was Separation Rapid, the point where the two Howland brothers and Dunn parted company with Major Powell and his party.

From our camp at the left side we could easily figure out a way to the upper plateau. Above that they would have a difficult climb as far as we could tell. That they did reach the top is well known. They met a tragic fate. The second day after getting out they were killed by some Indians — the Shewits Utes — who had treated them hospitably at first and provided them with something to eat. That night a visiting Indian brought a tale of depredations committed by some miners against another section of their tribe. These men were believed to be the guilty parties, and they were ambushed the next morning. Their fate remained a mystery for a year; then a Ute was seen with a watch belonging to one of the men. Later a Mormon who had a great deal of influence with the Indians got their story from them, and reported to Major Powell what he had learned. It was a deplorable and a tragic ending to what otherwise was one of the most successful, daring, and momentous explorations ever undertaken on this continent.

We find there is a current belief that it was cowardice and fear of this one rapid that caused these men to separate from the party. The more one hears of this separation, the more it seems that it was a difference of opinion on many matters, and not this one rapid, that caused them to leave. These men had been trappers and hunters, one might say pioneers, and one had been with Major Powell before the river exploration. They had gone through all the canyons, and had come through this far without a fatality. They had seen a great many rapids nearly as bad as this, and several that were worse,

if one could judge by its nature when we found it.   They
were not being carried by others, but had charge of one
boat.   They did smash one boat in Disaster Rapid in
Lodore Canyon, and at that time they claimed Major
Powell gave them the wrong signal.   This caused some
feeling.

At the time of the split, the food question was a serious
one.   There were short rations for a long time; in fact
there was practically no food.   After an observation,
Major Powell informed them that they were within forty-
five miles of the Virgin River, in a direct line.   Much
of the country between the end of the canyon and the
Virgin River was open, a few Mormon settlements
could be found up the Virgin Valley.   He offered them
half of the small stock of provisions, when they per-
sisted in leaving, but they refused to take any provisions
whatever, feeling sure that they could kill enough game
to subsist on.   This one instance would seem to be
enough to clear them of the stigma of cowardice.   The
country on top was covered with volcanic cinders.   There
was little water to be found, and in many ways it was
just as inhospitable as the canyon.   The cook had a
pan of biscuits, which he left on a rock for them, after
the men had helped the party lift the boats over the rocks
at the head of the rapid.   After landing in safety around
a bend which hid them from sight, the boating party
fired their guns, hoping they would hear the report, and

follow in the abandoned boat. It is doubtful if they could hear the sound of the guns, above the roar of the rapid. If they did, they paid no attention to it. The younger Howland wished to remain with the party, but threw his lot with his brother, when he withdrew.

While these men did not have the Major's deep scientific interest in the successful completion of this exploration, they undoubtedly should have stayed with their leader, if their services were needed or desired. It is more than likely that they were insubordinate; they certainly made a misguided attempt, but in spite of these facts it scarcely seems just to brand them as cowards. Two days after they left, the boating party was camped at the end of the canyons.

CHAPTER XXIII

THE first section of Separation Rapid was run the first thing in the morning, a manœuvre that was accomplished by starting on the left shore and crossing the swift centre clear to the other shore. This allowed us to reach some quiet water near a small deposit of rock and earth at the base of the sheer wall. Two feet of water would have covered this deposit; likewise two feet of water would have given us a clear channel over this second section. As it was, the rapid was rough, with many rocks very near the surface. Directly across from us, close to the left shore, was what looked like a ten-foot geyser, or fountain of water. This was caused by a rock in the path of a strong current rebounding from the shore. The water ran up on the side near the wall, then fell on all sides. It was seldom the water had force enough to carry to the top of a rock as large as that. This portage of the second section was one of the easiest we had made. By rolling a few large rocks around we could get a stream of water across our small shore large enough to float an empty boat with a little help, so we lightened them of the cargo and floated them through our canal. While running the third section the *Edith* was carried up on the sloping rock in the middle of the stream; she paused a moment, then came down like a shot and whirled around to the side without mishap. This made the thirteenth rapid in which both boats were lined or portaged. In three other rapids one boat was run through and one was portaged. Half of all these rapids were located in the Grand Canyon.

All this time we were anxiously looking forward to a rapid which Mr. Stone had described as being the worst in the entire series, also the last rapid we would be likely to portage and had informed us that below this particular rapid everything could be run with little or no inspection. Naturally we were anxious to get that rapid behind us. It was described as being located below a small stream flowing from the south. The same rapid was described by Major Powell as having a bold, lava-capped escarpment at the head of the rapid, on the right. We had not seen any lava since leaving Diamond Creek, and an entry in my notes reads, "we have gone over Stone's 'big rapid' three times and it is still ahead of us." The knowledge that there was a big rapid in the indefinite somewhere that was likely to cause us trouble seemed to give us more anxious moments than the many unmentioned rapids we were finding all this time. We wondered how high the escarpment was, and if we could take our boats over its top. We tried to convince ourselves that it was behind us, although sure that it could not be. But the absence of lava puzzled us. After one "bad" rapid and several "good" rapids we came to a sharp turn in the canyon. Emery was ahead and called back, "I see a little stream"; Bert joined with "I see the lava"; and the "Bold Escarpment Rapid," as we had been calling it for some time, was before us. It was more than a nasty rapid, it was a cataract!

What a din that water sent up! We had to yell to make ourselves heard. The air vibrated with the impact of water against rock. The rapid was nearly half a mile long. There were two sections near its head staggered with great rocks, forty of them, just above or slightly submerged under the surface of the water. Our low stage of water helped us, so that we did not have to line the boats from the ledge, eighty feet above the water, as others had done. The rapid broke just below the lower end of the sheer rock, which extended twenty feet beyond the irregular shore. The *Edith* went first, headed upstream, at a slight angle nearly touching the wall, dropping a few inches between each restraining stroke of the oars. Bert crouched on the bow, ready to spring with the rope, as soon as Emery passed the wall and headed her in below the wall. Jumping to the shore, he took a snub around a boulder and kept her from being dragged into the rapid. Then they both caught the *Defiance* as she swung in below the rock, and half the battle was won before we tackled the rapid.

Our days were short, and we did not take the boats down until the next day; but we did carry much of the camp material and cargo halfway down over ledges a hundred feet above the river. For a bad rapid we were very fortunate in getting past it as easily as we did. Logs were laid over rocks, the boats were skidded over them about their own length and dropped in again. Logs and boats were lined down in the swift, but less riotous water, to the next barrier, which was more difficult. A ten-foot rounded boulder lay close to the shore, with smaller rocks, smooth and ice-filmed, scattered between. Powerful currents swirled between these rocks and disappeared under two others, wedged closely together on top. Three times the logs were snatched from our grasp as we tried to bridge them across this current, and they vanished in the foam, to shoot out end first, twenty feet below and race away on the leaping water. A boat would be smashed to kindling-wood if once carried under there. At last we got our logs wedged, and an hour of tugging, in which only two men could take part at the same time, landed both boats in safety below this barrier. We shot the remainder of the rapid on water so swift that the oars were snatched from our hands if we tried to do more than keep the boats straight

H. LAUZON.   E. L. KOLB.   *Copyright by Kolb Bros.*

THE LAST PORTAGE. THE ROCKS WERE ICE–FILMED. NOTE POTHOLES.

with the current. That rapid was no longer the "Bold Escarpment," but the "Last Portage" instead, and it was behind us.

The afternoon was half gone when we made ready to pull away from the Last Portage. There were other rapids, but scarcely a pause was made in our two-hour run, and we camped away from the roar of water. The canyon was widening out a little at a time; the granite disappeared in the following day's run, at noon. Grass-covered slopes, with seeping mineral springs, took the place of precipitous walls; they dropped to 2500 feet in height; numerous side canyons cut the walls in regular sections like gigantic city blocks, instead of an unbroken avenue. Small rapids continued to appear, there were a few small islands, and divided currents, so shallow they sometimes kept us guessing which one to take, but we continued to run them all without a pause. We would have run out of the canyon that day but for one thing. Five mountain-sheep were seen from our boats in one of the sloping grassy meadows above the river. We landed below, carried our cameras back, and spent half an hour in trying to see them again, but they had taken alarm.

Placer claim locations and fresh burro tracks were seen in the sand at our last Grand Canyon camp, and a half mile below us we could see out into open country. We found the walls, or the end of the table-land, to be about two thousand feet high, with the canyon emerging at a sharp angle so that a narrow ridge, or "hogs-back," lay on the left side of the stream. Once out in the open, the walls were seen to be quite steep, but could be climbed to the top almost any place without trouble. Saturday, January the 13th, we were out of the canyon at last, and the towering walls, now friendly, now menacing, were behind us. Three hundred and sixty-five large rapids, and nearly twice as many small rapids, were behind us and the dream of ten years was an accomplished fact. But best of all, there were no tragedies or fatalities to record. Perhaps we did look a little the worse for wear, but a few days away from the river would repair all that. The boats had a bump here and there, besides the one big patch on the *Edith;* a little mending and a little caulking would put both the *Edith* and *Defiance* in first-class condition.

There is little of interest to record of our 175-mile run to Needles, California. It was a land of desolation — an extension of the Mojave Desert on the south, and the alkaline flats and mineral mountains of Nevada on the north, of Death Valley and the Funeral Mountains of California to the northwest — a burned-out land of grim-looking mountains extending north and south across our way; a dried-out, washed-out, and wind-swept land of extensive flats and arroyos; a land of rock and gravel cemented in marls and clay; ungraced with any but the desert plants, —

cactus and thorny shrubs, — with little that was pleasing
or attractive. A desert land it is true, but needing only
the magic touch of water to transform much of it into a
garden spot. Even as it was, a few months later it
would be covered with the flaming blossoms of the desert
growth, which seem to try to make amends in one or
two short months for nearly a year of desolation.

A wash ran along the base of the plateau from which
we had emerged. An abandoned road and ferry showed
that this had once been a well-travelled route. The
stream had a good current and we pulled away, only
stopping once to see the last of our plateau before a turn
and deepening banks hid it from view. We wondered
if the water ever dropped in a precipitous fall over the
face of the wall and worked back, a little every year, as
it does at Niagara. We could hardly doubt that there
were some such falls back in the dim past when these
canyons were being carved.

In the middle of the afternoon we passed a ranch or
a house with a little garden, occupied by two miners,
who hailed us from the shore. A half-mile below was the
Scanlon Ferry, a binding tie between Arizona, on the
south and what was now Nevada, on the north, for we
had reached the boundary line shortly after emerging
from the canyon. We still travelled nearly directly west.
The ferry was in charge of a Cornishman who also had
as pretty a little ranch as one could expect to find in

T

such an unlikely place. A purling stream of water, piped from somewhere up in the hills, had caused the transformation. The ranch was very homey with cattle and horses, sheep and hogs, dogs and cats, all sleek and contented-looking. The garden proved that this country had a warm climate, although we were not suffering from heat at that time. An effort was being made to grow some orange trees, but with little promise of success; there were fig trees and date-palms, with frozen dates hanging on the branches, one effect of the coldest winter they had seen in this section.

The rancher told us he could not sell us anything that had to be brought in, for it was seventy miles to the railroad, but we could look over such supplies as he had. It ended by his selling us a chicken, two dozen eggs, five pounds of honey, and ten pounds of flour, — all for $2.50. We did not leave until the next morning, then bought another jar of honey, for we had no sugar, and two-thirds of the first jar was eaten before we left the ferry.

We pulled away in such a hurry the next morning that we forgot an axe that had been carried with us for the entire journey. A five-hour run brought us to the mouth of the Virgin River, a sand-bar a mile wide, and with a red-coloured stream little larger than Cataract Creek winding through it. We had once seen this stream near its head waters, a beautiful mountain creek, that seemed to bear no relation to this repulsive-looking stream

that entered from the north. A large, flat-topped, adobe
building, apparently deserted, stood off at one side of the
stream. This was the head of navigation for flat-
bottomed steamboats that once plied between here
and the towns on the lower end of the river. They
carried supplies for small mines scattered through the
mountains and took out cargoes of ore, and of rock salt
which was mined back in Nevada.

It was here at the Virgin River that Major Powell
concluded his original voyage of exploration. Some of
his men took the boats on down to Fort Mojave, a few
miles above Needles; afterwards two of the party continued on to the Gulf. The country below the Virgin River had been explored by several parties, but previous to this time nothing definite was known of the
gorges until this exploration by this most remarkable
man. The difficulties of this hazardous trip were increased for him by the fact that he had lost an arm in
the Civil War.

It is usually taken for granted that the United States
government was back of this exploration. This was
true of the second expedition, but not of the first. Major
Powell was aided to a certain extent by the State College
of Illinois, otherwise he bore all the expense himself.
He received $10,000 from the government to apply on
the expenses of the second trip.

We felt that we had some reason to feel a justifiable

pride for having duplicated, in some ways, this arduous journey. It was impossible for us to do more than guess what must have been the feelings and anxieties of this explorer. Added to the fact that we had boats, tested and constructed to meet the requirements of the river, and the benefit of others' experiences, was a knowledge that we were not likely to be precipitated over a waterfall, or if we lost everything and succeeded in climbing out, that there were a few ranches and distant settlements scattered through the country.

But we had traversed the same river and the same canyons which change but little from year to year, and had succeeded beyond our fondest hopes in having accomplished what we set out to do.

The Black Mountains, dark and forbidding, composed of a hard rock which gave a metallic clink, and decorated with large spots of white, yellow, vermilion, and purple deposits of volcanic ashes, were entered this afternoon. The peaks were about a thousand feet high. The passage between is known as Boulder Canyon. Here we met two miners at work on a tunnel, or drift, who informed us that it was about forty miles to Las Vegas, Nevada, and that it was only twenty-five miles from the mouth of Las Vegas Wash, farther down the river, to this same town and the railroad.

Fort Callville — an abandoned rock building, constructed by the directions of Brigham Young, without

windows or roof, and surrounded by stone corrals —
was passed the next day. At Las Vegas Wash the river
turned at right angles, going directly south, holding with
very little deviation to this general direction until it
empties into the Gulf of California nearly five hundred
miles away. The river seemed to be growing smaller
as we got out in the open country. Like all Western
rivers, when unprotected by canyons, it was sinking in
the sand. Sand-bars impeded our progress at such places
as the mouth of the Wash. But we had a good current,
without rapids in Black Canyon, which came shortly
below, and mile after mile was put behind us before we
camped for the night.

An old stamp-mill, closed for the time, but in charge
of three men who were making preparations to resume
work, was passed the next day. They had telephone
communication with Searchlight, Nevada, twenty odd
miles away, and we sent out some telegrams in that way.

More sand-bars were encountered the next day, and
ranches began to appear on both sides of the river. We
had difficulty on some of these bars. In places the river
bed was a mile wide, with stagnant pools above the sand,
and with one deep channel twisting between. At Fort
Mojave, now an Indian school and agency, we telephoned to some friends in Needles, as we had promised
to do, telling them we would arrive about noon of the
following day. We made a mistake in not camping at

the high ground by the "fort" that night, for just below the river widened again and the channel turned out in the centre. It was getting dark and we had entered this before noticing which way it turned, and had a hard pull back to the shore, for we had no desire to camp out there in the quicksand. The shore was little more desirable. It was a marsh, covered with a growth of flags and tules, but with the ground frozen enough so that we did not sink. Our last camp — No. 76 — was made in this marsh. There we spent the night, hidden like hunted savages in the cane-brake, while an Indian brass band played some very good music for an officers' ball, less than half a mile away.

We were up and away with the sun the next morning. On nearing Needles, a friend met us on the outskirts of the town and informed us that they had arranged what he called an official landing and reception. At his request we deferred going down at once, but busied ourselves instead at packing our cargo, ready for shipping. Our friend had secured the services of a motion-picture operator and our own camera was sent down to make a picture of the landing, which was made as he had arranged.

We landed in Needles January 18, 1912; one month from the time of our start from Bright Angel Trail, with a total of one hundred and one days spent along the river. In that time our camps had been changed seventy-six times.

Copyright by Kolb Bros.

WATCHING FOR THE SIGNAL FIRE. MRS. EMERY AND EDITH KOLB.

Our two boats, highly prized as souvenirs of our twelve hundred mile trip, and which had carried us through three hundred and sixty-five big rapids, over a total descent of more than five thousand feet, were loaded on cars ready for shipment; the *Edith* to Los Angeles, the *Defiance* to the Grand Canyon.

Among other mail awaiting us was the following letter, bearing the postmark of Hite, Utah :

"KOLB BROS.,
    "DEAR FRIENDS :
        "Well I got here at last after seventeen days in Cataract Canyon. The old boat will stand a little quiet water but will never go through another rapid. I certainly played 'ring-a-round' some of those rocks in Cataract Canyon; I tried every scheme I had ever heard of, and some that were never thought of before. At the last rapid in Cataract I carried all my stuff over the cliff, then tried to line the boat from the narrow ledge. The boat jerked me into the river, but I did not lose my hold on the chain and climbed on board. I had no oars, but managed to get through without striking any rocks, and landed a mile and a half below the supplies. I hope the 'movies' are good.[1]
                            "Sincerely yours,
                                "CHAS. SMITH."

[1] See appendix, History of Cataract Canyon.

CONCLUSION. HOW I WENT TO MEXICO
CHAPTER XXIV

ON THE CREST OF A FLOOD

A WESTWARD-BOUND train was bearing me across the Mojave Desert one day in May. In a few swiftly passing hours we had made a six-thousand foot descent from the plateau with its fir and aspen-covered mountain, its cedar and piñon-clothed foot-hills, and its extensive forests of yellow pine. Crimson and yellow-flowered cactus, sage and chaparral, succeeded the pines. The cool mountains had given way to burned-out, umber-coloured hills, rock-ribbed arroyos, and seemingly endless desert; and the sun was growing hotter every minute.

If the heat continued to increase, I doubted if I would care to take a half-planned Colorado River trip down to the Gulf. Visions of the California beaches, of fishing at Catalina and of horseback rides over the Sierra's trails, nearly unsettled my determination to stop at Needles, on the California side of the river. This was my vacation! Why undergo all the discomfort of a voyage on a desert stream, when the pleasures and comforts of the Pacific beckoned? One thing was sure, if I was not successful in securing a boat at Needles, the very next train would find me on board, bound for the Western Slope. By mid-afternoon the chaparral had disappeared and only the cactus remained — the ocotilla, covered with a million flowers, wave upon wave of crimson flame, against the yellow earth. Violet-veiled mountains appeared in the west, marking the southern trend of the Colorado. The air was suffocating. The train-created wind was like a blast from a furnace; yet with the electric fans whirring, with blinds drawn and windows closed to keep the withering air *out*, it seemed a little less uncomfortable in the car, in spite of the unvitalized air, than under the scorching sun.

We were beside the Colorado at last. I had a good view of the stream below, as we crossed the bridge — the Colorado in flood, muddy, turbulent, sweeping onward like an affrighted thing, — repulsive, yet with a fascination for me, born of an intimate acquaintance with the dangers of this stream. The river had called again! The heat was forgotten, the visions of the coast faded, for me the train could not reach Needles, ten miles up the river, quickly enough.

With my brother, I had followed this stream down to Needles, through a thousand miles of canyon. I had seen how it carved its way through the mountains, carrying them on, in solution, toward the ocean. At last I would see what became of all these misplaced mountains.

I would see the tidal bore as it swept in from the Gulf. I had heard there were wild hogs which burrowed through the cane-brake. It may be that I would learn of a vessel at some port down on the Mexican coast, which I might reach and which would take me around the Lower California Peninsula. I felt sure there was such a port. No doubt I could have found books to tell me exactly what I would see, but too much information would spoil all the romance of such an adventure. It was all very alluring. With the spring flood on, the river could not help but be interesting and exciting, a pretty good imitation of the rapids, perhaps. If I could only secure a boat !

Half an hour later I was meeting old acquaintances about the hotel, connected with the station. The genial hotel manager, with the Irish name, was smilingly explaining to some newcomers that this was not hot; that "a dry heat at 110 degrees was not nearly as bad as 85 degrees back in Chicago," "and as for heat," he continued, "why down in Yuma" — then he caught sight of me, with a grin on my face, and perhaps he remembered that I had heard him say the same thing two years before, when it was even hotter; and he came over with outstretched hand, — calling me uncomplimentary names, under his breath, for spoiling the effect of his explanation; all which was belied by his welcome. It takes an Irishman to run a big hotel in the middle of the desert.

A few inquiries brought out the information that I

was not likely to get a boat. The stores did not keep them. I should have given my order two weeks before to an Indian who built boats to order at $2.00 a foot. This was a new one on me. Suppose a fellow wanted — well, say, about $15.00 worth. It would look something like a tub, wouldn't it? Perhaps it was to be the coast, for me, after all.

The Colorado River in flood is a terrible stream. Unlike the Eastern rivers, there are no populous cities — with apologies to Needles and Yuma — along its shores, to be inundated with the floods. Unlike the rivers of the South, few great agricultural districts spread across its bottoms. Along the upper seven hundred miles there are not a half-dozen ranches with twenty-five acres under cultivation. But if destructive power and untamed energy are terrible, the Colorado River, in flood, is a terrible stream.

After changing into some comfortable clothes I sauntered past the railway machine shops down to the river, and up to where a fight was being waged to save the upper part of the town from being torn away by the flood. For a month past, car after car of rock had been dumped along the river bank, only to disappear in the quicksands; and as yet no bottom had been reached. Up to this point the fight was about equal. The flood would not reach its crest until two or three weeks later.

Beyond a fisherman or two there were few men by the river. The workmen had finished their day's labour. A ferryman said that I might talk an Indian into selling his boat, but it was doubtful. My next job was to find such an Indian.

A big, greasy Mojave buck lay on an uncovered, rusty bed spring, slung on a home-made frame, before his willow and adobe home, close to the Colorado River. In answer to my repeated question he uncoiled and stretched the full length of his six foot six couch, grunted a few words in his native tongue to other Indians without a glance in my direction, then indifferently closed his eyes again. A young Indian in semi-cowboy garb, — not omitting a gorgeous silk handkerchief about his neck, — jabbered awhile with some grinning squaws, then said in perfectly understandable English, "He will sell his boat for $18.00. It is worth $30.00." This was decisive for an Indian. It usually takes a half-day of bickering to get them to make any kind of a bargain. I told him I would take it in the morning.

It was a well-constructed boat, almost new, built of inch pine, flat-bottomed, and otherwise quite similar in shape to the boats my brother and I had used on our twelve hundred mile journey through the canyons of the Green and Colorado rivers, — but without the graceful lines and swells that made those other boats so valuable to us in rapids. The boat was nearly new and

THE GRAND CANYON FROM THE HEAD OF BRIGHT ANGEL TRAIL.

Copyright by Kolb Bros.

well worth $30.00, as boat prices went in that town. Why he was willing to sell it for $18.00, or at the rate of $1.00 a foot, I could not imagine. It was the first bargain an Indian had ever offered me. But if I paid for it that evening, there were doubts in my mind if I should find it in the morning, so I delayed closing the bargain and went back again to inspect the boat.

That evening I inquired among my acquaintances if there was any one who would care to accompany me. If so I would give them passage to Yuma, or to the Gulf of California in Mexico, if they wished it. But no one could go, or those who could, wouldn't. One would have thought from the stories with which I was regaled, that the rapids of the Grand Canyon were below Needles, and as for going to the Gulf, it was suicide. I was told of the outlaws along the border, of the firearms and opium smugglers, who shot first and questioned afterward, and of the insurrectos of Lower California. The river had no real outlet to the ocean, they said, since the break into Salton Sea, but spread over a cane-brake, thirty miles or more in width. Many people had gone into these swamps and never returned, whether lost in the jungles or killed by the Cocopah Indians, no one knew. They simply disappeared. It was all very alluring.

My preparations, the next day, were few. I had included a sleeping bag with my baggage. It would come in equally handy whether I went down on the Colorado or up into the Coast Range. A frying-pan, a coffee-pot, a few metal dishes and provisions for a week were all I needed. Some one suggested some bent poles, and a cover, such as are used on wagons to keep off the sun. This seemed like a good idea; and I hunted up a carpenter who did odd jobs. He did not have such a one, but he did have an old wagon-seat cover, which could be raised or dropped at will. This was even better, for sometimes hard winds sweep up the river. The cover was fastened to the sides of the boat. The boat, meanwhile, had been thoroughly scrubbed. It looked clean before, but I was not going to take any chances at carrying Indian live-stock along with his boat. My surplus baggage was sent on to Los Angeles, and twenty-four hours after I had landed in Needles, I was ready to embark.

My experience in camping trips of various sorts has been that the start from headquarters occupies more time than any similar preparation. Once on the road, things naturally arrange themselves into some kind of a system, and an hour on the road in the evening means several hours gained the next morning. Added to this, there are always a number of loafers about railroad towns, and small things have a way of disappearing. With this in mind, I determined to make my start that evening, and at 7 P.M. on the 23d of May, 1913, I embarked on a six to eight mile an hour current, paced by cottonwood logs, carried down by the flood from the head waters in Wyoming, Utah, and Colorado.

When sailing on the unruffled current one did not notice its swiftness — it sped so quietly yet at the same time with such deadly intent — until some half submerged cottonwood snags appeared, their jagged, broken limbs ploughing the stream exactly like the bow of a motor-driven boat, throwing two diverging lines of waves far down the stream. One would almost think the boat was motionless, it raced so smoothly, — and that the snags were tearing upstream as a river man had said, the day before, "like a dog with a bone in his teeth." A sunken stone-boat, with a cabin half submerged, seemed propelled by some unseen power and rapidly dwindled in the distance.

So fascinating were these things that I forgot the approaching night. I first noticed it when the stream slackened its mad pace and spread over its banks into great wide marshes, in divided and subdivided channels and over submerged islands, with nothing but willow and fuzzy cattail tops to indicate that there was a bottom underneath. Here there was no place to camp had I wished to do so. Once I missed the main channel and had a difficult time in finding my way back in the dark. After two or three miles of this quiet current, the streams began to unite again, and the river regained its former speed. I was growing weary after the first excitement, and began to wish myself well out of it all and safely anchored to the shore. But I knew there was a level bank above the river close to the bridge, which would make a good camping place; so I rested on my oars, facing down the stream with eyes and ears alert for the treacherous snags. Then the stars began to appear, one by one, lighting up the cloudless sky; a moist, tropical-like breeze moved up the stream, the channel narrowed and deepened, the snags vanished, and the stream increased its swiftness.

And with eyes wide open, but unseeing, I dozed.

It was the lights of a passenger train crossing the bridge, just a short distance away, that made me realize where I was. The train thundered into the darkness; but louder than the roar of the train was that of the water directly ahead, and hidden in the impenetrable shadow over on the right shore was a noise much like that made by a Grand Canyon rapid.

Wide awake now, I pulled for the left, and after one or two attempts to land, I caught some willow tops and guided the boat to the raised bank. Beyond the willows was a higher ground, covered with a mesquite thicket, with cattle trails winding under the thorny trees. Here I unrolled my sleeping bag, then went up to interview the operator and the watchman, and to get a drink of clear water, for I had no desire to drink the liquid mud of the Colorado until it was necessary. In answer to a question I told them of my little ride. One of the men exclaimed, "You don't mean to say that you

came down on the flood after dark!" On being informed
that I had just arrived, he exclaimed: "Well I reckon you
don't know what the Colorado is. It's a wonder this
whirlpool didn't break you against the pier. You ought
to have brought some one with you to see you drown!"

CHAPTER XXV

FOUR DAYS TO YUMA

BEFORE sunrise the following morning, I had completed my few camp duties, finished my breakfast, and dropped my boat into the whirlpool above the bridge. My two friends watched the manœuvre as I pulled clear of the logs and the piers which caused the water to make such alarming sounds the night before; then they gave me a final word of caution, and the information that the Parker Bridge was sixty miles away and that Yuma was two hundred and fifty miles down the stream. They thought that I should reach Yuma in a week. It seemed but a few minutes until the bridge was a mile up the stream. Now I was truly embarked for the gulf.

By the time I had reached the spire-like mountainous rocks a few miles below the bridge, which gave the town of Needles its name, the sun was well up and I was beginning to learn what desert heat was, although I had little time to think of it as I was kept so busy with my boat. Here, the stream which was spread a mile wide above, had choked down to two hundred feet; small violent whirlpools formed at the abrupt turns in this so-called canyon and the water tore from side to side. In one whirl my boat was twice carried around the circle into which I had allowed it to be caught, then shot out on the pounding flood. Soon the slag-like mountains were passed and the country began to spread, first in a high barren land, then with a bottom land running back from the river. The willow bushes changed to willow trees, tall and spindly, crowded in a thicket down to the river's edge. The Chemehuevi Indians have their reservation here. On rounding an abrupt turn I surprised two little naked children, fat as butterballs, dabbling in a mud puddle close to the stream. The sight, coupled with the tropical-like heat and the jungle, could well make one imagine he was in Africa or India, and that the little brown bodies were the "alligator bait" of which we read. Only the 'gators were missing. The unexpected sight of a boat and a white man trying to photograph them started them both into a frightened squall. Then an indignant mother appeared, staring at me as though she would like to know what I had done to her offspring. Farther along were other squaws, with red and blue lines pencilled on their childlike, contented faces, seated under the willows. Their cotton garments, of red and blue bandanna handkerchiefs sewed together, added a gay bit of colour to the scene.

Below this were two or three cozy little ranch houses and a few scattered cattle ranches, with cattle browsing back in the trees. All this time it was getting hotter, and I was thankful for my sheltering cover. My lunch, prepared in the morning, was eaten as I drifted. Except in a few quiet stretches I did little rowing, just enough to keep the boat away from the overhanging banks and in the strong current.

The bottom lands began to build up again with banks of gravel and clay, growing higher with every mile. The deciduous trees gave way to the desert growths: the cholla, "the shower of gold," and the palo verde and the other acacias. Here were the California or valley-quail; and lean, long-legged jack-rabbits. Here too were the coyotes, leaner than the rabbits, but efficient, shifty-eyed, and insolent. One could admire but could hardly respect them.

I had entertained hopes of reaching Parker that evening, but supposed the hour would be late if I reached it at all. Imagine my surprise, then, when at half-past four I heard the whistle of a train, and another turn revealed the Parker bridge. I had been told by others that it had taken them three or four days to reach this point on a low stage of water. Evidently the high water is much better for rapid and interesting travel.

Here at the bridge, which was a hundred feet above the river, was a dredge, and an old flat-bottomed steamboat, a relic of a few years past, before the government built the Laguna dam above Yuma, and condemned the Colorado as a navigable stream. Those were the days which the Colorado steamboat men recall with as much fond remembrance as the old-time boatmen of the Mississippi remember their palmy days.

In spite of the fact that the boats were flat-bottomed and small, it was real steamboating of an exciting nature at least. At times they beat up against the current as far as the mouth of the Rio Virgin. In low water the channels shifted back and forth first choked with sand on one side of the stream, then on the other. While the total fall from Fort Mojave, a few miles above Needles, to the Gulf is only 525 feet, considerable of that fall came in short sections, first with a swift descent, then in a quiet stretch. Even in the high-water stage I was finding some such places.

Parker stood a mile back from the river, on top of the level gravelly earth which stretched for miles on either side of the river clear to the mountains. This earth and gravel mixture was so firmly packed that even the cactus had a scant foothold. The town interested me for one reason only, this being, that I could get my meals for the evening and the following morning, instead of having to cook them myself. After I had eaten them, however, there was a question in my mind if my own cooking, bad as it was, would not have answered the purpose just as well. The place was a new railroad town on an Indian reservation, a town of great expectations, somewhat deferred.

It was not as interesting to me as my next stop at Ahrenburg, some fifty miles below Parker. This place, while nothing but a collection of dilapidated adobe buildings, had an air of romance about it which was missing in the newer town. Ahrenburg had seen its day. Many years ago it was a busy mining camp, and the hope is entertained by the faithful who still reside in its picturesque adobe homes that it will come back with renewed vigour. Here at Ahrenburg I met a character who added greatly to the interest of my stay. He was a gigantic, raw-boned Frenchman, at that time engaged in the construction of a motor boat; but a miner, a sailor, and a soldier of fortune in many ways, one who had pried into many of the hidden corners of the country and had a graphic way of describing what he had seen. I was his guest until late that night, and was entertained royally on what humble fare he had to offer. We both intended to renew our acquaintance in the morning, but some prowling Mexicans near my boat, croaking frogs, and swarms of mosquitos gave me a restless night. With the first glimmer of daylight I was up, and half an hour later I was away on the flood.

This was my big day. The current was better than much of that above; I was getting used to the heat, and,

Copyright by Kolb Bros.

THE CORK SCREW: LOWER END OF BRIGHT ANGEL TRAIL.

instead of idly drifting, I pulled steadily at the oars.
The river twisted back and forth in great loops with the
strong current, as is usual, always on the outside of the
loops, close to the overhanging banks. I would keep
my boat in this current, with a wary lookout over my
shoulder for fallen trees and sudden turns, which had
a way of appearing when least expected. At some such
places the stream was engaged at undermining the banks
which rose eight and ten feet above the water. Occasional
sections, containing tons of earth and covered with tall,
slender willow trees, would topple over, falling on the
water with the roar of a cannon or a continued salute of
cannons; for the falling, once started, quite often extended
for half a mile down the stream. At one such place
eighteen trees fell in three minutes, and it would be safe
to say that a hundred trees were included in the extended
fall. The trees, sixty feet high, resembled a field of
gigantic grass or unripened grain; the river was a reaper,
cutting it away at the roots. Over they tumbled to be
buried in the stream; the water would swirl and boil,
earth and trees would disappear; then the mass of leaf-
covered timber, freed of the earth, would wash away to
lodge on the first sand-bar, and the formation of a new
island or a new shore would begin.

Then again, the banks were barren, composed of
gravel and clay, centuries older than the verdure-covered
land, undisturbed, possibly, since some glacial period de-

posited it there. But a shifting of the channel directed the attack against these banks. Here the swift current would find a little irregularity on the surface and would begin its cutting. The sand-laden water bored exactly like an auger, in fast-cutting whirls. One such place I watched for a half-hour from the very beginning, until the undermined section, fourteen feet high, began to topple, and I pulled out to safety, but not far enough to escape a ducking in the resulting wave.

Below this, instead of a firm earth, it was a loose sand and gravel mixture twenty feet above the river. Here for half a mile the entire bank was moving, slowly at the top, gathering speed at the bottom. While close to this I heard a peculiar hissing as of carbonated water all about me. At first I thought there were mineral springs underneath, but found the noise was caused by breaking air bubbles carried under the stream with the sands. All this day such phenomena continued, sliding sand-banks and tumbling jungles. In these latter places some cattle had suffered. Their trails ran parallel with the stream. No doubt they had one or two places where they drank cut down to the stream. Knowing nothing of the cutting underneath, they had been precipitated into the flood, and now their carcasses were food for swarms of vultures gathered for an unholy feast.

What powerful, graceful birds these scavengers are,

stronger than the eagle even, tireless and seemingly motionless as they drift along searching every nook and cranny for their provender ! But aside from a grudgingly given tribute of admiration for their power, one has about as much respect for them as for the equally graceful rattlesnake, that other product of nature which flourishes in this desert land.

The bird life along this lower part of the river was wonderful in its variety. The birds of the desert mingled with those of the fertile lands. The song-birds vied with those of gorgeous plume. Water-birds disported themselves in the mud-banks and sloughs. The smaller birds seemed to pay little attention to the nearness of the hawks. Kingfisher perched on limbs overhanging the quiet pools, ready to drop at the faintest movement on the opaque water; the road-runner chased the festive lizard on the desert land back of the willows. Here also in the mesquite and giant cactus were thrush and Western meadow-larks and mocking-birds mimicking the call of the cat-bird. Down in the brush by the river was the happy little water-ousel, as cheerful in his way as the dumpy-built musical canyon wren. The Mexican crossbill appeared to have little fear of the migrating Northern shrike. There were warblers, cardinals, tanagers, waxwings, song-sparrows, and chickadees. Flitting droves of bush-tit dropped on to slender weeds, scarcely bending them, so light were they. Then in a minute

they were gone. In the swamps or marshes were countless red-winged blackbirds.

The most unobservant person could not help but see
birds here. I had expected to find water-fowl, for the
Colorado delta is their breeding place; but I little expected to find so many land birds in the trees along the
river. Instead of having a lonesome trip, every minute
was filled with something new, interesting, and beautiful,
and I was having the time of my life.

I camped that night at Picachio, — meaning the
Pocket, — eighty miles below Ahrenburg. This is still
a mining district, but the pockets containing nuggets
of gold which gave the place its name seem to have all
been discovered at the time of the boom; the mining now
done is in quartz ledges up on the sides of grim, mineral-
stained hills. I was back in the land of rock again, a
land showing the forces of nature in high points of foreign
rock, shot up from beneath, penetrating the crust of the
earth and in a few places emerging for a height of two
hundred feet from the river itself, forming barren islands
and great circling whirlpools, as large as that in the
Niagara gorge, and I thought, for a while, almost as
powerful. In one I attempted to keep to the short side
of the river, but found it a difficult job, and one which
took three times as long to accomplish as if I had allowed
myself to be carried around the circle.

Then the land became level again, and the Chocolate

Mountains were seen to the west. A hard wind blew across the stream, so that I had to drop my sunshade to prevent being carried against the rocks. This day I passed a large irrigation canal leading off from the stream, the second such on the entire course of the Colorado. Here a friendly ranchman called to me from the shore and warned me of the Laguna dam some distance below. He said the water was backed up for three miles, so I would know when I was approaching it.

In spite of this warning, I nearly came to grief at the dam. The wind had shifted until it blew directly down the stream. The river, nearly a mile wide, still ran with a powerful current; I ceased rowing and drifted down, over waves much like those one would find on a lake driven by a heavy wind. I saw some high poles and a heavy electric cable stretched across the stream, and concluded that this was the beginning of the dam. I began to look ahead for some sign of a barrier across the stream, far below, but I could see nothing of the kind; then as I neared the poles it suddenly dawned on me that there was no raised barrier which diverted all the water through a sluice, but a submerged dam, over which the flood poured, and that the poles were on that dam.

My sail-like sunshade was dropped as quickly as I could do it, and, grabbing the oars, I began to pull for the California shore.

It was fortunate for me that I happened to be comparatively near the shore when I began rowing. As it was, I landed below the diverting canal, and about a hundred yards above the dam. On examination the dam proved to be a slope about fifty feet long. A man in charge of the machinery controlling the gates told me that the dam lacked seven feet of being a mile wide, and that approximately seven feet of water was going over the entire dam.

Great cement blocks and rocks had been dropped promiscuously below the dam to prevent it from being undermined. Even without the rocks it was doubtful if an uncovered boat could go through without upsetting. The great force of the water made a trough four or five feet lower than the river level, all water coming down the slope shooting underneath, while the river rolled back upstream. On two occasions boatmen had been carried over the dam. In each case the boat was wrecked, but the occupants were thrown out and escaped uninjured. I could not help but be amused, and feel a little uncomfortable too, when I saw how nearly I came to being wrecked here, after having escaped that fate in the rapids of the canyons.

I ran my boat back to the diverting canal, then rowed down to the massive cement gates, which looked to me like a small replica of some of the locks on the Panama Canal. With the help of an Indian who was ready for a job my boat was taken out, rolled around the buildings on some sections of pipe, and slid over the bank into the canal below the gates.

In spite of a desire to spend some time inspecting the machinery of this great work, — which, with the canal and other improvements, had cost the government over a million dollars — I immediately resumed my rowing. It was mid-afternoon, and measured by the canal, which was direct, it was twelve miles to Yuma. But I soon learned that great winding curves made it much farther by the river. In some cases it nearly doubled back on itself. The wind had shifted by this time and blew against me so hard that it was almost useless to attempt rowing. In another place there were no banks, and the water had spread for three miles in broken sloughs and around half-submerged islands, the one deep channel being lost in the maze of shallow ones. With these things to contend with it was dusk long before I neared the town, the twelve miles having stretched to twenty. Finally I saw a windmill partly submerged. Some distance away was a small ranch house also in the water. The house, with lights in the upper story, was a cheering sight; the windmill looked out of place in the midst of all this desolation of water. Soon other houses appeared with lights showing through the windows. Once I lost my way and spent a half hour in getting back to the right channel.

Somewhere in the dark, I never knew just when, I

passed the mouth of the Gila River. In a similar way, in broad daylight I had passed the Bill Williams Fork above Ahrenburg.

At last I neared the town. I could discern some buildings on top of a small hill, evidently one of the back streets of Yuma. After tying my boat, I hid my small load in some mesquite trees, then climbed the hill and passed between two peculiar stone houses dark as dungeons. They puzzled me from the outside, but when once past them, I was no longer in doubt. I had entered the open gateway leading to the courtyard of the Yuma penitentiary. No wonder the buildings looked like dungeons. This was a new experience for me, but somehow I had always imagined just how it would look. I was considering beating a retreat when a guard hailed me and asked me if I was not lost. With the assistance of the guard, I escaped from the pen and found my way to the streets of Yuma, just four days after leaving the Needles bridge.

CHAPTER XXVI

ACROSS THE MEXICO BORDER

"MEXICO is a good place to keep away from just at present." This was the invariable answer to a few casual inquiries concerning what I would be likely to meet with in the way of difficulties, a possible companion for the voyage to the Gulf, and how one could get back when once there. I received little encouragement from the people of Yuma. The cautions came not from the timid who see danger in every rumour, but from the old steamboat captains, the miners, and prospectors who knew the country and had interests in mineral claims across the border. These claims they had lost in many cases because they had failed for the last two years to keep up their assessment work. There were vague suggestions of being stood up against an adobe wall with a row of "yaller bellies" in front, or being thrown into damp dungeons and held for a ransom.

The steamboat men could give me little information about the river. The old channel had filled with silt, and the river was diverted into a roundabout course little more than a creek in width, then spread over the whole delta. The widely spread water finally collected into an ancient course of the Colorado, known as the Hardy or False Colorado. As nearly as I could learn no one from Yuma had been through this new channel beyond a certain point called Volcanic Lake. Two or three parties had come back with stories of having attempted it, but found themselves in the middle of a cane-brake with insufficient water to float a boat. With a desire to be of real assistance to me, one old captain called a Yuma Indian into his office and asked him his opinion, suggesting that he might go along.

"Mebbe so get lost in the trees, mebbe so get shot by the Cocopah," the Indian replied as he shook his head.

The captain laughed at the last and said that the Yuma and Cocopah Indians were not the best of friends, and accused each other of all sorts of things which neither had committed. Some Mexicans and certain outlawed whites who kept close to the border for different reasons, and the possibilities of bogging in a cane-brake were the only uncertainties. In so many words he advised me against going.

Still I persevered. I had planned so long on completing my boating trip to the Gulf, that I disliked to abandon the idea altogether. I felt sure, with a flood on the Colorado, there would be some channel that a flat-bottomed boat could go through, when travelling with the current;

but the return trip and the chances of being made a target for some hidden native who had lived on this unfriendly border and had as much reason for respecting some citizens of the United States as our own Indians had in the frontier days, caused me considerable concern. I knew it was customary everywhere to make much of the imaginary dangers, as we had found in our other journeys; but it is not difficult to discriminate between sound advice and the croakings which are based on lack of real information. I knew this was sound advice, and as usual I disliked to follow it. At last I got some encouragement. It came from a retired Wild West showman, — the real thing, one who knew the West from its early days. He laughed at the idea of danger and said I was not likely to find any one, even if I was anxious to do so, until I got to the La Bolso Ranch near the Gulf. They would be glad to see me. He thought it was likely to prove uninteresting unless I intended to hunt wild hogs, but that was useless without dogs, and I would have trouble getting a gun past the custom officers. His advice was to talk with the Mexican consul, as he might know some one who could bring me back by horseback.

In the consul I found a young Spaniard, all affability, bows, and gestures; and without being conscious of it at first I too began making motions. He deplored my lack of knowledge of the Spanish language, laughed at any

x

suggestion of trouble, as all trouble was in Eastern Sonora, he said, separated from the coast by two hundred miles of desert, and stated that the non-resident owner of the La Bolsa cattle ranch happened to be in the building at that moment. In a twinkling he had me before him and explained the situation. This gentleman, the owner of a 600,000-acre grant, and the fishing concession of the Gulf, stated that the ranch drove a team to Yuma once a week, that they would bring me back; in the interval I must consider myself the guest of the Rancho La Bolsa. The consul gave me a passport, and so it was all arranged.

In spite of the consul's opinion, there were many whispered rumours of war, of silent automobiles loaded with firearms that stole out of town under cover of the night and returned in four days, and another of a river channel that could be followed and was followed, the start being made, not from Yuma, but from another border town farther west. A year before there had been an outbreak at this place of certain restless spirits, — some whites included, — and they went along the northern line of Mexico, sacking the ranches and terrorizing the people. The La Bolsa ranch was among those that suffered. The party contained some discharged vaqueros who were anxious to interview the ranch foreman, but fortunately for him he was absent. Then they turned south to Chihauhau and joined the army of Madero. War, to them, meant license to rob and kill. They were not insurrectos, but bandits, and this was the class that was most feared.

Meanwhile I had not given up the idea of a possible companion. Before coming to Yuma I had entertained hopes of getting some one with a motor boat to take me down and back, but there were no motor boats, I found. The nearest approach to a power boat was an attempt that was being made to install the engine from a wrecked steam auto on a sort of flat-bottomed scow. I heard of this boat three or four times, and in each case the information was accompanied by a smile and some vague remarks about a "hybrid." I hunted up the owner, — the proprietor of a shooting gallery, — a man who had once had aspirations as a heavy-weight prize fighter, but had met with discouragement. So he had turned his activities to teaching the young idea how to shoot — especially the "Mexican idea" and those other border spirits who were itching for a scrap.

The proprietor of the shooting gallery drove a thriving trade. Since he had abandoned his training he had taken on fat, and I found him to be a genial sort of giant who refused to concern himself with the serious side of life. Even a lacing he had received in San Francisco at the hands of a negro stevedore struck him as being humorous. He did not seem to have much more confidence in his "power boat" than the others, but said I might talk with the man who was putting it together, ending with the remark "Phillipps thinks he can make her run, and he has always talked of going to the Gulf."

On investigation I found Al Phillipps was anxious to go to the Gulf, and would go along if I would wait until he got his boat in shape. This would take two days. Phillipps, as he told me himself, was a Jayhawker who had left the farm in Kansas and had gone to sea for two years. He was a cowboy, but had worked a year or two about mining engines. In Yuma he was a carpenter, but was anxious to leave and go prospecting along the Gulf. Phillipps and I were sure to have an interesting time. He spoke Spanish and did not fear any of the previously mentioned so-called dangers; he had heard of one party being carried out to sea when the tide rushed out of the river, but as we would have low tide he thought that, with caution, we could avoid that.

At last all was ready for the momentous trial. The river bank was lined with a crowd of men who seemed to have plenty of leisure. Some long-haired Yuma Indians, and red and green turbaned Papagos, gathered in a group off a little to one side. A number of darkies were fishing for bullheads, and boys of three colors besides the Mexicans and a lone Chinaman clambered over the trees and the boats along the shore.

It was a moment of suspense for Phillipps. His

reputation as an engineer and a constructor of boats hung in the balance. He also had some original ideas about a rudder which had been incorporated in this boat. Now was his chance to test them out, and his hour of triumph if they worked.

The test was a rigid one. The boat was to be turned upstream against an eight-mile current with big sand-waves, beginning about sixty feet from the shore, running in the middle of the river. If the engine ran, and the stern paddle-wheel turned, his reputation was saved. If she was powerful enough to go against the current, it was a triumph and we would start for the Gulf at once.

On board were Phillipps, a volunteer, and myself. Before turning the boat loose, the engine was tried. It was a success. The paddle-wheel churned the water at a great rate, sending the boat upstream as far as the ropes would let her go. We would try a preliminary run in the quiet water close to the shore, before making the test in the swift current. The order was given to cast off, and for two men, the owner and another, to hold to the ropes and follow on the shore. The engine was started, the paddle-wheel revolved, slowly at first but gathering speed with each revolution. We began to move gently, then faster, so that the men on shore had difficulty in keeping even with us, impeded as they were with bushes and sloping banks. Flushed with success, the order was given to turn her loose, and we gathered in the ropes. Now we were drifting away from the shore, and making some headway against the swift current. The crowd on shore was left behind.

But as we left the bank the river increased in speed, and the boat gradually lost. Then she stood still, but began to turn slowly, broadside to the current. This was something we had not foreseen. With no headway, the rudder was of no avail. There was no sweep-oar; we had even neglected to put an oar on the boat. With pieces of boards the stranger and I paddled, trying to hold her straight, but all the time, in spite of our efforts, she drifted away from the land and slowly turned. A big sand-wave struck her, she wheeled in her tracks and raced straight for a pier, down the stream.

About this time our engineer began having trouble with his engine. At first we feared it would not run, now it seemed it would not stop.

A great shout went up from the shore, and a bet was made that we would run to the Gulf in less than a day. A darky boy fell off a boat in the excitement, the Indians did a dance, men pounded each other and whooped for joy. Then a bolt came loose, and the engine ran away. Driving-rod and belts were whirled "regardless," as the passenger afterwards said, about our heads.

Then the crash came. Our efforts to escape the pier were of no avail. I made a puny effort to break the impact with a pole, but was sent sprawling on the deck. Al tumbled headlong on top of the engine, which he had stopped at last, our passenger rolled over and over, but we all stayed with the ship. Each grabbing a board, we began to paddle and steered the craft to the shore.

With the excitement over, the crowd faded away. Only two or three willing hands remained to help us line the craft back to the landing. The owner, who had to run around the end of the bridge, came down puffing and blowing, badly winded, at the end of the first round. Without a word from any one we brought the boat back to the landing.

Al was the first to speak.

"Well, what are you going to do?" he asked.

"Me? I'm going to take my boat and start for the Gulf in ten minutes. I'll take nothing that I cannot carry. If I have to leave the river I will travel light across the desert to Calexico. I think that I can get through. If you want to go along, I'll stick with you until we get back. What do you think about it?"

It was a long speech and a little bitter perhaps. I felt that way. The disappointment on top of the three days' delay when time was precious could not be forgotten in a moment. And when my speech was said I was all through.

Al said he would be ready in half an hour. Our beds were left behind. Al had a four-yard square of canvas for a sail. This would be sufficient covering at night in the hot desert. We had two canteens. The provisions, scarcely touched before arriving here, were sufficient for five days. I was so anxious to get started that I did not take the time to replenish them in Yuma, intending to do so at the custom-house on the Arizona side, twelve miles below, where some one had told me there was a store. I counted on camping there. After a hurriedly eaten luncheon we were ready to start, the boat was shoved off, and we were embarked for Mexico.

Half an hour later we passed the abandoned Imperial Canal, the man-made channel which had nearly destroyed the vast agricultural lands which it had in turn created. Just such a flood as that on which we were travelling had torn out the insufficiently supported head-gates. The entire stream, instead of pushing slowly across the delta, weltering in its own silt to the Gulf, poured into the bottom of the basin nearly four hundred feet below the top of this silt-made dam. In a single night it cut an eighty-foot channel in the unyielding soil, and what had once been the northern end of the California Gulf was turned into an inland sea, filled with the turbid waters of the Colorado, instead of the sparkling waters of the ocean. Nothing but an almost superhuman fight finally rescued the land from the grip of the water.

A short distance below, just across the Mexican line, on the California side, was the new canal, dug in a firmer soil and with strongly built gates anchored in rock back from the river.

Half a mile away from the stream, on a spur railway, was the Mexican custom-house. I had imagined that it would be beside the river, and that guards would be seen patrolling the shore. But aside from an Indian fishing, there was no one to be seen. We walked out to the custom-house, gave a list of the few things which we had, assured them that we carried no guns, paid our duty, and departed. We had imagined that our boat would be inspected, but no one came near.

The border line makes a jog here at the river and the Arizona-Mexico line was still a few miles down the stream. We had passed the mouth of the old silt-dammed Colorado channel, which flowed a little west of south; and we turned instead to the west into the spreading delta or moraine. About this time I remarked that I had seen no store at the custom-house and that I must not neglect to get provisions at the next one or we would be rather short.

"We passed our last custom-house back there." Al replied, "That's likely the last place we will see until we get to the ranch by the Gulf."

No custom-house! No store! This was a surprise. What was a border for if not to have custom-houses and inspectors ? With all the talk of smuggling I had not thought of anything else. And I could tell by Al's tone that his estimation of my foresight had dropped several degrees. This was only natural, for his disappointment and the jibes still rankled.

At last we were wholly in Mexican territory. With the States behind, all of our swiftly running water had departed, and we now travelled on a stream that was nearly stagnant. All the cottonwood logs which had finally been carried down the stream after having been deposited on a hundred shores, found here their final resting place. About each cluster of logs an island was forming, covered with a rank grass and tules.

Ramified channels wound here and there. Two or three times we found ourselves in a shallow channel, and with some difficulty retraced our way. All channels looked alike, but only one was deep.

Then the willow trees which were far distant on either shore began to close in and we travelled in a channel not more than a hundred feet wide, growing smaller with every mile. This new channel is sometimes termed the Bee River. It parallels the northern Mexico line; it also parallels a twenty-five mile levee which the United States government has constructed along the northern edge of this fifty-mile wide dam shoved across the California Gulf by the stream, building higher every year. Except for the river channel the dam may be said to reach unbroken from the Arizona-Sonora Mesa to the Cocopah Mountains. The levee runs from a point of rocks near the river to Lone Mountain, a solitary peak some distance east of the main range. This levee, built since the trouble with the canal, is all that prevents the water from breaking into the basin in a dozen places.

We saw signs of two or three camp-fires close to the stream, and with the memory of the stories haunting us a little we built only a small fire when we cooked our evening meal, then extinguished it, and camped on a dry point of land a mile or two below. I think we were both a little nervous that night; I confess that I was, and if an unwashed black-bearded individual had poked his head out from the willows and said, "Woof!" or whatever it is that they say when they want to start up a jack-rabbit, we would both have stampeded clear across the border. In fact I felt a little as I did when I played truant from school and wondered what would happen when I was found out.

Daybreak found us ready to resume our journey, and with a rising sun any nervousness vanished. What could any one want with two men who had nothing but a flat-bottomed boat?

All the morning we travelled west, the trees ever drawing closer as our water departed on the south, running through the willows, arrow-weed, and cat-tails. Then the channel opened into Volcanic Lake, a circular body of water, which is not a lake but simply a gathering together of the streams we had been losing, and here the water stands, depositing its mud. All the way across it had no depth but a bottomless mud, so soft it would engulf a person if he tried to wade across.

On the west there was no growth. The shore was nothing but an ash-like powder, not a sand, but a rich soil blown here and there, building in dunes against every obstruction, ever moving before the wind. Here were boiling, sputtering mud pots and steam vents building up and exhausting through mud pipe-stems, rising a foot or two above the springs. Here was a shelter or two of sun-warped boards constructed by those who come here crippled with rheumatism and are supposed to depart, cured. Here we saw signs of a wagon track driven toward Calexico, the border town directly north of the lake. The heat was scorching, the sun, reflected from the sand and water, was blistering, and we could well imagine what a walk across that ash-like soil would mean. Mirages in the distance beckoned, trees and lakes were seen over toward the mountains where we had seen nothing but desert before; heat waves rose and fell. Our mouths began to puff from the reflected sun, our faces burned and peeled, black and red in spots. There was no indication of the slightest breeze until about three o'clock, when the wind moved gently across the lake.

We had skirted the northern part of the circle, pass-

ing a few small streams and then found one of the three
large channels which empty the lake. As it happened
we took the one on the outside, and the longest. The
growth grew thicker than ever, the stream choked down
to fifty feet. Now it began to loop backward and forward and back again, as though trying to make the longest and crookedest channel possible in the smallest space.
The water in the channel was stagnant, swift streamlets
rushed in from the tules on the north, and rushed out
again on the south. It was not always a simple matter
to ascertain which was the main channel. Others just
as large were diverted from the stream. Twice we
attempted to cut across, but the water became shallow,
the tules stalled our boats, and we were glad to return,
sounding with a pole when in doubt.

Then we began to realize that we were not entirely
alone in this wilderness of water. We saw evidence of
another's passage, in broken cat-tails and blazed trees.
In many places he had pushed into the thickets. We
concluded it must be a trapper. At last, to our surprise,
we saw a telephone equipment, sheltered in a box nailed
on a water-surrounded tree. The line ran directly
across the stream. Here also we could see where a boat
had forced a way through, and the water plants had been
cut with a sharp instrument. What could it be? We
were certain no line ran to the only ranch at the Gulf.
We had information of another ranch directly on the bor-

der line, but did not think it came below the levee, and as far as we had learned, there were no homes but the wickiups of the Cocopah in the jungles. It was like one of those thrilling stories of Old Sleuth and Dead Shot Dick which we read, concealed in our schoolbooks, when we were supposed to be studying the physical geography of Mexico. But the telephone was no fiction, and had recently been repaired, but for what purpose it was there we could not imagine. After leaving the lake there was no dry land. At night our boat, filled with green tules for a bed, was tied to a willow tree, with its roots submerged in ten feet of water. Never were there such swarms of mosquitos. In the morning our faces were corrugated with lumps, not a single exposed spot remaining unbitten.

The loops continued with the next day's travel, but we were gradually working to the southwest, then they began to straighten out somewhat, as the diverted streams returned. We thought early in the morning that we would pass about ten miles to the east of the coast range, but it was not to be. Directly to the base of the dark, heat-vibrating rocks we pulled, and landed on the first shore that we had seen for twenty-four hours.

Here was a recently used trail, and tracks where horses came down to the water. Here too was the track of a barefooted Cocopah, a tribe noted for its men of gigantic build, and with great feet out of all proportion to their size. If that footprint was to be fossilized,

Copyright by Kolb Bros.

ZOROASTER TEMPLE: FROM THE END OF BRIGHT ANGEL TRAIL.

future generations would marvel at the evidence of some gigantic prehistoric animal, an alligator with a human-shaped foot. These Indians have lived in these mud bottoms so long, crossing the streams on rafts made of bundles of tules, and only going to the higher land when their homes are inundated by the floods, that they have become a near approach to a web-footed human being.

Our stream merely touched the mountain, then turned directly to the southeast in a gradually increasing stream. Now we began to see the breeding places of the water-birds of which we had heard. There was a confusion of bird calls, sand-hill cranes were everywhere; in some cases with five stick-built nests in a single water-killed tree. A blue heron flopped around as though it had broken a wing, to decoy us from its nest. The snowy white pelican waddled along the banks and mingled with the cormorants. There were great numbers of gulls, and occasional snipe. We were too late to see the ducks which come here, literally by the million, during the winter months. There were hawks' nests in the same groups of trees as the cranes, with the young hawks stretching their necks for the food which was to be had in such abundance. And on another tree sat the parent hawks, complacently looking over the nests of the other birds, like a coyote waiting for a horse to die. At Cocopah Mountain a golden eagle soared, coming down close to the ground as we rested under the mesquite. Then as we travelled clear streams of water began to pour in from the north and east, those same streams we had lost above, but cleared entirely of their silt. Now the willows grew scarce, and instead of mud banks a dry, firm earth was built up from the river's edge, and the stream increased in size. Soon it was six or seven hundred feet wide and running with a fair current. This was the Hardy River. We noticed signs of falling water on the banks as though the stream had dropped an inch or two. In a half-hour the mark indicated a fall of eight inches or more; then we realized we were going out with the tide. A taste of water proved it. The river water was well mixed with a weak saline solution. We filled our canteens at once.

We saw a small building and a flagpole on the south shore, but on nearing the place found it was deserted. A few miles below were two other channels equally as large as that on which we travelled, evidently fed by streams similar to our own. There were numerous scattered trees, some of them cottonwood, and we saw some grazing cattle. We began to look for the ranch house, which some one had said was at the point where the Colorado and the Hardy joined, and which others told us was at the Gulf.

CHAPTER XXVII

THE GULF OF CALIFORNIA

THAT the head of the Gulf of California has a big tide is well known. Choked in a narrowing cone, the waters rise higher and higher as they come to the apex, reaching twenty-five feet or over in a high tide. This causes a tidal bore to roll up the Colorado, and from all reports it was something to be avoided. The earliest Spanish explorers told some wonderful tales of being caught in this bore and of nearly losing their little sailing vessels.

This was my first experience with river tides. It was somewhat of a disappointment to me that I could not arrange to be here at a high tide, for we had come at the first quarter of the moon. Out on the open sea one can usually make some headway by rowing against the ebb or flow of the tide: here on the Colorado, where it flowed upstream at a rate of from five to eight miles an hour, it was different. When we reached the head of the tide, it was going out. Unfortunately for us the day was gone when the current began to run strong. It hardly seemed advisable to travel with it after dark. We might pass the ranch, or be carried against a rock-bound coast, or find difficulty in landing and be overwhelmed by the tidal bore. So when darkness fell we camped, pulling our boat out in a little slough to prevent it from being carried away. Evidently we were too near the headwaters for a tidal bore, for at eleven P.M. the waters turned and came back as quietly as they ran out.

We launched our boat before the break of day, and for four hours we travelled on a good current. The channel now had widened to a half-mile, with straight earthy banks, about fifteen feet high. Still there was no sign of a ranch, and it began to look to us as if there was little likelihood of finding any.

The land was nearly level and except for a few raised hummocks on which grew some scattered trees, it was quite bare. This was not only because it did not get the life-giving water from the north, but because at times it was submerged under the saline waters from the south. Near the shores of the river, and extending back for fifty feet, was a matted, rank growth of grass; beyond that the earth was bare, baked and cracked by the burning sun. This grass, we found, was a favorite resort of rattlesnakes. We killed two of them, a large one and a vicious little flat-headed sidewinder.

All this land was the south rim of the silt dam, which extended from the line of cliffs or mesa on the east to the mountains on the west. The other rim, a hundred feet higher, lay at least fifty miles to the north. Here was the resting-place of a small portion of the sediment carved away by the Colorado's floods. How deep it is piled and how far it extends out under the waters of the Gulf would be hard to say.

We felt sure that we would get to the Gulf with this tide, but when the time came for it to turn we were still many miles away. There was nothing to do but to camp out on this sun-baked plain. We stopped a little after 9.30 A.M. Now that we were nearing the Gulf we were sure there would be a tidal bore. As we breakfasted a slight rushing sound was heard, and what appeared to be a ripple of broken water or small breaker came up the stream and passed on. This was a disappointment. With high water on the river and with a low tide this was all the tidal bore we would see.

In four hours the water rose fourteen feet, then for two hours the rise was slower. Within three feet of the level it came. The opposite side, rounded at the edges, looked like a thread on top of the water, tapered to a single silken strand and looking toward the Gulf, merged into the water. To all appearances it was a placid lake spread from mountain to mesa.

Our smaller canteen was still filled with the fresh water secured the evening before. The other had been emptied and was filled again before the return of the tide, but considerable taste of the salt remained. What we did now must be done with caution. So far we had not seen the ranch. We were in doubt whether it was somewhere out on the coast or back on one of the sloughs passed the evening before. We had heard of large sail-boats being hauled from Yuma and launched by the ranch. This would seem to indicate that it was somewhere on the Gulf. We had provisions sufficient for one day, one canteen of fresh water, and another so mixed with the salt water that we would not use it except as a last resort.

A little after 3.30 P.M. the tide changed; we launched our boat and went out with the flood. As we neared the mouth of the stream we found that the inrush and outrush of water had torn the banks. Here the river spread in a circular pool several miles across. It seemed almost as if the waters ran clear to the line of yellow cliffs and to the hazy mountain range. Then the shores closed in again just before the current divided quite evenly on either side of a section of the barren plain named Montague Island. We took the channel to the east.

Our last hope of finding the ranch was in a dried-out river channel, overgrown with trees. But although we looked carefully as we passed, there was no sign of a trail or of human life. Some egrets preened their silken feathers on the bank; sand-hill cranes and two coyotes, fat as hogs and dragging tails weighted with mud, feasted on the lively hermit-crabs, which they extracted from their holes — and that was all.

The sun, just above the lilac-tinted mountains, hung like a great suspended ball of fire. The cloudless sky glared like a furnace. Deep purple shadows crept into the canyons slashing the mountain range. The yellow dust-waves and the mirages disappeared with the going down of the sun. Still we were carried on and on. We would go down with the tide. Now the end of the island lay opposite the line of cliffs; soon we would be in the Gulf.

So ended the Colorado. Two thousand miles above, it was a beautiful river, born of a hundred snow-capped peaks and a thousand crystal streams; gathering strength, it became the masterful river which had carved the hearts of mountains and slashed the rocky plateaus, draining a kingdom and giving but little in return. Now it was going under, but it was fighting to the end. Waves of yellow struggled up through waves of green and were beaten down again. The dorsal fins of a half-dozen sharks cut circles near our craft. With the last afterglow we were past the end of the island and were nearing the brooding cliffs. Still the current ran strong. The last vestige of day was swallowed in the gloom, just as the Colorado was buried 'neath the blue. A hard wind was blowing, toward the shore; the sea was choppy. A point of rocks where the cliffs met the sea was our goal. Would we never reach it? Even in the night, which was now upon us, the distance was deceptive. At last we neared the pile of rocks. The sound of waters pounding on the shore was heard, and we hurriedly landed, a half-mile above it, just as the tide turned.

The beach was a half-mile wide, covered with mud and sloughs. There was no high shore. But an examination showed that the tide ran back to the cliffs. One of us had to stay with the boat. Telling Phillipps to get what sleep he could, I sat in the boat, and allowed the small breakers which fox-chased each other to beat it in as the tide rose.

An arctic explorer has said that having an adventure means that something unexpected or unforeseen has happened; that some one has been incompetent. I had the satisfaction of knowing that the fault of this adventure, if such it could be called, was mine. Here we were, at our goal in Mexico, supposed to be a hostile land, with scant provisions for one day. It was a hundred miles along the line of cliffs, back to Yuma. So far, we had failed to find the ranch. It was not likely that it was around the point of rocks. We knew now that the Colorado channel was fifteen miles from the mouth of the river, and was not a slough as we had supposed. Doubtless the ranch was up there. Our best plan was to return to the head of the tide, going up the Colorado, then if we did not find the ranch we would abandon the boat, snare some birds, keep out of the scorching heat, and travel in the morning and evening. Two active men should be able to do that without difficulty.

So the hours passed, with the breakers driving the boat toward the line of cliffs. When it had reached its highest point, I pulled into a slough and tied up, then woke Al as we had agreed. While I slept, he climbed the cliffs to have a last look. An hour after daybreak he returned. Nothing but rock and desert could be seen. We dragged the boat down in the slime of the slough until we caught the falling tied. Then Al rigged up his sail. With the rising sun a light breeze blew in from the Gulf. Here was our opportunity. Slowly we went up against the falling tide. Then as the breeze failed, the tide returned. Fifty feet away a six foot black sea bass floated; his rounded back lifted above the water. With the approach of the boat he was gone. The sharks were seen again.

Two hours later we had entered the mouth of the river carried by the rising tide. Several miles were left behind. Another breeze came up as the tide failed, and the sail was rigged up again. Things were coming our way at last. Al knew how to handle a boat. Running her in close to the top of the straight falling banks I could leap to the land, take a picture, then run and overtake the boat, and leap on again.

Then the wind shifted, the tide turned, and we tied

up, directly opposite the point where we had camped the afternoon before. It was the hottest day we had seen. Whirlwinds, gathering the dust in slender funnels, scurried across the plains. Mirages of trees bordering shimmering lakes and spreading water such as we had come through below Yuma were to be seen, even out towards the sea. Then over toward the cliffs where the old Colorado once ran we saw a column of distant smoke. Perhaps it was a hunter; it could hardly be the ranch. As we could do nothing with the boat, we concluded to walk over that way. It was many miles distant. Taking everything we had, including our last lunch, we started our walk, leaving a cloth on a pole to mark the point where our boat was anchored. But after going four miles it still seemed no nearer than before, so we returned. It was evening. The water was drinkable again; that was something to be thankful for. By ten o'clock that night the tide would come up again. After dark we found that our boat was being beached. So we ran it down and began pulling it along over a shoal reaching far out from the shore. As we tugged I was sure I heard a call somewhere up the river. What kind of a land was this! Could it be that my senses were all deceiving me as my eyes were fooled by the mirage? I had heard it, Al had not, and laughed when I said that I had. We listened and heard it again, plainly this time, "Can't you men find a landing? We have a good one up here," it said.

We asked them to row down, advising them to keep clear of the shoal. We waded out, guided by their voices, in the pitch darkness and neared the boat.

One shadowy form sat in either end of a flat-bottomed boat. There was a mast, and the boat was fitted for two oarsmen as well. Evidently the load was heavy, for it was well down in the water. The sail cloth was spread over all the boat, excepting one end where there was a small sheet-iron stove, with a pan of glowing wood coal underneath. The aroma of coffee came from a pot on the stove. As I steadied myself at the bow I touched a crumpled flag, — Mexican, I thought, — but I could not see. Both figures sat facing us, with rifles in their hands, alert and ready for a surprise. Smugglers! I thought; guns, I imagined. They could not see our faces in the dark, neither could we distinguish theirs. Judging by their voices they were young men. I thought from the first that they were Mexicans, but they talked without accent. They could see that we carried no arms, but their vigilance was not relaxed. They asked what our trouble was and we told them of the beached boat, what we had been doing, and why we were there. They said they were out for a little sight-seeing trip down in the Gulf. They might go to Tiburone Island. One of them wondered if it was true that the natives were cannibals. He said he would not care about being shot, but he would hate to be put in their stew-pot. We asked them how much water they carried. A fifteen-gallon keg was all. They hoped to get more along the coast. It is quite well known there is none. They professed to be uninformed about the country, did not know there was a ranch or a tidal bore, and thanked us for our information about the tides, and the advice to fill their keg when the water was lowest, which would be in half an hour. They could not sell any provisions, but gave us a quart of flour.

As we talked an undermined bank toppled over, sounding like shots from a gun. One cocked his rifle on the impulse, then laughed when he realized what it was. Just before we parted one of them remarked, "You came through the Bee River four days ago, near a telephone, didn't you?" "Yes, but we didn't see any one," I replied.

"No? But we saw you!" And we felt the smiles we could not see.

They said the large ranch had some Chinamen clearing the highest ground, and building levees around it to keep the water out. The telephone and a motor boat connected the different ranches. Their advice to us was to keep to the river, not to look for the ranch, but to get on the telephone and raise a racket until some one showed up.

Then we parted to go to our respective landings, with mutual wishes for a successful journey. The boat was pulled down. The tide was on the point of turning, but

TEN MILES FROM THE GULF OF CALIFORNIA. COMING UP ON A TWENTY–FOOT TIDE.

SUNSET ON THE LOWER COLORADO RIVER.

it would be an hour before there would be any strength to it. I went to shore and built a fire of some driftwood, for the long stand in the water had chilled me. Al stayed with the boat. Earlier in the day, I cautiously shook the sticks loose from the matted grass, fearing the rattlers which were everywhere. In this case nothing buzzed. But I had no sooner got my fire well started when a rattler began to sing, roused by the light and the heat, about twenty feet away. My fire was built beside one of the many sloughs which cut back through the grass and ended in the barren soil. These sloughs were filled with water when the tide was in and made ideal landing places, especially if one had to avoid a big tidal bore. Getting on the opposite side of the fire, I tossed a stick occasionally to keep him roused. Soon another joined, and between them they made the air hum. By this time I was thoroughly warmed and felt that the boat would be the best place for me. Carefully extinguishing my fire, I went down to the river just as the tide returned.

Without any sign or call from the shore we were carried up with the tide. We were both weary but I dared not sleep, so I merely kept the boat away from the shores and drifted, while Phillipps slept. I had picked out a guiding star which I little needed while the current was running strong, but which would give us our course when the tide changed, for we could be carried out just as easily.

But an hour after we left our camp another light appeared, growing larger and larger. It was one of two things. Either my fire was not extinguished, or a match thrown down by one of the others had fired the deep dry grass. I consoled myself that it could not spread, for the sloughs and the barren soil would cut it off. I had a grim satisfaction when I thought of the snakes and how they would run for the desert land. This was a real guiding star, growing larger and larger as we were carried up the stream. I slept on shore when the tide would take us no farther. Phillipps got breakfast. We were now about three miles from the slough. After breakfast we alternately towed the boat, for there was no wind to carry us up this morning, and two hours later arrived at the diverging streams. Near by we saw some mules showing evidence of having been worked. It was clear now that the ranch was near. There was still a chance that we would take the wrong stream. Over on the opposite side was a tall cottonwood tree. This I climbed, and had the satisfaction of seeing some kind of a shed half a mile up the east stream. The land between proved to be a large island. As we neared the building two swarthy men emerged and came down to the shore. "Buenas dias," Al called as we pulled in to the landing.

"Buenas dias, Señor," they answered with a smile.

They were employees of the Rancho La Bolso, which was a half-mile up the stream.

Did we make the big fire which had burned until morning?

Our answer seemed to relieve their minds.

What would we do with our boat? It was theirs to do with as they pleased. Leading two horses from out of the building, they mounted and told us to climb on behind, and away we rode across some water-filled sloughs. Hidden in the trees we came to the buildings — three or four flat-topped adobe houses. Some little brown children scattered to announce our coming.

As we dismounted two white men approached. "Why, hello, Phillipps!" the ranch boss said when he saw my companion. "This is a long walk from Yuma. You fellows are just in time to grub!"

THE END

APPENDIX

THE parties who have made extended voyages through one or more of the canyons of the Green and Colorado rivers, and the order of their leaving, according to Dellenbaugh, are as follows:

Major J. W. Powell left Green River, Wyoming, May 24, 1869; arrived at the Virgin River with five of his party, six in all, Aug. 30, 1869 — was met there by some Mormons who had been ordered to be on the lookout by Brigham Young. The party were distributed as follows:

The boats : 1. *Emma Dean.* J. W. Powell, John C. Sumner, Wm. H. Dunn.

2. *Kitty Clyde's Sister.* Walter Powell, G. Y. Bradley.

3. *No Name.* O. G. Howland, Seneca Howland, Frank Goodman.

4. *Maid of the Canyon.* Wm. R. Hawkins, Andrew Hall.

Notes. F. Goodman left the party at the Mouth of the Uinta. The *No Name* was wrecked in Lodore Canyon. O. G. Howland, Seneca Howland, and Wm.

H. Dunn left the party when about twenty-five miles from the mouth of the Grand Canyon, and were killed by the Shewits Utes near Mt. Dellenbaugh. Sumner and Hall went on down to the Gulf of California.

The second Powell expedition left Green River, Wyoming, May 22, 1871, taking advantage of the high water, which is desirable on the Green River. They arrived at the Mouth of the Paria, Oct. 22, 1871. Starting again from the Paria (Lee's Ferry) Aug. 17, 1872, they passed through Marble Canyon and nearly 100 miles of the Grand Canyon, reaching the mouth of Kanab Canyon Saturday, Sept. 7, 1872. Here the voyage was discontinued on account of high water, rising higher each day. The crews of this party were distributed as follows:

1871.   1. *Emma Dean.*   J. W. Powell, S. V. Jones, F. S. Dellenbaugh, J. K. Hilliers.

2. *Nellie Powell.*   A. H. Thompson, John F. Steward, F. M. Bishop, F. C. A. Richardson.

3. *Canonita.*   E. O. Beaman, W. Clement Powell, Andrew C. Hatton.

Notes.   Richardson left in Brown's Park; Beaman, Steward, and Bishop at the end of the first season. The boats had been badly pounded, the *Nellie Powell* very much so, and she was left at Lee's Ferry. The party proceeded as follows:

1872. 1. *Emma Dean.*   J. W. Powell, S. V. Jones, F. S.
          Dellenbaugh, J. K. Hilliers.
       2. *Canonita.* A. H. Thompson, W. Clement
          Powell, A. C. Hatton.

H. M. Hook with fifteen miners in crude boats left
Green River, Wyoming, June 1, 1869. H. M. Hook and
one other were drowned in Red Canyon, and the expedition was abandoned.

Earlier parties to attempt descent: 1825 — Wm.
H. Ashley and party to Brown's Park. 1849 — Wm. L.
Manly and party to Uintah Valley. The name D.
Julian, Mai 1836, occurs carved in the walls in Labyrinth
Canyon, and again in Cataract Canyon. No further
record at present.

BROWN-STANTON

This expedition left Blake (Green River, Utah) May
25, 1889, 16 men with 6 boats (very light). The entire
party was Frank M. Brown, chief, Robert Brewster
Stanton, chief engineer, John Hislop, C. W. Potter,
T. P. Rigney, E. A. Reynolds, J. H. Hughes, W. H. Bush,
Edward Coe, Edward ————, Peter Hansborough,
Henry Richards, G. W. Gibson, Charles Porter, F. A.
Nims, T. C. Terry.

Notes. Brown, Hansborough, and Richards were
drowned in Marble Canyon. The expedition was tem-

z

APPENDIX

porarily abandoned in lower Marble Canyon. Hughes, Terry, and Rigney left at Glen Canyon, Reynolds left at Lee's Ferry, and Harry McDonald joined the party.

STANTON

Stanton re-outfitted with heavy boats, 22 feet long, and began the second trip in Glen Canyon. This party included R. B. Stanton, Langdon Gibson, Harry McDonald, Elmer Kane, John Hislop, F. A. Nims, Reginald Travers, W. H. Edwards, A. B. Twining, H. G. Ballard, L. G. Brown, and James Hogue. They entered the head of Marble Canyon Dec. 28, 1889, and finished at tide water in the Gulf of California, Apr. 26, 1890. One boat wrecked in the Grand Canyon. Purpose of trip, survey for a railroad.

Notes. Nims had a fall in Marble Canyon, which broke his leg. He was taken out over a 1700-foot wall and carried over the plateau to a point where he could be hauled out by wagon. McDonald left the expedition near the upper end of the Grand Canyon, Hogue and one other left at Diamond Creek.

GALLOWAY

Nathan Galloway left Green River, Wyoming, in the autumn of 1895 and went to Lee's Ferry. Late in 1896 N. Galloway and Wm. Richmond left Henry's Fork, Wyoming, and reached Needles, Feb. 10, 1897. Galloway passed down as far as the Uintah Valley five times, and through Desolation and Gray canyons seven times, through Cataract three times, and the Grand Canyon, once before making the trip with Julius F. Stone. Galloway was a trapper.

FLAVELL

On Aug. 27, 1896, George F. Flavell and one companion, name unknown, started from Green River, Wyoming, and went to Yuma, Arizona, which was reached Dec. 1896. They had one boat; flat-bottomed. Little is known about this expedition. Prospector or trapper?

RUSSELL-MONNETTE

Charles S. Russell, E. R. Monnette, and Bert Loper, in three steel boats, left Blake (Green River), Utah, Sept. 20, 1907. Russell and Monnette reached Needles in Feb. 1908 with one boat. Purpose, prospecting.

Notes. Loper's boat was punctured in the lower end of Cataract Canyon, and he held up to repair while the others continued to prospect as far as Lee's Ferry. After a long wait they proceeded with the trip. Loper arrived shortly after, but discontinued the trip when he found he was left behind. A second boat was lost in the Hance Rapid. The third boat was torn away from them, while lining it in the Hermit Creek Rapid. They climbed the granite, and followed a trail which took them to the camp of L. Bouchre, a prospector. The boat was found the next day with three holes in its side, in a whirlpool five miles below the Hermit Creek Rapid. The boat was repaired and the voyage completed to Needles.

STONE

Julius F. Stone of Columbus, Ohio, accompanied by Nathan T. Galloway, Chas. S. Sharp, S. S. Denbeudorff, and R. A. Cogswell (Photographer), outfitted with four flat-bottomed boats, left Green River, Wyoming, Sept. 12, 1909, and reached Needles Nov. 15, 1909, with all boats in good condition, and with the remarkable record for Stone and Galloway of having brought their two boats through without an upset.

Notes. Sharp discontinued the trip at Glen Canyon, and one boat was left at this place. Purpose, photographic exploration.

KOLB

On Sept. 8, 1911, Emery C. Kolb, James Fagin, and Ellsworth L. Kolb, outfitted with two flat-bottomed boats, left Green River and arrived at Bright Angel Trail, Nov. 16, 1911. James Fagin left the party at the mouth of Lodore Canyon. On Dec. 19, Herbert Lauzon joined the party at the Grand Canyon for the trip to Needles ; Ernest V. Kolb was taken along for a twenty-five mile ride to the end of the Bass Trail. Lauzon finished the trip at Needles with the Kolb brothers, Jan. 18, 1912. Purpose, moving pictures and photographs. In May, 1913, E. L. Kolb made the trip from Needles to the Gulf, travelling on the high water and making the 400-mile run in 8 days.

THE HISTORY OF CATARACT CANYON

J. S. Best and party left Green River, Utah, July 10, 1891. Wrecked in Cataract Canyon. No lives lost.

There are incomplete records of nine parties who have attempted to pass through Cataract Canyon, and who undoubtedly met with fatalities. On two occasions a single member escaped and reached the Hite ranch in a famished condition.

John Vartan, an Armenian prospector, lost his boat and barely succeeded in escaping. His clothes were made into a rope by which he dropped from a ledge to a canyon, through which he reached the Land of Standing Rocks. He was found after weeks of exposure, during which time he lived on plants and roots. He was nursed back to life, but never gave a very clear account of his experiences.

A. G. Turner, the Glen Canyon prospector, made a successful passage through the rapids of this canyon in 1907.

The Stone expedition found a wrecked boat and fresh tracks of three persons, one of these being a boy's tracks, on the shore. No further trace of them has been discovered.

Charles Smith wrote us that he succeeded in getting through after we saw him in 1911.

In 1912 Smith and Galloway combined and passed through in safety. Near Dark Canyon they found the decomposed body of a man on a rock in mid-stream. From odors, they judged there were other bodies in other places not far from this find.

Just before this book goes to press we have received two letters, one from Mr. J. F. Stone, stating that Galloway had died a natural death. Another letter is from John Hite, informing us that his brother Cass Hite was dead. In the same letter he states that Smith left Blake, Utah, for the third time, in November, 1913, and had never showed up at his home. Later he and Loper found half of his wrecked boat. A full heart pays tribute to the memory of Smith.

So it goes on from year to year. Judging by these experiences it would seem that the carefully planned expeditions, especially those with covered boats containing air chambers, succeed in getting through.

The writer believes that a passage can be made through Cataract Canyon, in low water, without being compelled to run more than one or two bad rapids, if great

care is taken while crossing from one shore to the other
between the rapids.   With a light canvas boat, or
with a canoe in the hands of experts, it might be possible
to avoid them all, but I would not care to be so quoted,
as I am a little uncertain about the two last bad rapids.
This would not be possible in Marble or the Grand
Canyon. The last mentioned contains many rapids as
bad as any in Cataract Canyon. We find that all those
who have made successful passages are infatuated with
their type of boat. All we will claim for our type, which
came to us through Stone and Galloway, is that three
expeditions have used this type of boat, and they all
— with the exception of one in perfect condition left by
Stone's party with Hite — finished at Needles. But
whether made of steel, wood, or canvas, all boats should
be decked as much as possible to keep out the powerful
waves, and should contain large air chambers. Rowlocks, oars, paddles, and ropes should be carefully guarded
against breakage and loss.

The flood stage on the Colorado River, about 300,000
cubic second feet, exceeds that on the St. Lawrence River
at Niagara Falls, which carries about 250,000 cubic second
feet. The descent in many rapids on the Colorado equals
that of any section of the St. Lawrence, excepting Niagara
Falls. In the low water stage, the rapids lose much of
their strength of current and violence of waves, and the
flow is only a small fraction of the flood stage.

The deepest canyons of the Green and Colorado rivers, their length, approximate depth, and the fall of the river are as follows. These figures are compiled from "A Canyon Voyage," U. S.G. S. maps, and other sources.

	LENGTH IN MILES	GREATEST DEPTH IN FEET	APPROXIMATE DESCENT
Flaming Gorge ⎤			
Horseshoe ⎟	35		
Kingfisher ⎟			
Red ⎦		2700	350
Lodore	20½	2700–3000 [1]	425
Whirlpool	14	2200	140
Split Mountain	9	2000	90
Desolation	97	2700	⎫ 550 [2]
Gray	36	2000	⎭
Cataract	41	2700–3000 [3]	430
Marble	65½	3500	480
Grand Canyon	217	5000–6000 [4]	1850

The entire distance from Green River, Wyoming, to the tide water is something over 1600 miles. The descent is a little over 6000 feet. About 4300 feet of this descent occurs in 500 miles of the canyons listed above; 2330 feet comes in Marble Canyon and the Grand Canyon, the two combined making an unbroken canyon of 283 miles.

[1] Peaks close to the canyon reach a height of 3000 ft. above the river.

[2] The upper half of Desolation Canyon has no rapids.

[3] Maps give depth as 2700 ft. We believe some walls are higher.

[4] Greatest depth on the south side of the Grand Canyon is near 5000 ft., on the north rim about 6000 ft.

THE following pages contain advertisements of a few of the Macmillan books on kindred subjects

California

By MARY AUSTIN

With illustrations in color by SUTTON PALMER.

Cloth, 12mo, boxed, $4.00 net

That Mrs. Austin has a subject worthy of a fluent pen and that she is fully qualified to do justice to it no one will deny. There have been books about California before, but none of them written with so real an appreciation of its wonders as this one in which the grandeur of the state has been so vividly presented. Not only does Mrs. Austin know California, she loves it. Her volume will serve as a guide to the many tourists who will be visiting the coast during the coming exposition, a guide which is neither formal nor stilted, but interpretative, replete with beautiful descriptions of beautiful spots. It will be none the less interesting reading to those who have never seen the places and have no prospect of doing so. Mr. Palmer's colored pictures are a splendid supplement to the text.

A Wanderer in Venice

By E. V. LUCAS

Author of " A Wanderer in Holland," " A Wanderer in Paris," etc.

With illustrations in color and in black and white.

Decorated cloth, 12mo, $1.75 net; leather, $2.50 net

Mr. Lucas's "Wanderer" books have made many friends. Much of the charm of Florence, London, Paris, and Holland has been caught by him and transferred to the printed page along with bits of their histories, interesting anecdotes and legends. To these four volumes Mr. Lucas now adds one on Venice. What a place of hidden treasure that wonderful city is to one of Mr. Lucas's very original genius all who have read the preceding works in this series can easily understand. And Mr. Lucas has fully realized his opportunities. The book is, perhaps, the most fascinating of all. With its colored illustrations and its black and white plates, with its no less vivid and appreciative text, it is a publication which no one who has ever been to Venice should overlook, while to those who have not been it will open up new vistas of undreamed-of beauties.

THE MACMILLAN COMPANY

Publishers   **64-66 Fifth Avenue**   **New York**

With Poor Immigrants to America

By STEPHEN GRAHAM

Author of " With the Russian Pilgrims to Jerusalem," "A Tramp's Sketches," etc.

Illustrated. Cloth, 8vo, boxed, $2.50 net

" We collected on the quay at Liverpool — English, Russians, Jews, Germans, Swedes, Finns, all staring at one another curiously and trying to understand languages we had never heard before. Three hundred yards out in the harbor stood the red-funneled Cunarder which was to bear us to America." These words describe the beginning of the colorful travels of which Mr. Graham writes in this book. Mr. Graham has the spirit of the real adventurer. He prefers people to Pullmans, steerage passage to first cabin. In his mingling with the poorer classes he comes in contact intimately with a life which most writers know only by hearsay, and interesting bits of this life and that which is picturesque and romantic and unlooked for he transcribes to paper with a freshness and vividness that mark him a good mixer with men, a keen observer and a skillful adept with the pen.

Panama: The Canal, The Country and The People

By ARTHUR BULLARD (Albert Edwards)

Revised Edition with Additional Chapters and New Illustrations

Decorated cloth, 8vo, boxed, $2.00 net

Not only has Mr. Bullard revised such material of the first edition of his book as has been retained in the present issue, but he has added to that several chapters. These have to do largely with the canal since its completion. This work has probably enjoyed greater popularity than any other volume on Panama, a fact due, no doubt, to its comprehensiveness. It is not confined to any one matter. There are descriptions of the natural beauties of the locality, discussions of the customs and life of its inhabitants and sections devoted to the canal, its history, construction and those concerned with it. Besides the new text there are also many new and fascinating illustrations.

THE MACMILLAN COMPANY

Publishers   64-66 Fifth Avenue   New York

Japan To-day and To-morrow

By HAMILTON W. MABIE

Author of " American Ideals, Character and Life "

Illustrated. Decorated cloth, 12mo, boxed, $2.00 net

The purpose of this volume is to convey a clear and definite impression of the spirit of the Japanese people — what they are interested in and what we may expect of them in the future. Pursuant to its aim, it offers chapters on the manners and habits of the Japanese, their family life, their love of art and of nature and their attitude toward religion. Their historical development is very lightly sketched and their education and political development somewhat more fully. No American is perhaps better fitted to write such a book as this than Dr. Mabie. As lecturer to Japan on the Carnegie Peace Endowment a year or so ago he had splendid opportunity for a close study of the country and its people. Added to this is his power of clearly analyzing that which he sees and of expressing his thought in English that it is a pleasure to read.

Southern Italy and Sicily

By F. MARION CRAWFORD

New edition in two volumes. With many half tone illustrations in the text and 31 photogravures

Decorated cloth, 8vo, $5.00 net

This book is a rare combination of text and pictures. Mr. Crawford and Mr. Brokman, the illustrator, worked together in an almost ideal fashion. The vivid description of the one and the sympathetic drawings of the other make a narrative of travel set off now and then by a bit of history that is of most fascinating interest. Every Crawford admirer as well as every lover of the beautiful in books will wish to add this edition, which may truly be called the *edition de luxe,* to his library.

THE MACMILLAN COMPANY

Publishers   64–66 Fifth Aveuue   New York

GRAND
CANYON
ASSOCIATION